New South Women

PLCMC

The Public Library of Charlotte and Mecklenburg County
in Association with John F. Blair, Publisher

New South Women

Twentieth-
Century Women
of Charlotte, North Carolina

by Mary Kratt

Appendix by Mary Davis Smart

*The paper in this book meets the guidelines
for permanence and durability of the
Committee on Production Guidelines for Book Longevity
of the Council on Library Resources.*

Library of Congress Cataloging-in-Publication Data
Kratt, Mary Norton.
New South women : twentieth century women of Charlotte, North
Carolina / by Mary Kratt ; appendix by Mary Davis Stuart.
         p.   cm.
Includes bibliographical references and index.
ISBN 0-89587-250-1 (alk. paper)
1. Women—North Carolina—Charlotte—Biography. 2. Women—North
Carolina—Charlotte—History—20th century. I. Title.
HQ1439.C43 K73 2001
305.4'092'275676—dc21
2001037671

To
the memory of Hannah Blair Withers,
who insisted that the story of Charlotte women
was the only one to write,
and to Mary Manning Boyer, historian

Contents

Preface

*R*eviewing pre-1950s histories of Charlotte, North Carolina, you might think notable women were rare. In fact, you might doubt that women made up half the population, because they are largely absent except for Mrs. "Stonewall" Jackson of Charlotte. And even her veneration as a widow of prominence is largely attached to the career of her husband, a remarkable maverick Confederate general.

In each of my books I have tried to balance the scales with the truer story, which is that women were here in strength, both of numbers and character. Very simply and with creative determination, they were highly original and courageous. They made Charlotte and the region quite a different place.

This book focuses on Charlotte women of the twentieth century, the years 1900–2000, and was commissioned by the Women of the Year Award Committee 1954–2001, with the support of the Public Library of Charlotte and Mecklenburg County, the Knight Foundation, and other generous gifts. The inclusion of all women in the century whose lives and activities were significant was not possible. For this, the author begs forgiveness, and hopes that the work of all women continues to bear fruit in hopeful memory and tribute.

The book's purpose is to tell a *representative* story of women of the century, guided by the motto of the National Association of Colored Women's Clubs (founded 1896), a motto which serves in the year 2001 and beyond for women of every color, class, and background:

"Lifting as we climb."

Mary Kratt
Charlotte, 2001

Brief Chronology of National Events
Important to Charlotte women

1848 The First Women's Rights Convention is held in Seneca Falls, New York. Demand for women's suffrage is presented.

1893 Colorado allows women to vote; the first state in the nation to do so.

1919 Nineteenth Amendment, passed by Congress, is ratified by the required three-fourths of the states in 1920. North Carolina did not ratify it.

1923 The Equal Rights Amendment is introduced in Congress.

1954 In *Brown v. Board of Education*, Supreme Court declares that separate but equal facilities for the races are unconstitutional.

1960 Birth control pills are approved and available in 1961.

1961 President John F. Kennedy appoints Eleanor Roosevelt chair of the first President's Commission on the Status of Women.

1963 Author Betty Friedan publishes her groundbreaking book, *The Feminine Mystique.*

1964 Civil Rights Act is passed by Congress. It includes Title VII, prohibiting discrimination in employment on the basis of race, color, religion, national origin, and sex.

1966 National Organization for Women (NOW) is founded.

1970-71 *The Female Eunuch* by Germain Greer, *Sexual Politics* by Kate Millett, and *Woman Power* by Celestine Ware are published. Media attention to women's movement gears up.

1972   Equal Rights Amendment passes both houses of Congress with ratification by three-fourths of states required.

Roe v. Wade decision by U.S. Supreme Court establishes women's right to abortion.

1973   *Our Bodies, Ourselves: A Book by and for Women*, created by the Boston Women's Health Collective, is published.

1974   Domestic workers are covered by the minimum-wage law.

1982   Equal Rights Amendment is unable to garner the necessary number of states for ratification.

1983   Sally Ride becomes first U.S. woman in space.

1984   Geraldine Ferraro runs for U.S. vice president.

1987   Congress declares March "Women's History Month."

1988   Methodists create a gender-neutral hymnal.

1989   African-American Barbara Harris is ordained as first female bishop in Episcopal Church.

1991   Clarence Thomas's Supreme Court confirmation hearings center on accusations of sexual harrassment.

1992   EMILY'S List, the Women's Campaign Fund, and other groups raise money for a record number of women running for electoral office.

1994   Supreme Court rules that blocking the entrance to an abortion clinic is illegal.

1995   Glass Ceiling Commission reports white men hold 95 percent of senior management positions.

1999   U.S. women's soccer team wins World Cup trophy.

Elizabeth Dole, North Carolina native, announces run for U.S. Presidency.

2000   First Lady Hillary Rodham Clinton wins election to U.S. Senate from New York.

Acknowledgements

Grateful thanks for the generous and patient assistance of the Archives Staff of UNC Charlotte; Robin Brabham; Marilyn Bradbury, Foundation of the Carolinas; Mecklenburg County Bar Association; staff of Robinson-Spangler Carolina Room at PLCMC; Mecklenburg County Board of Elections; Jack Claiborne; Tom Hanchett; Dot Hodges; Mary Klentz, League of Women Voters; Bob Anthony, North Carolina Collection, UNC Chapel Hill; Lily Bezner; Mary Boyer; Phil Busher; Carolyn DeMerritt; Wardie Martin; Peaches McLean Deal; Sally McMillan; Dan Morrill; Sally Robinson; Carolyn Sakowski; Marcia Simon; Mary Davis Smart; staff of the Museum of the New South; Elizabeth Dumbell Stiles for editing this project; and Don Sturkey.

CHAPTER ONE

*W*hen expert sharpshooter Annie Oakley performed in 1901 in Charlotte's Latta Park with Buffalo Bill Cody's Wild West Show, most Charlotte women were church-going stay-at-home housewives with many children. Or they may have worked outside the home as millworkers, teachers, shopgirls, laundresses or domestics. And the millworkers, laundresses, or domestics also were likely to have had numerous children.

By 1900, the American pot began to boil.

What followed was an unprecedented era of progressive new ideas and unimagined energies. Positive change was slow for the status of women and for African-Americans, but almost every other facet of life would never be the same after the inventions and reforms soon to come.

Vice President "Teddy" Roosevelt suddenly became president of the United States when President William McKinley was shot and killed by an assassin in

1901. A former governor of New York state and the first president who saw the federal government as protector of the public interest, Roosevelt brought the same zeal to the presidency as he showed when he charged up San Juan Hill in the Spanish-American War. He began an era of continuous reform that affected all Americans. A few of these reforms were his trust-busting enforcement of the Sherman Anti-trust Law, the passing of the Pure Food and Drug Act, the creation of national parks and forests, intervention in labor struggles, and setting interstate rate standards to curb unfair and arbitrary rail transport fees. The rash of reform infected the whole country under Roosevelt, and Charlotte, North Carolina, was no exception.

Charlotte looked like a busy, muddy town in 1900. And she was growing. Lawyer Julia Alexander described the Square, the center of town, in the early decades of the century: "From Independence Square, electric lines are reaching out in every direction along wide avenues lined on either side with beautiful shade trees, and over well-kept streets. Suburban sections . . . are rapidly building up . . . Dilworth, Elizabeth Heights, Piedmont Park, and Myers Park are especially attractive . . . Belmont, Highland Park, Atherton, and Chadwick are among the progressive urban mill settlements."

In 1900, the town of Charlotte had about 18,000 black and white citizens, while in the county on hundreds of rural farms, workers raised cotton, food, and cattle. Mecklenburg County's 55,000 included the city population clustered densely around the ridgeline crossroads of Trade and Tryon Streets. Locals called this crossroads The Square. Blacks and whites lived intermingled uptown, some in frame houses, some along alleys, others in large, rambling residences which encompassed a whole block for one family's stable, yard, garden, and mansion.

Charlotte's first cotton mill started in 1881 and by 1900, joined hundreds of other textile mills in the region where girls and women with their families left the hardscrabble mountain and Piedmont Carolina farms and came to work in cotton mills of Charlotte, Gastonia, and Lancaster. In a month in the cotton mill, a young girl could earn as much as her tenant-farmer father saw in an entire year.

The development of hydroelectric power around 1900, which harnessed Piedmont rivers to run factories and cotton mills, created many mill villages and towns clustered around outlying railroad stops, cotton gins, a bank, livery stable, and general store. Although many did, cotton mills no longer had to huddle at the edge of riverbanks, relying on water wheels and turbines, but could receive power from electric lines.

Inventions such as the telephone, telegraph, typewriter, electric streetcar, and the automobile changed life radically. Radio and silent movies were yet to come, but gossip, newspapers, and dime novels were plentiful.

The traditional image of woman's role was that of homemaker, a passive, domestic wife who upheld the morals of society. The female on a pedestal removed from baser instinct was entrenched in the popular mind, but this was soon to change. All over the country, young, educated women and men of the middle class saw themselves as reformers of industry, government, health and education issues, rightful shakers of the formerly rigid rules of society.

Women in particular became involved in reform issues of health and temperance, and concerns about prostitution, lynching, and child labor. They joined or created organizations to correct obvious wrongs within their own communities and to aid people whose troubles touched their own comfortable lives. Charlotte women did this, following much publicized reforms like Jane Addams' social experiment at Hull House in Chicago, which pushed to improve living conditions in the industrial districts of that city.

In New York City, the Henry Street Settlement House pioneered social reforms initiated by Lillian Wald, one of the first public health nurses and a leader in the child welfare movement. In 1904, she formed the National Child Labor Committee. Women, many of whom were educated, well-to-do reformers, trained in these highly organized, female-led settlement houses like Hull House or Henry Street and spawned a staunch coterie of workers and leaders for child labor reform and the women's suffrage movement. Charlotte may have been well removed geographically from these cities, but the publicity and influence engendered by these female reformers was known throughout the country.

In the South, despite the overriding ideals of chivalry and white women's exalted, restricted place in society, women not surprisingly edged first into reform via their own church organizations. The safe-sounding missionary society, a staple of southern churches, consistently met local and regional needs under the benevolent umbrella of religion. This respectable, time-honored tradition had proved most effective in Charlotte. The Women's Christian Temperance Union battled the evils of alcohol, which most often threatened the lives of women and children when husbands and fathers poured their paychecks into drink, causing abuse and poverty.

The ardent, organized anti-lynching effort pushed by women elsewhere, gained momentum as lynchings of black men in the South continued to be common occurrences. These whispered-about events were sedately reported in small newspaper notices, but often were not actively prevented. In Charlotte newspapers, one does not find headlines about women in the early part of the century who were organizing for the prevention of lynching nor for the prevention of child labor. In Charlotte, many upper- and middle-class women were do-gooders and also married to, or in the churches of, or neighbors and friends to mill owners. Consequently, cotton mill labor reform seemed a rare topic for discussion, least of all action.

But women were at work to be sure. The creative energy of five young, single women of Charlotte in 1896 had been just a hint of the good works to come with the turn of a new century. Their venture was the first edition of a women's newspaper in North Carolina.

They wrote and produced a "Women's Mecklenburg Declaration of Independence Edition" of *The Charlotte Observer* with the enthusiastic aid of the *Observer's* editor J.P. Caldwell. To do this, they infiltrated the newspaper's male domain. Reporters seemed "unruffled by the unaccustomed presence of women in the office." Mamie Bays edited the edition with the aid of Sallie Whisnant, business manager; Eva Liddell, advertising; Adele Brenizer, circulation; and Laura Wadsworth, illustration. Miss Whisnant in her phaeton drawn by her horse "Dusty" called on prospective advertisers, while Lilly Long wrote historical pieces aided by Mrs. "Stonewall" Jackson and her sister Harriet Irwin.

The sisters Irwin and Jackson were two of Charlotte's most prominent and visible women of society and accomplishment during the late 1800s. Mary Anna Morrison Jackson (1831–1915) was the town's premier arbiter of taste and style. It was generally accepted that "no social occasion was complete without her." First regent of the Charlotte chapter of the Daughters of the American Revolution (DAR), which she founded, she spent many years writing a biography of her husband, the celebrated Confederate general called "Stone-wall." U.S. Presidents and Confederate soldiers visiting town paid tribute in her parlor. Hers was a military funeral in 1915.

Her sister Harriet Morrison Irwin (1828–97) was an architect and writer who patented her plan in 1869 as H.M. Irwin, titled "Improvement in the Con-struction of Houses." She devised an unusual hexagonal house form with "hex-agonal or lozenge-shaped rooms," building one at 912 West Fifth Street and in several other Charlotte locations.

A third notable woman, Rachel Jones Holton (1813–1905), rivaled the sisters' accomplishments. When her husband Thomas, who edited a Charlotte daily newspaper called *The North Carolina Whig*, died in a buggy accident, Rachel took over and published the paper herself in the difficult years prior to and during the Civil War.

Even though no women are recorded as holding Charlotte public office prior to 1900 (nor could they vote), they occasionally had made a decorous political outburst, such as their call for a public park in 1876. But the board of aldermen's minutes that steamy July night show that their request "for the benefit of the citizens, was on motion, referred to the Cemetery Committee" where it understandably died. Not until 1890 did Charlotte have a small up-town space designated as a "Park" and that was on federal property on West Trade Street. The women wanted a place for their children to play other than the streets or the cemetery.

But this first women's edition of the *Observer* ambitiously set out to chronicle some of these local women's accomplishments in various fields. Women's achievements, wit and humor, music and art, literature and religion were fea-tured along with a photo of Charlotte's first woman cyclist and her bicycle. Mrs. John Van Landingham's article on "Women in Profession" focused on Charlotte pioneer physician Dr. Annie Alexander.

When the first copy came off the press late at night, editor Bays said, "We stayed there until after twelve o'clock and Sallie Whisnant went home with me and we talked all night. We were too excited and we were all back at the *Observer* building on South Tryon Street the next morning before five o'clock."

The edition appeared naturally on Charlotte's most hallowed local holi-day, Mecklenburg Declaration of Independence Day, May 20. This was the day "held dear and celebrated," the women wrote, "by Mecklenburg sons and daughters in memory of their forefathers who through great trials made this a free country by throwing off the British yoke."

The five women were highly embarrassed when their pictures appeared on the front page, but the drawing of Miss Liberty, which had been planned for and chosen, "was unusable because of engravers' changes made in Washington, D.C." The ads touted pianos, hotels, shops selling cloth, elegant shoes, and gauze underwear, and one drugstore, which advertised medicines including "French brandy, Topaz sherry wine, and Port wine sold for strictly medicinal purposes." The landmark women's edition was sold on Charlotte streets and to subscribers and also on trains connecting in Charlotte. A Lenoir man bought a copy on the train because he recognized the picture of his wife's friend on the front page.

Ironically, the women's edition was a money-making project, the proceeds to benefit the Young Men's Christian Association and its Woman's Auxiliary. They cleared $706.25 and were "overjoyed for that splendid amount for the work of the YMCA."

While many northern women had rallied and organized around the issue of the abolition of slavery, Charlotte women organized early to lend medical aid to Civil War soldiers. Subsequently they created war memorials in Charlotte to honor eminent historical figures and events or those who died in battle in all wars involving American troops.

Jane Wilkes wrote a concise account in 1896 of a seminal organized effort by the women of Charlotte. "The first Hospital in Charlotte was established by the ladies, in a large building used as the wash-house for the Military Institute, now the Graded School. Here all arrangements were made for the care of the passing soldiers. Every day two members of the hospital association went there with supplies . . . and gave their time and strength to the nursing and caring for our men." This Hospital Association had engaged three Charlotte women, two white and one black, to go to Yorktown and nurse "our North Carolina men through measles, camp fever, etc."

Women's efforts continued postwar with fundraising at concerts, suppers, tableaux, and charades to raise money for soldiers' burials and a Civil War Monument. Wilkes wrote the text on the only Charlotte confederate monument, an obelisk in Elmwood Cemetery.

The remarkable and pertinent fact here is primarily the character of Jane Smedburg Wilkes (1827–1913). A New Yorker from a prominent family, she married another well-to-do New Yorker, John Wilkes, in 1854 and they moved to Charlotte, arriving via train, ferry, and stagecoach from South Carolina, since there was no train from the north directly into Charlotte. Their purpose in this adventure was to supervise their families' mining and flour milling properties in the Charlotte area. For four years, they lived about two miles from the center of town near the long-established St. Catherine Flour Mills. Their first child was born at home in the winter of 1855. The Wilkes family also owned the St. Catherine Gold Mine. Their second child Isabella was born the next year at sea on the U.S.S. *Roanoke* off Sandy Hook, New Jersey.

The couple "accepted the destiny of their adopted South" and both became town leaders, she in relief and humanitarian work, he in business with his Mecklenburg Iron Works and as a leader in St. Peter's Episcopal Church. They moved to town to an elegant house on West Trade Street. Jane wrote an account of the Confederate Navy Yard, which had taken over the initial site of Wilkes' iron works on East Trade Street. The Wilkes' northern ties could have isolated and ostracized them from the town during the Civil War, but they had entered within a few years the essential heart and fabric of the town. In the late nineteenth century, she raised funds to provide a proper burial and a memorial to 169 Civil War soldiers of Mecklenburg County who had been buried locally in mass graves. It was to this tall Elmwood Cemetery monument bearing the text written by Jane Wilkes that Mrs. "Stonewall" Jackson led children and townspeople with garlands of flowers on each Confederate Memorial Day for many years.

Jane Wilkes' genteel organizing and fundraising efforts led to St. Peter's Home and Hospital (begun 1876), Charlotte's first public hospital, and to the Good Samaritan Hospital (opened 1891), North Carolina's first black hospital and one of the first in the South. The latter effort took many years and was supported by funds solicited in the many letters Jane Wilkes wrote to northern friends, among them financier J.P. Morgan who gave $200.

For nearly 60 years and into the early twentieth century, Wilkes was one of Charlotte's most prominent women, working in her garden, giving away her abundant flowers, and rising to large needs confronting citizens irrespective of race, heritage, or economics. As a northern patrician of Scots and Swedish descent and the granddaughter of a wealthy Swedish iron merchant, she successfully adopted Charlotte and its people and their institutions, so much so that at her funeral in 1913, the *Charlotte Evening News* reported, "Never in the history of the Church and seldom in the history of the city has there been such a gathering. The rich and the poor, white and black, came together to pay the tribute of appreciation to this great woman. The seats on the south aisle were reserved for the colored people and they were filled to overflowing."

Dr. Charles M. Strong in his medical history of the county wrote of her, "When a hospital was a small thing in the eyes of the profession, it was a great building in the heart of this good woman. . . . For many years she felt responsible for the deficit at St. Peter's or at Good Samaritan and in one way or another, managed to keep the books in some sort of balance. Any one wishing to put up a million dollar memorial hospital in Charlotte, should put a marble statue of Mrs. Jane R. Wilkes just inside the front door."

Wilkes organized the North Carolina branch of the Women's Auxiliary to the Board of Missions of the Episcopal Church and was its presiding officer for many years. Her interest in hospitals could have had several origins. The pioneering war work in nursing by Florence Nightingale in the Crimean War (1853–56) was well publicized. Also, of Jane Wilkes's own nine children, two died in infancy, another died quite young, and a son died at age 18. One member of Jane's church recalled that she "always wore black and a little white linen cap," noting that she found it "interesting to know how saints look."

In 1921, a year after the Nineteenth Amendment to the Constitution gave women the right to vote, Jane Wilkes became one of the first three Charlotte women to hold public office. They were appointed to the school commission. Her *Charlotte Evening News* obituary called her "one of Charlotte's most useful women . . . [who worked] in season and out of season for causes which appealed to her sense of justice and charity." But Wilkes and her Episcopalian friends were not alone in directing their energies toward hospitals. In 1906, the Sisters of Mercy, including Sister Mary Dolores, Mother Mary Bride, Mother Mary Raphael, and Sister Mary Alphonse were a few of the many who organized what would become Mercy Hospital with a capacity of 25 beds in a wooden

Jane Smedburg Wilkes (1827–1931) is celebrated as "godmother of Charlotte hospitals" for her fundraising, founding, and long support of the town's first hospital for whites, St. Peter's Home and Hospital (1877), and also the region's first hospital for African-Americans, Good Samaritan (1891). From a wealthy New York family, she settled in Charlotte as the 27-year-old bride of fellow New Yorker, industrialist John Wilkes. She was one of the city's first female public officials (Charlotte School Commission 1921).

building on East First Street, behind St. Peter's Roman Catholic Church.

Around 1900, Jane Wilkes's pioneering work and influence was paralleled by a demure yet daring young woman, Annie Lowrie Alexander (1864–1929), a female pioneer in a professional field. She was a Mecklenburg County native, who in 1884 received her diploma at Woman's Medical College in Philadelphia. She earned the distinction of being the first licensed female physician to practice medicine in the South.

"Dr. Annie" was a descendant of a prominent Scots-Irish family who settled Mecklenburg in colonial times. Her father, Dr. John Brevard Alexander (1834–1911), described seeing a female patient die because the patient was too shy to allow herself to be examined by a male doctor. He went home and urged 14-year-old Annie to become a doctor and help such women. After education by her father and a private tutor, young Annie entered Woman's Medical College in Philadelphia.

In letters to her father from medical school, she wrote in the summer of 1884 about her fascination with surgery. "I have performed seven operations. . . . I think I will make a surgeon. . . . I would like to study about five years more before I go to practicing, then I would be plenty young, only 25. . . . I can't decide where to locate when I leave Philadelphia. I've thought of Baltimore, Atlanta, and Jacksonville, but there will be obstacles wherever I locate. My success will depend on my ability and the liberal views of the people among whom I will be.

"I feel and imagine I look very professional sometimes, especially when I am operating. . . . Do you remember how I quaked when you said, 'I must take off that colored girl's finger.' Her mother brought her to the house for you to see her finger . . . I thought I would never be able to put a knife on human flesh." She described her task for the next day at 12:30, to remove a tumor from a woman's back, so large "the tumor cannot be covered by one hand."

After a year as intern at her alma mater, she was an assistant teacher of anatomy in Baltimore at the Woman's Medical College, simultaneously practicing private medicine in that city. In 1887 she came back to North Carolina after receiving her license in 1885 from the Maryland Board of Medical Examiners. In her class of 100 candidates, she was the only woman and earned the

Mecklenburg County native Dr. Annie Lowrie Alexander (1864–1929) returned to Charlotte in 1887 after medical education in Philadelphia and New York, to become the first woman licensed to practice medicine in the South. She served on the staffs of Charlotte hospitals and World War I's Camp Greene, was the Queens College physician, and funded the education of numerous young women. Her patients primarily were women and children seen at her home and office at 410 North Tryon Street.

COURTESY OF THE ROBINSON-SPANGLER CAROLINA ROOM, PUBLIC LIBRARY OF CHARLOTTE AND MECKLENBURG COUNTY highest grade. Later she did postgraduate work in the New York Polyclinic. One report says that some of Dr. Annie's relatives, when they learned of her intention to be a physician, refused to speak to her or even to say her name.

The newspaper notice appeared in 1887 in Charlotte, "A nice young female physician, Miss Annie Lowrie Alexander, has located in this city ready to practice among women and children and consult about female disorders generally. . . . She has been educated in the best medical schools of the country. Her office is at Mrs. Lathan's nearly opposite the post office." Two years later she made a 10-dollar down payment on a house at 410 North Tryon Street where she lived, kept office hours, and later added rooms so patients could stay over. By 1900, her elderly parents had moved from their family home in Cornelius where Dr. Annie grew up, and joined her on North Tryon Street. Her patient records available in archives show that her patients were women and children. Dr. Annie served on the staffs of Presbyterian and St. Peter's Hospitals and was for 23 years the physician for Charlotte's Presbyterian College for Women (later Queens College).

But her early days were not easy ones according to an essay in her handwriting in 1900: "There are eight women practicing in the state, one of whom is a negro." Perhaps referring to her own experience, she wrote: "This pioneer woman in North Carolina was received with cold indifference by the professions and open curiosity by the laity. . . . It was more than two years before she was self-supporting."

She states that there was great opposition to a woman doctor's being admitted to the professional associations. "When her name was read out as having passed the examination successfully, she quietly walked up to the desk and signed the constitution and payed [sic] the fee. The members were astonished into silence or their southern galantry [sic] forbade their further action in the matter."

Dr. Annie's speeches and essays praise women's involvement in progressive clubs and civic reform. She wrote in the 1920s, "Women nowadays . . . can no more be withheld from her public duty than she can be exempt from taxes." She was convinced that "hospitals, asylums, prison reforms, and reformatories need and have the influence of woman's power. Women through Women's Clubs, Civic Leagues, Betterment Associations, Settlement Associations have done great good in civic improvement in city, town and country parks, settlement work, schools, nature study, social aid, educational work, and municipal reform."

During World War I, when Charlotte housed an army training camp at Camp Greene, she was appointed acting surgeon and became a first lieutenant in the army working for the U.S. Health Service. In this capacity she held medical inspection of thousands of local schoolchildren and discovered a large number of cases of trachoma in one city school. Those children were immediately removed from school and treated, preventing permanent eye damage and further contagion.

She remained single and assisted in the education of many nieces and nephews. Records also reveal her underwriting the medical education of young Chinese women to become physicians in 1920–22. A letter in 1920 from the executive secretary of the executive committee of the Foreign Missions of the Presbyterian Church U.S. thanks her and states, "you will have the joy of training a competent young woman for what I trust will be a magnificent service in China."

Although Dr. Annie was only an honorary member of the North Carolina Medical Society and of the Southern Medical Society, she apparently proved herself in her hometown. In Charlotte beginning in 1909, she served the first of several terms as president of the Mecklenburg Medical Society and gave medical reports to their gatherings as other physicians did, also serving as vice president of the Women's Physicians of the Southern Medical Association. As an Alexander, she also was a member, as prominent Charlotte women often were, of the Daughters of the American Revolution and the United Daughters of the Confederacy (UDC). She was noted for her "femininity, gentle manners and cultured womanhood." In 1929, at age 65, she died of pneumonia contracted from a patient. Her obituary described "a demureness and a humility, a seeking of not her own that glorified her in the esteem of her people."

One of Dr. Annie's continuing involvements had been as physician and board member of the Florence Crittenton Home, living out her contention that "it is only through organization that any great reform can be done, and the public conscience can only be aroused through organized effort."

Charlotte's Crittenton Home's earliest name was "The Home for Fallen Women" and its goal was to provide shelter for unwed girls who became pregnant. At first, girls averaging 18 years of age were sent to homes outside

Charlotte and payment made for an assistance fee and railroad expenses. In 1903, a young woman died in Charlotte after swallowing crushed glass in desperation over her situation and this event precipitated local efforts to help and provide for such women.

After visiting the girl in the hospital just before her death, Charlotte newspaper reporter Isaac Irwin Avery challenged Charlotteans: "Fallen women! These are the human beings that the Florence Crittenton Mission wishes to save by establishing a rescue home in this city. The charity undertakes a task desperately hard, for since man was born he has placed furthest from redemption women who have sinned. . . . If you would reform a man you pat him on the back and make him sit at your table; but you would visit a fallen woman secretly, and you would consider yourself good if you kept reproach and lashing pity from showing in your eyes. Adopt a new plan here, give the unfortunates a kindness that does not patronize and a sympathy that is not feigned. . . . If you are going to do this hazardous thing, then, in God's name, go the limit in love."

Author and teacher Rose Leary Love recalled seeing girls near her own neighborhood of Brooklyn, white girls who had become prostitutes and were subjects of public scorn and curiosity by both black and white neighbors. In her memoir of early twentieth-century uptown streets in Second Ward, Love recalls that her mother, a teacher at Myers Street School, and her lawyer father warned their children about Springs Alley, advising never to go near this alley or pass through it. "But when we went to the corner grocery," she writes, "we would often see some of these unfortunate young white women who had come to buy at the store. Most of them looked to be quite young and were often very pretty. They were always dressed in expensive negligees or some other fancy dress. Cosmetics were usually applied too heavily to their faces and nearly all of them had a white poodle dog trailing behind them. They often gave you a friendly smile, but they seldom spoke to you. We were told that one or more of the most lavishly decorated homes belonged to the madam or the person who seemed to be in charge of the younger ones." When one of these girls or any unmarried girl became pregnant, she faced a serious dilemma.

Charlotte's Crittenton Home was one of many organized after a visit by Charles Crittenton, who established such a home in 1883 in New York City as a memorial to his daughter who died at age four. But in 1903 and for many decades after, the attitude toward unwed mothers was one of shame and ostracism. Avery described naïve young women who arrived by train hoping to get a job or connect with a cousin who may have already left town. Such girls frequently disappeared, he said, into "Springs Alley" where their lives turned into despair. Not surprisingly, no such address is listed in the city directory of that era.

The Charlotte Crittenton group built a large house in 1905 at 523 North McDowell Street at the corner of East Ninth Street. "Our aim is to give shelter and protection to young girls when the first misstep is made, in order to help them reconstruct their lives; to keep the mother and baby together, and to send them from the Home with an equipment and attitude that will make them worthwhile citizens." The girls received medical treatment, prenatal care, and training in baby care and home economics. Immediately after the home's opening, applications came to fill all spaces available. The home received very few gifts of money, but lots of clothes and supplies. So many dignitaries attended its opening and crowded onto the speakers' platform, the platform fell at what had formerly been called the "Home for Fallen Women." The location served until the 1940s when the home moved to a site adjacent to Charlotte Memorial Hospital. The original building became the Hotel Alexander, one of the few places where black entertainers, such as Louis Armstrong, could stay when visiting Charlotte.

Another extremely beneficial institution had its origins about this same time. In the decade prior to 1900, Charlotteans interested in reading and literature formed a subscription library above a bookstore in the center of town at 22 South Tryon Street, the books available to persons who would pay 50 cents a month. Librarian Bessie Lacy Dewey was a primary fixture as hostess, keeping it open even during evenings, "so that a pleasant place of resort may always be accessible to members." An early assistant to Dewey compared the atmosphere to "one of those famous London literary clubs where visitors would come in for a book and remain to talk with their literary friends for hours . . . those present would vie in recognizing quotations and the [Shakespearean] characters quoted." When Dewey died, eight upper-class women who had been the library's regular patrons tried to collect overdue fees and contributions to pay the library's debts, but not until alderman Thomas S. Franklin garnered support in New York from the Andrew Carnegie Corporation, did the library get on solid footing.

Part of the agreement with Carnegie, who generously funded the building and some operating fees, was the requirement that the city provide a public library to serve blacks. Aldermen in 1904 bought a lot at the corner of Brevard and East Second Streets, in the heart of Charlotte's vigorous black neighborhood of Brooklyn. Lydia Schencks was appointed librarian for the new, brick 2,500-square-foot building. This well-used library was surrounded by several black churches and black professionals' businesses and homes. At the large, classical library for whites uptown at the corner of East Sixth and North Tryon Streets, Annie Smith Ross was the first librarian. She had studied library work in Atlanta and incorporated the radical idea of creating separate adult and children's reading areas. She helped to organize and served as the first president of the North Carolina Library Association, bringing its first conference to Charlotte in 1904, writes Pat Ryckman in her history of the Charlotte library.

Among the "radical" organized diversions around 1900, book clubs were quite popular. These study groups, which were organized and attended separately by both black and white women, usually met in the daytime while husbands were away at work and while maids, housekeepers, or relatives tended the children. Following a national trend, they met in members' homes and had a prepared program leader and presentation on history, art, or literature followed by lunch or by afternoon refreshments. In one, the hostess had to restore order by ringing a silver dinner bell to quiet the talking ladies. Officers were elected, the annual monthly program topics were chosen, and this data was sometimes printed in small booklets for distribution. Copies of these and some of the early minute books can be found in the Robinson-Spangler Carolina Room of Charlotte's main public library.

The secretary of one of these book clubs wrote that if you looked out the window you would see "upon the hours of three or four, here and there, some women with quick and interested steps wending their way to the elegant home of Mrs. L.C. Johnston." A few members were in their teens, many in their early 30s and some older.

A 1902 edition of the *Charlotte News* and *The Times Democrat* lists names of book clubs: Virginia Dare Book Circle, Over the Tea Cups, Les Lettres, and the Grace King (after a popular southern novelist of the day whose theme was portrayal of both black and white women). The earliest Charlotte book club, the Cranford (begun in 1892, and still active more than a century later), seems to have adopted its name from a popular novel *Cranford* by British novelist and humanitarian Elizabeth Gaskell, whom contemporaries classed with the Brontes and George Eliot. Other book clubs were named the Eclectic (1894), Sorosis (1896), Athenae, May Afternoon, and Bessie Dewey.

The Virginia Dare historian notes that "even more than its social aspect, they valued planned study." But it was also true, she says, "Women know how to talk, not only about something, and a talkative woman never pauses at any social gathering. But whoever saw a dozen men make conversation out of nothing?" And in the early 1900s when many of these book clubs began, there were serious political concerns as well. "Women could not vote at the time, but they made their opinions known and were not without influence." One Virginia Dare club secretary recorded one member's departure to New York to study art and two others who left to become missionaries. The 1902 listing also chronicles missionary societies, a married women's club, and several clubs named for days of the week.

Employment options for Charlotte's young middle- or upper-class white women at the time were primarily missionary, teacher, nurse, wife, or mother. Bloss Lucas, who was unmarried, taught china ware painting in a studio behind her home. Single young women over 25, who were often called spinsters, remained at home, and, as was expected of unmarried daughters, nursed family members and elderly parents. There were few other options, so book clubs were adventurous diversions in the days before autos, radio, or television, a time when travel usually meant bicycle, horse-drawn cart or buggy, or train. *Cranford Profiles* note that one member and her husband spent Sunday afternoons memorizing the shorter catechism.

For black women and men who were barred from most parks, restaurants, and public entertainments, church and neighborhood were the focus of activity. Rose Leary Love writes that "church entertainments and church programs of a more intellectual order helped provide the people with wholesome bits of recreation and information."

At book club meetings in white neighborhoods, Convere Myers Jones always carried out her program theme in "décor and refreshments with clever interpretation" delighting guests with her "expression and flair." After her study of England and its cathedrals, members found their lunch places marked with a miniature cathedral. At another meeting, each found a hand-painted picture of her own home at her plate. When they studied Verdi, she invited musicians to come and perform. Once she recorded as secretary how "two pretty angels came bearing Christmas fruit cakes and delicious homemade wine." And there is the Cranford story of little Edna, age eight, who calls, "Mother, there's a lady downstairs to see you. She asked for you by name, so I put her in the front room." After greeting the visitor, Edna's mother scolded her, "Edna, my friends are 'ladies.' Book salesmen or anyone else is a woman."

Another story included in the Cranford Club history describes member Mabel Wright Dawson, who taught piano. She was unable to find help to "do the floors" in time for the piano recital. In desperation, she said, "God, if you will send me someone to do the floors, I will give up my glass of sherry at lunch." Four days before the piano recital for her pupils at her home, a man came by seeking work. The floors done, she gave up sherry, and switched to port.

In 1914, the Virginia Dare women studied the just-opened Panama Canal and in 1920–21, just after the passage of the Nineteenth Amendment giving women the right to vote for the first time, voting and women were hot topics: "Heroines of Modern Progress" (Susan B. Anthony, Jane Addams and Mary Baker Eddy); "Beautiful Women" (Cleopatra and Mary Stuart); "Women Before the Public Eye" (Madame Marie Curie and Lady Astor); "Heroines of Shakespeare;" and "Women in Literature." In 1933, the topics included "Emancipation" and "Outstanding Women in Politics?" The sarcastic question mark was part of the latter program's title. And every year or so thereafter, there was at least one program concerned with women's rights.

Separate institutions and activities for blacks and whites had been the custom prior to 1900 in Charlotte as in the rest of the South, but men, women, and children of both races were to become far more divided with the passing of the Jim Crow laws around 1900 in North Carolina and also in other states. In this action, legislation required a whole series of degrading changes and division for blacks who had formerly had civic freedoms and privileges, such as voting and office holding as well as open seating in buses or trains.

Women, regardless of color, still could not vote. Although organized efforts had begun in 1848 at Seneca Falls, New York, women who owned considerable property, held responsible positions in many benevolent organizations, wrote important books which were read and acclaimed nationwide, still were not able to go to the ballot box on election day to cast their votes for local or national officials. Author Edith Wharton could not vote. Nor could scientist Marie Curie who won the Nobel Prize in 1903. Suffrage efforts were still linked in people's minds with the abolition efforts of 50 years before when women organized, traveled, and spoke to aid the anti-slavery cause.

CHAPTER TWO

*I*t is hard to imagine that a woman like Susie Harwood Van Landingham of New England, Atlanta, and now Charlotte, an educated, wealthy business-woman in her own right, was not allowed to vote for public office anywhere in America in 1907. This was the year she arrived in Charlotte with her new husband John Van Landingham, a well-connected Charlotte cotton broker and former business manager of *The Charlotte Observer*.

Susie Van Landingham (ca. 1867–1937) had owned and operated the Majestic Hotel on Peachtree Street in Atlanta from the late 1880s until the early 1900s. She had been YWCA president in Atlanta from the late 1880s until the early 1900s where the YW focused on training and counseling young women in health and legal matters. In Charlotte, she kept her Atlanta contacts and became involved in cultural, church, charity, and patriotic activities, particularly with the Red Cross and as a leader in the group to determine the relocation site for the U.S. Mint building. At its new location, it would become the Mint Museum of Art.

Van Landingham's local, state, and national activities with the DAR led to her role as speaker at numerous convocations and dedications of historic markers, often funded and placed by the DAR. She was a charter member of the Mecklenburg DAR chapter, the oldest chapter in the state. Her speeches and essays are collected in her book, *Glowing Embers*, in which she writes of women, political ethics, historical figures, North Carolina literature, southern culture, and suffrage. Her talk on "Civic Responsibility" applauded and publicized the view of Frenchman Max O'Rell, who proposed a new coat of arms with this motto for the United States: "Make way for the women." O'Rell declared "the most interesting woman in the world is the American woman . . . free, easy, perfectly natural. There is not in the world a woman to match her in a drawing-room. They are clever, they can talk, they can think . . . are original and superbly independent."

Van Landingham also praised the addition of educational institutions for women in Charlotte and North Carolina such as the new State Normal and Industrial College in Greensboro to train young women for jobs, later to be called Women's College, and subsequently UNC Greensboro. With the expansion of business and business machines such as the telephone and typewriter, young women were flocking to urban areas such as Charlotte, leaving the farm and large families of siblings not far behind.

To educate these young women early in the century, Charlotte's colleges included Elizabeth College (1896–1915), Presbyterian College for Women (which moved from uptown and became Queens College in 1914), and King's Business College (beginning in 1901) with commercial and business courses for both sexes. Young black women attended Scotia Seminary (founded by Presbyterians in 1867 in nearby Concord, North Carolina) where many were trained as teachers. Scotia later became Barber-Scotia College (1932) and was subsequently affiliated with Johnson C. Smith University, whose president for a time served both institutions. Many young, white Baptist daughters rode the train east to attend the new Baptist Female University in Raleigh (later Meredith College) when it began in 1899. Young Episcopalians attended Saint Mary's School in Raleigh (founded 1842).

Generations of young women in the nineteenth century had traveled to learn at Salem Female Academy, which was the earliest academy for educating young women in the region, begun by the Moravians in Winston-Salem in 1802. It soon became one of the best schools for women in the South.

Just north of Charlotte but still in Mecklenburg County, a young woman lived at the turn of the century in the tiny college village of Davidson. Her father, William Joseph Martin, was a faculty member at Davidson College, a chemistry professor noted for his acute "ability to distinguish between essential and non essential matters." His daughter Mary took him as her mentor, according to biographer Emily Herring Wilson. Mary's mother, Letitia Costin Martin, was closely involved in the mission-minded Presbyterian Ladies Benevolent Society of their church and often invited Presbyterian missionaries to dine in their home. Mary admired the missionaries enormously, and as a child, decided to be one. She graduated from Statesville Female College 20 miles up the road. Returning home, she took some of the courses offered by the North Carolina Medical College, which operated privately in the town of Davidson. "They wouldn't let me study anatomy or go in dissecting rooms where the naked cadavers were lying about. It would have been highly unladylike," she said. She enrolled at the Woman's Medical College in Philadelphia, the only women's medical school in the country, graduated, interned, and served as a college physician. Returning to Davidson at the then-spinsterly age of 29 she met Eustace Sloop, who was completing a two-year medical course at the college. "I stopped calling him Sloop and began to call him 'Doctor.'" She had known him earlier as a student of her father's at parties at her parents' house. Both Sloop and Mary planned to be medical missionaries.

After her internship at the New England Hospital for Women and Children in Boston, Dr. Mary Martin worked for a year as the physician at Agnes Scott College in Atlanta. When Sloop finished his medical education at Jefferson Medical College in Philadelphia, they were married in 1908 in Blowing Rock. Immediately after the ceremony, they rode horseback to the mountain village of Plumtree where Sloop had recently set up practice. Their life became one of practicing medicine together, not in the foreign mission fields as they had initially expected, but in the rough and impenetrable wilderness of western North Carolina's mountains where there were no roads or trains, telephones or electricity, and certainly no hospitals. Fortunately, Mary was an experienced horsewoman and she said later, "we were both tough as pine knots." It would be a hard life most of the time, "primitive, often lonely, always challenging."

Dr. Mary Martin Sloop waited many nights for "Doctor" to come home drenched or frost-bitten on horseback. He would have been called to deliver a baby or perform surgery in a remote cabin high across mountains on slick paths which required fording numerous swift creeks. Often she went with him and they found the cramped, smoky cabins full of family and animals to be so dim and dangerous for surgery that they performed surgery outside under a tree. When he was away, she treated patients in the ramshackle office. Often patients arrived on makeshift stretchers or by oxcart. She wrote in 1957, looking back at her life, "Life was daring us. Life was dealing out the cards. I would pick up my hand and play it. And I'd have fun, too, doing it."

The acute needs of the mountain people, especially those of the children, for clothing, books, education, and manual training had been a constant concern of the Sloops in Plumtree. These worries continued when they moved their practice in 1911, closer to where most of their patients lived in the Linville Valley. Before long they had organized a school in Crossnore, and Mary wrote thousands of letters to her friends in Charlotte and elsewhere describing the children's needs for clothes, Sunday school supplies, and books. Soon boxes and trunks from her benevolent network of friends and family arrived. In time she organized the building of dormitories where mountain students could come and board and go to school. It became the well-known Crossnore School. She saw high school education as the only prevention for the very early marriages which were so prevalent.

Someone called her a "steam engine in skirts." She knew how to plan and present needs and have them accepted. For many years, she relentlessly raised funds and lobbied for a compulsory school law. She traveled many times to Raleigh to ask for roads into the backcountry for the extremely isolated counties, which had no access to any road. As funds finally came, the students and mountain people built the buildings themselves. And no one worked harder than Dr. Mary. She tapped her DAR friends who listed Crossnore as an "approved school" to receive funds, since Mary was from a DAR family. Several buildings were built by DAR funds. When the checks from the DAR arrived periodically, Mary declared them a "miracle and thanked her children for making it happen by their prayers." One of the DAR friends who helped Crossnore was Susie Harwood Van Landingham. The whole desperate effort was an early example of energetic and creative networking.

Eventually Crossnore School provided 11 grades of education by trained teachers nine months of the year. The school fostered the revival of weaving skills as a cottage industry for women to earn a livelihood. In her 40-year crusade, Dr. Mary Martin Sloop worked toward getting a state law passed to raise the compulsory age for school attendance to 16, and pressured the legislature and governor "to provide paved roads, modern agricultural assistance and training, and more effective law enforcement against moonshiners for Avery and adjoining counties." For her work, she was named American Mother of the Year. With author LeGette Blythe, she wrote her story as a book, *Miracle of the Hills*.

The clear call by Dr. Mary Martin Sloop and the direct conduit of aid received by Crossnore from women in the Carolinas, their churches, and organized societies, particularly from Charlotte, show the kind of remarkable power which these organized women could muster.

One of the large American forces for beneficial work was the Woman's Club. The Charlotte Woman's Club had a remarkable beginning. (Note that Woman, not Women, was the phrasing in these early days of the century. Woman was the term of choice, as in Elizabeth Cady Stanton's *The Woman's Bible* published in New York in two volumes 1895, 1898.)

For many years, Charlotte women's civic efforts were largely confined to church work or to the acceptable territory of family, friends, or close neighbors. Public attitudes considered women who engaged in public enterprises to be distinctly unfeminine and that such acts were unseemly for well-bred ladies. But with the national rise of the woman's club movement in the 1890s and early 1900s, North Carolina clubs for women saw rapid growth. Historian Glenda Riley writes that these clubs "focused on cultural and literary activities, the reform of social conditions within their own communities, the opening of new jobs and careers for women, and the achievement of woman suffrage. . . . Club women often saw the community as a larger home in which they functioned." Their benevolent efforts swept with the large broom of "municipal housekeeping."

Charlottean Agnes Wilkes read a letter from her sister in Hartford, Connecticut. "You should organize a Mother's Club," her sister insisted. When the sister visited, she helped organize a club to help young Charlotte mothers learn how to train their children physically, mentally, and spiritually. One woman, when asked to serve as club secretary and parliamentarian, was alarmed when the discussion turned to studying parliamentary procedure in order to set up and run the club properly, "Why, my husband would never let me belong to anything where they studied parliamentary law!" She did not return for four months.

In a few years, the scope of the group widened past issues of child training, specifically to work toward making Charlotte a better, safer place for raising children. *Observer* columnist Mrs. J.A. Yarbrough wrote that the women "felt the inner stirrings of undeveloped powers. . . . First tolerated as a passing fad, the club movement gained influence and respect," and reached a status of responsibility and usefulness.

After visiting woman's clubs in Ohio, Charlotte's prominent Mrs. F.C. Abbott told her Charlotte group, "There are health laws, school matters, and social influence which you should investigate and discuss. The purpose of right motherhood and fatherhood is to leave in the world a mortal better than its parent." So in 1901, the Study Club for Mothers enlarged its membership to 25 and formed the Charlotte Woman's Club. In 1903, it joined the North Carolina Federation of Women's Clubs. Such was the women's zeal, that E.D. Latta was persuaded to donate the land for a clubhouse. Tycoon James B. Duke and industrialist D.A. Tompkins gave donations to the club's work, solidifying its social and civic prominence and success.

On E.D. Latta's land gift, the Woman's Club built an outstanding two-story clubhouse at 1001 East Morehead Street seating 400. Architect Charles C. Hook designed it in appealing Italian Regency revival design. It served as an impressive setting for concerts, recitals, banquets, and speeches by national figures such as Eleanor Roosevelt, authors, and distinguished visitors throughout the twentieth century. Besides such events, the club's key contribution to the city and its citizens was fostering the birth of such organizations as the YWCA, PTA, Travelers' Aid Society, the North Carolina Federation of Music Clubs, and the League of Women Voters. The club established the first Charlotte kindergarten, home economics programs in public schools, brought the first public health nurses to Charlotte, and gave vital support to the public library and to the creation of the Mint Museum of Art.

Of major benefit to young women who arrived in Charlotte to work but had no place to stay was the founding of the YWCA in 1902. The Woman's Club with Mrs. Walter Liddell as president, organized its beginning. Their intention was to open a boarding department for young women away from home. This first YWCA residence for working women opened on West Trade Street and moved to East Trade Street in 1914.

Other examples of the club's ongoing work were providing scholarships for female high school graduates, creating a loan closet of wheelchairs and hospital beds for families of invalids, donating books to penitentiaries, raising funds to conquer tuberculosis, and staffing the World War I and II bus and railway aid stations for servicemen and travelers. Later efforts included cancer control programs and services to needy families and children. Historian Dan Morrill wrote of the Woman's Club's vital emergence, "While retaining the refinement and grace associated with womanhood, the members committed themselves to a posture of public advocacy."

One Charlottean, Laura Holmes Reilley (1861–1941), became so well known for her work in woman's clubs on the local, state, and national level that she was the first North Carolina woman to be listed in *Who's Who in America*. A St. Louis native, she and her husband settled in Charlotte in 1890. She raised six children as well as public consciousness. Her concern with politics, history, and culture along with her leadership abilities led her to the early presidency of the Woman's Club (1903–8, 1922–24), and on to national offices in that organization. But voting rights were her primary interest. She was an organizer of the North Carolina Suffrage Association, a charter member of the Equal Suffrage League, and was appointed by Governor Locke Craig to the Southern Suffrage Conference in New Orleans in 1914 where she was elected vice president.

And like most well-connected prominent women of the time, she also rose in the ranks of the DAR, the Colonial Dames, the Society of Mayflower Descendants, and the Mint Museum of Art. She organized locally the Needlework Guild of America. Concerned with the new medium of the movies, she was first president and an organizer of the Better Films Committee of Charlotte, and a member of the advisory committee for the participation of women in the New York World's Fair in 1939.

At this time, concern for child labor issues was a natural issue for churchwomen, who pushed for legislative protection of thousands of women and child laborers in the southern textile and tobacco industries. Mill owners and industrialists such as D.A. Tompkins and publisher David Clark argued that parents should decide if and when their children should work, not the federal government. Strong national publicity appeals to farm workers strengthened the opposition to anti-child labor legislation. But a child labor law took effect in 1917. Again in 1934, strikes locally failed, but the events, writes historian Thomas C. Hanchett, "helped Congress to pass the Fair Labor Standards Act in 1938 ending child labor and establishing a U.S. minimum wage." Both acts helped women, even though many were opposed.

Nationally, black woman's clubs were denied membership in the General Federation of Woman's Clubs. But black women in Charlotte often played out the traditional female role of "morals keepers" within their own communities. Many black women worked full-time to help support their families, often taking in laundry on a regular basis from client families or working six or more days a week as a cook, nurse, or domestic for white families.

One black woman who rose from the ranks to national prominence was Mary McLeod Bethune, who was in the Charlotte area as a student at Scotia College. The daughter of slaves, she was to become an important African-American leader and educator, president of the National Association of Colored Women and founder, in 1935, of the National Council of Negro Women. The council coordinated 20 national and 95 local organizations of approximately 850,000 African-American women looking out for their concerns during the New Deal. These programs advanced during the New Deal under Roosevelt addressed relief for women's economic problems and job training.

One of the skills most admired and in demand in Charlotte in the early 1900s was that of seamstress. An expert seamstress' work in creating dresses for ladies and children is well remembered by Charlotte families. In many cases, the seamstress would be scheduled to arrive at the family home, take fittings, and sometimes set up her sewing machine and stay several days until her work was done, or to take the work home and bring the new clothes back for final alterations. The selection of ready-to-wear clothing found in local stores was limited. Skilled seamstresses, both black and white, were much sought after.

Floretta D. Gunn in a remembrance published in *The Charlotte Observer*, recalls seamstresses who were her neighbors on North Myers Street in First Ward in the 1920s. A black seamstress hired by a white family "was given car fare of five cents each way and was paid about two dollars a day to make as many garments as possible. Other families took their material to seamstresses' homes. We lived next door to Daisy Jones. We watched a surrey pull up in front of her house. The chauffeur helped the white customer to the gate and waited until she had completed her business with Mrs. Jones. My sister and I proudly wore the necklaces of empty spools of thread strung on a cord given us by Mrs. Daisy." Popular catalogs from Sears Roebuck, McCall's, and Montgomery Ward had dress patterns and printed sketches of clothing which listed the type of cloth, trimmings, and thread suggested.

Surreys brought customers at regular intervals to another well-known seamstress, Ms. Jennie Pethel, at her home. "Mrs. Sally Hoskins made clothes for Mrs. Stonewall Jackson. Mrs. Hoskins was told that if she wished to attend the funeral [of Mrs. Jackson], she would have to sit in the balcony of the First Presbyterian Church. She went."

Teacher and author Rose Leary Love, who grew up in Charlotte's Brooklyn neighborhood in Second Ward, wrote about the skill of her own neighbors, housewives who were "specialists with the needle, and people from the best sections of the city were thrilled when they could secure their sewing assistance. Some seamstresses went out to sew; others had the work brought to them. I remember Bertha, our next door neighbor, who could make the tiniest stitches and do the most beautiful smocking I have ever seen. Women from some of the most prosperous homes in Charlotte would beg her to make their baby clothes and children's dresses.

Seamstresses proved so vital to the social success and self-esteem of Charlotte women and girls that those who possessed sewing skills and the fine art of dressmaking were in great demand. Cecilia Wilson, a seamstress, was well known for her dress designs around 1900.

"At one time, most mothers in Brooklyn seldom thought of buying store-bought clothes for their children. Sewing machines would hum late into the night as mothers made clothes for the families."

Equally in demand were those women who hired out as cooks. Leary writes of many black women who worked as cooks "in private homes in the city and in large institutions such as hotels, schools, and hospitals. Some had special training. Others had been trained at the feet of their mothers. Their training, coupled with their innate ability to season and beautify foods, made their services in great demand."

CHAPTER THREE

*E*arly in the twentieth century, two exceptional young women chose to follow a novel path within an esteemed male profession. In doing so, they gained a strong, respected foothold in public life. Two female lawyers, who were among the first in North Carolina, had set up their practices separately and at different times in Charlotte. The first was a Mecklenburg daughter, Julia McGehee Alexander (1876–1957). She was admitted to the bar in 1914 after her schooling at Mary Baldwin College and then at UNC Chapel Hill where she studied law and was president of her class. She continued her studies at the University of Michigan and at Columbia University Law School in New York. She became accustomed to breaking new ground. She was the second woman to be licensed to practice law in North Carolina, the first woman to enter independent law practice in the state, and the first Mecklenburg woman to serve as a representative to the North Carolina House of Representatives (1925–27).

Her law office in 1916 was at the popular Latta Arcade, subsequently on West Third Street, and in the 1930s, in her combined home and office at 600 North Tryon Street. So passionate was she about history that she wrote many articles including a history of Mecklenburg County as well as two books, *Charlotte in Pictures and Prose* (1906) and *Mothers of Great Men* (1916). In writing the latter, she noted the difficulties in finding sources relating the lives of her subjects, the mothers of George Washington, John Ruskin, John and Charles Wesley, and St. Augustine.

Although Alexander was defeated in her run for mayor, she must have done a fine job in the State House because Charlotte elected another woman to succeed her. Carrie McLean (1873–1948), Charlotte's second female lawyer, was elected a North Carolina state representative (1927–29) and distinguished herself by introducing a bill to foster the merger of the municipal governments of Charlotte and Mecklenburg County, an idea whose fruition in the year 2000 had still not come. She worked successfully against a bill to criminalize the teaching of evolution, which neighboring Tennessee had enforced with the sensational Scopes trial in 1925.

To attain her law license, she read law when she was in her 40s, but she made the best score in her 1918 exam class of almost 100 applicants. She later studied at Columbia University, practiced with the law firm of Tillett and Guthrie, and then practiced alone. Male colleagues often asked her to write briefs for their cases. She was a charter member of the Charlotte Business and Professional Women's Club, and was in 1925 the first woman president of the Mecklenburg County Bar. Alexander and McLean were only two of an impressive array of talented women on the Charlotte scene in that era.

Anna Forbes Liddell no doubt raised Charlotteans' eyebrows when she preferred to be called Forbes instead of Anna. With Suzanne Bynum of Asheville, she organized in Charlotte in 1913 the first meeting of the Equal Suffrage League in North Carolina. A year later she was on the suffragettes' float which processed with both decorum and defiance in the annual May 20th parade celebrating the Mecklenburg Declaration of Independence. She was, after all, from one of Charlotte's first families. Her father presided over the Liddell Company, manufacturing textile machinery in extensive machine shops along North Tryon Street where Liddell Street remains to this day.

Suffrage Float. On May 20, 1914, these daring young Charlotte women advocated "Votes for Women." Their plucky political statement rode among many traditional floats, such as Ivey's and the Boy Scouts in the annual celebrations and parade honoring the Mecklenburg Declaration of Independence of May 20, 1775. At the time of this parade, no American woman, white or black, had the right to vote although suffragettes had campaigned for over 50 years. Six years after this photograph, the Nineteenth Amendment to the U.S. Constitution granted votes for women.
COURTESY OF MUSEUM OF THE NEW SOUTH

Forbes Liddell was a writer who, after attending Charlotte's Queens College, wrote freelance for *The Charlotte Observer* and *The New York Evening Post*. She and her friends edited a special suffrage issue of the *Observer*. Leaving Charlotte in 1915, she graduated with honors from UNC in 1918, moved to New York City to work in publishing for McGraw-Hill, and in 1924 was one of the first two women to receive a doctor of philosophy degree at UNC Chapel Hill. She became a distinguished professor of philosophy at Florida State and a lifelong advocate of women's rights. In her wheelchair in later years, she appeared at a rally in 1978 to admonish Florida legislators for not ratifying the Equal Rights Amendment.

Young Gladys Tillett didn't make headlines the day she marched in the parade down Tryon Street carrying the suffragist flag. In fact, her name wasn't even in the newspapers, although she was from a very prominent North Carolina family and not a Charlottean at the time. That day, May 20, 1914, Gladys Avery was a college junior, soon to be student body president at North Carolina College for Women (later UNC Greensboro).

The Charlotte Observer reported that the parade was "the most spectacular feature" of the annual anniversary celebration of the Mecklenburg Declaration of Independence, Charlotte's favorite holiday for speeches, dignitaries, and hoopla. The parade even outshone noted attendees such as U.S. Vice President Thomas R. Marshall and his wife who "added her amiable charms to the magnificent occasion." Decorated floats followed a military guard, numerous bands, Boy Scouts, and students, all led by mounted police and the pre-eminent Queen Charlotte float drawn by six horses.

Sandwiched in between floats representing Colonial Dames, Ivey's department store, the Daughters of the Confederacy, and the Mecklenburg Chapter of the DAR, was the yellow and white float of the North Carolina Equal Suffrage League. Atop the float were "Miss Suzanne Bynum, organizer of the league standing with suffrage banner in hand; Miss Julia McNinch at table writing; and Misses Mary Belle Palmer and Anna Forbes Liddell, Bessie Simmonds, Catherine McLaughlin, and Jane Stillman." Twenty-three-year-old Gladys probably walked alongside or behind with her banner, accompanied by other brave friends. The climate for woman's suffrage in 1914 was unfriendly. Woodrow Wilson, elected U.S. President in 1912 and in 1916, had used his position against woman's suffrage as part of his campaign platform. Charlotte lawyer Cameron Morrison, elected North Carolina governor in 1920, did likewise. Both candidates were successful. The right to vote was an unpopular idea even though women had been working actively and quite publicly throughout the country for equal voting rights since the pre-Civil War Seneca Falls Conference in New York in 1848.

But Gladys Avery of Morganton had conviction, spunk, and a heritage of political activism. In colonial times, her paternal great-grandfather Waightstill Avery was Charlotte's first lawyer, a framer of the Mecklenburg Resolves in 1775, and the first attorney general of North Carolina. Her maternal great-

Gladys Avery Tillett (1892–1984) of Morganton carried the suffragist flag as a college girl in Charlotte's 1914 parade, then came to live in the city in 1919. From a family of political leaders for generations, she was a leader in her city, state, and nation as a Democratic Party activist in Charlotte, founder of the Mecklenburg League of Women Voters (LWV) in 1920 and head of the state LWV, the first female speaker to address the Democratic Party National Convention, a presidential appointee to the U.N.Commission on the Status of Women, and president of ERA United in 1975.

grandfather was a state senator, her lawyer father was a judge and later a North Carolina Supreme Court justice. Both parents were keen on politics and often took Gladys with them to Washington to observe Congress in session. Politics was the family menu for dinner table talk.

She also had a mentor. Harriet Elliott was Gladys' college history and political science professor, and Elliott invited her own mentor, prominent suffragist Dr. Anna Howard Shaw to speak on the Greensboro campus. When Governor Locke Craig spoke at Gladys' college where she was the first student body president, he addressed Gladys directly saying he knew that "this lovely young lady is not for votes for women." She covered her smile with her white lace handkerchief, but that night she and classmates marched and burned the governor in effigy.

Gladys' college president was a progressive thinker himself and sent her and two other students to New York City to participate in settlement house work. This was social reform work popular with young, educated progressives of the era, particularly young upper-class women. He told the students before they left, "Girls, you're going up north, and they may be more assertive than you are, and whatever you are asked to do, show them how well you can do it. You are all good executives." Gladys recalled, "No matter what they asked us to do, we did it." On campus Gladys had organized the first Student Government Association. Her life as an ace organizer had just begun.

After graduating with a degree in political science and quickly earning another bachelor's degree at UNC Chapel Hill, she married Charlotte lawyer Charles W. Tillett, Jr. in 1917 and settled in Charlotte. Tillett was from a prominent family and his father was a Charlotte lawyer of note. In Charlotte, she pitched right in working to organize suffragists and she joined her husband's enthusiasm for the Democratic party.

The decade was a yeasty time for suffragettes. Energetic local and state groups led the ferment as the National American Woman's Suffrage Association (NAWSA) became the nation's largest voluntary organization. It encompassed the voices of two million women across America, pushing for federal suffrage legislation. In 1917 Alice Paul of Massachusetts, who formed the National Woman's party, initiated 24-hour pickets of the White House. The women were arrested, jailed, and force-fed to prevent hunger strikes. This created startling headlines. Their signs in front of Wilson's White House read "Kaiser Wilson," "How Long Must Women Wait for Liberty!" Perhaps most challenging to a nation just entering World War I in Europe was the women's ardent claim on several signs which read "Democracy Begins at Home." This countered the slogan promoting entry into World War I, "Make the World Free for Democracy." The disturbing headlines showing riots, arrests, and hunger strikes of imprisoned women brought strong pressure of public opinion against Wilson.

President Wilson changed his mind. Suffrage strategies finally paid off thanks to highly public marches, speeches, and picketing. Some Congressional candidates had been defeated in their home states because of their anti-suffrage position and many wives of male voters kept up a staunch pro-vote lobby at their dinner tables. When Wilson suggested that Democrats in the House of Representatives vote for the suffrage amendment, "one very ill representative was carried in on a stretcher to cast his vote, while another came from the deathbed of his suffragist wife to cast his," writes historian Glenda Riley. The tally had one vote over the necessary two-thirds majority needed. Women streamed into the halls singing "Praise God from whom all blessings flow." Soon the Senate also passed the measure.

When the Nineteenth Amendment to the Constitution, which guaranteed to women the right to vote, was ratified and became law in 1920, Gladys Avery Tillett (1892–1984) voted for the first time in a national or local election. That same year she organized the Charlotte chapter of the League of Women Voters, the first county-wide league in North Carolina. She became its president and later state president of the organization committed to social reform, education of woman as citizens, and the elimination of laws which discriminated against women. Author Emily Herring Wilson writes of Tillett, "What she joined, she organized and led."

In 1924, she became campaign chair for lawyer Carrie McLean of Mecklenburg County, who in 1927 was the second woman from this county elected to the North Carolina legislature. Tillett's attendance at the first national meeting of the League of Women Voters in Baltimore taught her to "Get in the political party of your choice and work for the things you believe in." At home while raising a family, she worked door-to-door in her precinct encouraging women to register to vote. The Baltimore sessions had taught her how to hold public candidates' forums, so she organized the first such candidates' meetings focusing on a Charlotte mayoral race. When she herself ran for vice chair of the Mecklenburg County Democratic party, the party chairman objected, saying "But Gladys, your Daddy was a judge!" At that time, for a southern lady, this was considered quite sufficient. Gladys knew better.

In the South, quiet techniques worked best, and Gladys was born to them. Always a lady, she took her father's advice and lived by it: "Be pleasant, be patient, and be persistent." Working politically as a female in her affluent neighborhood among prominent upper-class residents and in other sections of Charlotte, she learned to tailor her approach. In Myers Park she served sherry and A&P store cinnamon swirls to society ladies. But her courteous southern manner did not cloak her consistent message of equality: "No woman is free until all women are free. . . . The land of the free refers to men and the home of the brave to women." After serving as an organizer and Democratic party official, in 1936 and 1940 she took a post as nationwide director of the speakers bureau of the women's division of the Democratic National Committee, finding hundreds of outstanding speakers for women's groups all over the country. In this way she became friends with Eleanor Roosevelt, exchanging letters and visiting her home in Hyde Park. Both women shared a fervent advocacy for human rights: Roosevelt, as international voyager and spokeswoman for her husband, President Franklin Delano Roosevelt, and for her own humanitarian causes; Gladys from the grassroots moving up into national circles. Once when Mrs. Roosevelt was in Charlotte, she heard Gladys Tillett was in the audience and she said, "I want Gladys" and she hiked to the balcony to see her.

When Gladys was introduced to FDR, the aide said, "Mr. President, I want to tell you what her husband said—that when you listed the campaign contributors and put them down, i.e. 'Mr. Casper Whitney, $2,000' etc., Mr. Tillett wanted you to put down as his contribution 'Charles W. Tillett, his wife.'" FDR laughed heartily. It was true. Because Charles Tillett, who was as interested in politics as Gladys and was a noted writer and lobbyist for bills, supported and encouraged her in far-flung ventures. One particular job needed Gladys in Washington D.C. one summer, so Gladys took their teen-age daughter Gladys to Washington with her and they completed the task together.

Eleanor Roosevelt was a consummate role model for many American women in Charlotte and elsewhere. This example from *Notable American Women: The Modern Period* shows why. "At a 1939 Birmingham meeting inaugurating the Southern Conference on Human Welfare, she placed her chair so that it straddled the black and white sides of the aisle, thereby confounding local authorities who insisted on segregation. She resigned in the same year from the Daughters of the American Revolution after they denied the black artist Marian Anderson permission to perform at Constitution Hall. Instead, and in part through Eleanor Roosevelt's intervention, Anderson sang to 75,000 people from the Lincoln Memorial."

Eleanor Roosevelt campaigned strongly for an anti-lynching bill and argued for desegregation in the armed services and defense employment. Americans either loved her or hated her, but her intrepid politics and sense of justice inspired women in Charlotte and beyond. Once opposed to suffrage for women, she came to embrace it and became for many "the first woman of the world." No wonder that Gladys Tillett looked to her as well as her professor as mentors in the period of the late 1930s and the busy decades to follow.

Mary Myers Dwelle (1891–1975) caught it from her parents, who took her to art galleries and talked about "what was best," instilling in the young girl a love of art and the beautiful (flowers, gardens, buildings, trees). When they lived on East Trade Street in a home that encompassed an entire block near McDowell Street, she recalls that her father, John Springs Myers, took "several of us for a Sunday afternoon ride in mother's surrey. He drove up Trade Street across Independence Square and on to the Post Office, with the branch U.S. Mint adjoining. He stopped in front of the Mint and said, 'That is a beautiful building! Shall we paint the house this shade?' It was a light olive-green then. 'Oh yes, Papa, let's do!' He traveled a lot and knew what was beautiful." The incident opened Mary Myers Dwelle's young eyes to architecture and color and lighted a spark which was to see fruition in an ambitious effort to save the Mint decades later and make it North Carolina's first museum of art.

Dwelle's father and her brother-in-law George Stephens developed Myers's 1,200 acres of farmland along Providence Road into Myers Park. Here Myers

Arts leader Mary Myers Dwelle (1891–1975) grew up in Charlotte when the U.S. Mint on West Trade, designed by William Strickland, was the town's handsomest, most important nineteenth-century building. When the federal government dismantled the Mint to enlarge the post office, Dwelle with lawyer Julia Alexander led efforts in 1932 toward relocation of the building's numbered pieces and its reconstruction as the first art museum in North Carolina, the Mint Museum of Art (opened 1936). Dwelle is shown with Gainsborough's portrait of Queen Charlotte of England, the city's namesake.

COURTESY OF MINT MUSEUM OF ART

incorporated the many hundreds of trees he had planted for pleasure along the sand clay roads of his farmland and in his own lawn. Dwelle's own sense of beauty and of historic preservation was called on one day in the 1930s when she hosted Lelia Mechlin, president of the American Federation of the Arts in Washington. Dwelle had arranged for her to address the Charlotte Woman's Club that day. Although it was sleeting, she took Mechlin to see the classical 1836 Mint building, which the federal government was in the process of demolishing to replace with a modern post office. As they looked, the roof was being torn off. Mechlin decided to change her speech topic and she spoke instead on the subject: "You Should Save That Building."

"That turned the wheel," said Dwelle. "We raised $200 at the luncheon— then $3, $10, $50. My mother said she didn't know what my father would think about me begging for money that way. But we got enough to pay for the stones. About $2,500 in all." Charlotteans recall how as schoolchildren, they gathered nickels and dimes. Lawyer Julia Alexander and many vocal citizens made speeches to rally support and gather funds. Soon leaders succeeded in buying the stones and other Mint materials which were numbered and stored. Dwelle aimed to get help from the New Deal and the federal WPA program, which had just been created to hire out-of-work citizens during the Great Depression. To do this, she traveled many times to Raleigh to see the woman in charge of WPA projects. The program finally provided labor to erect the building on donated land with donated assistance from Charlotte architect Miles Boyer. More funds had to be raised at a critical stage in the reconstruction, but the Mint Museum of Art opened in October 1936 in a region which was still in the throes of severe economic depression.

Dwelle continued her involvement with the Mint and in philanthropy toward art and artists. Her interest in Charlotte history propelled her to write two books about the life of Queen Charlotte of England (1744–1818) for whom the city of Charlotte is named, and another non-fiction book, *Round about in England*. *The Charlotte Observer* published several of her interesting, colorfully detailed accounts of life in late nineteenth and early twentieth century Charlotte. Until her death in 1975, Dwelle continued her public and behind-the-scenes work, which culminated in the 1968 naming of the main gallery at the Mint, the Mary Myers Dwelle Gallery. From her hospital room in 1970, she wrote librarian Mary Louise Phillips at the Public Library, "I have an idea that Charlotte would like an article on a Myers Park Cotton Plantation." In her home on Hempstead Place near the Mint, she preserved the original color of the old Mint building on the living room walls.

While Dwelle and Tillett were organizing and promoting worthy causes from affluent homes in prestigious Eastover and Myers Park, other concerns enveloped Eudora Blakeley, a young divorcee who returned home with her child to live with her parents in the lower Providence farm area. Her ex-husband did not have a job and could not help, so one morning in the early 1930s, Eudora set out for uptown Charlotte to find a job. This was a brave act in the middle of the Great Depression. In 1933, joblessness hit a record 25% of the labor market in the United States.

She landed a job at *The Charlotte News* as secretary to the publisher, but a cost-cutting effort merged her job with another woman's. "She had been working there a long time and I was young and inexperienced. So I went to the *Observer* to apply and I remember well insisting on applying to the publisher, which was unheard of. They had a personnel person and they said 'You go see him.'

"But I said 'I really want to see Mr. Johnson, the publisher, if I may.' And when Mr. Johnson asked me why I didn't go see Mr. Allen, I said, 'In this day and time, the only way to get what you want is to go see the person at the top.' He sort of liked that and he hired me. Not as his secretary then, but in the circulation department." Later she became the publisher's secretary for 19 years, married the sports editor, Wilton Garrison, and years later as Eudora Garrison, was well known as the *Observer's* food editor, Sunday columnist, and author of two cookbooks.

Life was different also in this era for the thousands of women and girls who worked in the Charlotte area's numerous cotton mills.

By the age of 17 and a half, Edna Pearl Yandell had quit school after the eighth grade, married, clerked in two drugstores, worked in three textile mills, and had become a skilled textile worker in the weave room of Charlotte's Louise Mill. That year, 1923, she moved to the Hoskins Mill operated by the Hoskins-Chadwick Company in northwest Charlotte at Gossett and Hoskins Road. She liked her job as smash hand and would remain in that work for several decades. She became quite skillful at "picking out" and "smashing" broken sections of cloth being woven on looms in the mill weave room. She liked setting up the cloth, "drawing" the broken threads for continued weaving on the looms. Her life is representative of the many young women who outnumbered men in Charlotte-area mills, and on whose backs the thriving 1920s and 1940–50s textile economy was built.

She recalls starting in a mill beside her father, working for no pay as he taught her the work. Then after a year, working 12-hour days and half-day Saturdays, she was a full-fledged cotton mill worker. At the Highland Park Mill in North Charlotte, her family lived in one of the many identical mill houses since both she and her husband had jobs in the mill. Wearing home-made gingham dresses made from cloth woven at the mill and purchased at the mill store, she attended Brady's school provided by the mill for children whose parents worked at the mill. In Charlotte, she learned and endured the term "linthead" because of the cotton lint which stuck in mill workers' hair.

When she married, her name became Edna Hargett. She had a baby in her eighteenth year and returned to 12-hour day millwork five weeks later. A black woman cared for her baby, did her housecleaning, cooking, washing and iron-ing, and handed the baby to her three times a day when at nine and 12 and three o'clock Hargett was allowed by the mill foreman to come home briefly to breast-feed the baby. "I wanted to have children," Hargett recalls, "but I didn't want to have one that quick."

Hargett recalled how an unmarried girl's pregnancy in the mill commu-nity made the girl an outcast. Speaking of a girl who had an illegitimate preg-nancy, she said, "Your parents didn't want you to speak to them or nothing. People didn't associate with them, because they'd disgraced." As a consequence of such disapproval, many young unmarried women must have, despite pres-sure from boyfriends, practiced restraint out of fear of shame and village dis-approval. Hargett recalls, "There was very few of them that had babies."

Without birth control, pacifiers, or disposable diapers, without running water, prepared baby foods or infant seats, and with only coal fireplaces or oil or wood stoves for heat or cooking, women's lives were difficult. The black woman who helped her stayed on with Hargett through the birth of two more sons until all three children were old enough to attend school. By the 1930s, Hargett recalls that officials shortened the work day to eight hours and at some point labor laws required that women workers have some semblance of a seat to sit on occasionally during the day, such as a cotton box or a wide belt strung between the looms. Not until the 1940s and the arrival of a union does Hargett recall official breaks for 15 minutes in their day, although she recounts girls lingering in the bathroom to tell lengthy jokes and stories. The foreman would

Textile mill worker Ida Warren Wallace, born 1893, worked in the weave room at the large cotton mill, the Highland Park #1 in North Charlotte. She lived nearby at 606 E. 15th Street. She stands beside her niece, Shirley Bass, about 1938 in the Highland Mill #1 neighborhood. Early twentieth-century women, children, and whole families, often including grandparents, uncles, and aunts worked in Charlotte-area mills and lived in mill villages surrounding them.

COURTESY OF MUSEUM OF THE NEW SOUTH

come and bang on the door to get them back to work. Before these breaks, they ate standing up, "eating with one hand and jerking the loom with the other."

By the 1930s, Hargett recalls that without a union or seniority, "You just worked when the boss man told you to work." Working eight hours a day, she still had a day's work at home when the children were in school and she no longer had help. "We'd come home and do a washing and had to wash on a board outdoors and boil your clothes and make your own lye soap. And then you'd have time to go visit the sick in the community." The drudgery continued. She got up at five because she had to be at work at six. "Then you had to wash your hands in an old wash basin because you didn't have water in the house. You had to carry your water from a pump two or three doors down. And in wintertime it was awful cold. We had electricity all through the week at night, but just one day a week, on Thursday, we was allowed to do our ironing . . . here at Hoskins in the 1930s."

Quilting bees. Corn huskings. Gathering to shuck a neighbor's harvested corn, white and yellow corn. "Every time you'd find a red ear, you'd get to kiss a girl." Hargett was not a quilter. Hargett's hand was damaged in the mill machinery, leaving her with a crooked finger. She described cotton mill work: "In a way it was dangerous, but it was work I enjoyed." She liked repairing a bad section of cloth, "a good feeling to know I done my job right."

The weave room was "a loud, noisy place, awful dusty and linty," and hot, very humid with windows that could not be raised. Humidity was desirable and was fostered to keep the cotton threads damp so they would run through the looms smoothly without breaking. This was a consistent climate in Piedmont Carolina mills and was accepted by the workers.

An unacceptable situation led Hargett to divorce her husband. Her family kept losing their mill housing because her husband would not show up for work for days at a time. Mill workers' entire families, often including aunts, uncles, grandparents and children, were expected to work in exchange for housing. "If you quit your job, you'd lose your house." Hargett's skill at her job was such, however, that as a single parent, the mill made exception for her and granted her a mill house. "They'd not let a woman hold a house. They let me." When her husband, whom she later divorced, quit his job, the foreman said, "Well, Bill you know you are going to have to empty the house." Bill said, "Yes, I have to hunt a place somewhere."

The mill official asked about Bill's wife, Edna Hargett, "Where's Edna at?"

He answered, "She's working over at Louise [the Louise Mill near Central Avenue and Hawthorne Lane]. The official, Mr. Quickard, said, "If you bring her over here and let her work for me, I'll give you a house." So she did and they got a house. "I could always find a job if I wanted to quit and go to another mill."

Hargett was asked if she chose to stop having children. She said there was no kind of birth control and people didn't talk about that at all. She said most mill people she knew had four or five children. She wanted a daughter, but couldn't have one. "I had trouble carrying the last one, and I was put to bed several times. So after that they said I'd have to have a clean hysterectomy, so I did."

Hargett felt she became an adult the day she married and left her parents' house. "I knowed Daddy couldn't fuss with me, scold and all . . . was my own boss then." She had always wanted to be a stenographer and had gone to night classes three nights a week when her parents lived in Charleston briefly. Because she had asthma, doctors advised her parents that she needed a drier climate than low-country South Carolina, so they moved to Burlington, where there was no place to continue her night courses in stenography. She worked in a dimestore, then her parents moved the family to Charlotte. "When I was 16, old enough to work around machinery, they put me in the mill." She was disappointed, but remembers, "It wasn't a matter of how I felt; it's what I had to do, but I had to work to help because the wages were so cheap then . . . around 16 dollars a week in the mill then."

A woman in the 1930s from nearby Belmont, North Carolina, just west of Charlotte, had responded to President Franklin Roosevelt's repeated radio invitation urging the American people to write to him. She wrote enclosing a pay stub totaling $4.20, her weekly earnings, asking Roosevelt, "How can we live on that?"

Hargett recalls that during the Great Depression of the 1930s, the mills ran on short time, often alternating workers, and "we worked every day we could." If you had money, "you could go to the store and get a pound of liver for a nickel and a loaf of bread for a nickel, a bag of potatoes for about a dime. . . . If you didn't have money, you had to do without. Everybody had a garden back then. So we all had to depend on our gardens. We made it through by raising most of it." The shorter hours had a lasting effect on mill workers, succeeding in accomplishing what years of agitation had failed, that of reducing the average number of hours worked for all workers and particularly women. "In 1933, forty hours became the National Recovery Administration standard for the normal work week. And in the textile industry, where hours had been particularly long, they declined by 25 to 28 percent," reports Alice Kessler-Harris in *Out to Work: A History of Wage-Earning Women in the United States.*

Of Hargett's siblings, two became mill workers, one a housewife, another a Navy bandmaster. Of her own three sons, one became a pharmacist, another a mechanic, and one retired from the Air Force. Hargett herself married three times, divorced, and was widowed. Hargett knew some people had been critical of her getting a divorce, acting disapprovingly as they did "about illegitimate children, but I'd tell them to tend to their own business. . . . Still I believe my happiest days has been in the mill . . . Hoskins-Chadwick . . . looked after us just like we was one of the family. And Highland Park did, too." A three-room house rented for 90 cents a week. Hoskins allowed a sick worker to remain in a mill house until he was able to go back to work, taking two weeks' rent out of pay at the time to catch up back rent.

At Chadwick-Hoskins, "they had one of the little three-room houses left for our clubhouse, and they had a home economy woman come down and teach us how to do these things, and we really enjoyed that. She'd teach us how to cook and to make clothing and little crafts that she knew.

"They was trying to teach us women to be more self-sufficient, because we had to work in the mill and then do our home work too. We couldn't take courses to learn these different things, and they came in there . . . try out a new recipe, teach us how to re-do a little furniture. And whenever a woman got pregnant, we'd always shower her, and that was a big occasion; you'd get to go to a shower. Anybody married, we'd give them a shower, and that was another big occasion to go and carry a gift. But that's just about all the activities we had."

The Great Depression underlined the consistent habit of thrift among mill families. Hargett recalls, "My stepmother would can and make syrup peaches and dried apples. We raised our own pork. And we had a cow for milk and butter. Then we had a chicken that laid our eggs." This food was not for sale but to feed her family. Her father raised bees to get honey for sweetening and for sale. One female co-worker kept stealing her snuff, so Hargett put cayenne pepper in it. The woman's mouth burned and she had to run back and forth to the water fountain and the boss got suspicious of something amiss, but she "never did steal no more of my snuff."

The mill houses were filled with white people. Hargett recalls that there were "not many blacks living in mill villages. Most of them lived on farms. The sweep person was white people, but the scrubbers were usually black people. And the ones that did the bathroom work were black."

One Charlotte widow with four mill worker daughters found her daughters were laid off or fined "when they would not go out with the Boss men." They found other jobs at another mill, the Highland Park Manufacturing Co., but complained that "all the time they was working there the overseer was after one of them . . . to slip off from me at night and meet him and because she would not give him dates . . . he discharged all of them at this mill." The harshness of this prompted the widow to write to President Franklin Roosevelt: "I am writing you to see if there is not some one that can put a stop to this practis [sic] in Mills so as it will be a decent place for decent people to work in." Many southern women with heartbreaking problems wrote FDR hoping for assistance.

Alice Evitt, born in 1898, was about nine years older than Hargett, and she began hanging around near her father and her sisters at their work, learning the knack of the job. Her family, including the children, worked in the Highland Park Mill #3 in North Charlotte. She recalls that their work began at seven in the morning with a half-hour for lunch, when they came home for sandwiches and returned to work until six. "Back then when you could go in the mill, I liked to put up the ends and spin a little bit, so when I was 12 years old, I wanted to quit school. My daddy didn't want me to quit, and he said, 'Well, if you quit school, you've got to go to work.'

"So I just quit and went to work. I was 12 years old. The first day I went,

I run two sides, 12 and a half cents a side, 25 cents a day, from six until six, took 45 minutes for dinner. I loved it. I enjoyed it." She continued mill work and spinning for many years. Her sister worked in the same mill until 1964. Evitt recalls many children worked in the mill during the day and went to school nearby at night. When she was older, after her day at the mill, she like most women of the era canned fruits and vegetables in season since they had no freezers. Canned goods were costly or unavailable. In order to eat, they and most American women had to do a lot of canning, preserving for winter the fruit and vegetables they had raised or purchased by the bushel. "I'd can a heap when I'd go home. You didn't have freezers then." Evitt canned on her old wood stove even after she got a kerosene stove. "I just liked 'em better." She canned blackberries, beans, tomatoes, wild strawberry preserves, cabbage slaw ("stew it up and keep it"). "We raised our own meat" and fixed Irish potato dumplings and kraut dumplings, ham bone dumplings. "And we sold a lot of hams and things."

Willie Mae Honnecutt, born in 1887, was another Highland Park weaver who began mill work at 13. She recalls that her sister was delivered by an "old maid woman," a midwife called "Old Lady Massey." "Mama didn't have no doctor. Didn't have no doctors much for women then."

One female millworker in the 1930s was so stressed by the constant increase of her mill workload that she sighed, "They kept on adding until I had three jobs . . . more than I could do, so I had to quit. I thought I would get me a cow and stay at home with the children."

CHAPTER FOUR

$\mathcal{T}$he women described in the previous chapter leapt into the fervor of World War I, which enveloped Charlotte particularly, since Camp Greene, an army training camp, laid welcome siege to the city with 30,000 to 60,000 troops during 1917–18. Everyone in Charlotte joined in the war effort. It was impossible to ignore the uniformed troops all over uptown, in streetcars, and the dramatic war news daily in the local newspapers.

Charlotte women still could not vote or serve their country as soldiers, but they were enlisted in other ways reported in the papers: "The women are gardening and canning and working as they have never done before making supplies for hospitals and camps." An urgent call went out for knitted goods. Charlotte's quota was 1,500 sweaters, 1,500 mufflers, and the same number of sets of wristlets and pairs of socks to keep soldiers warm in Europe and in the frigid tents at Camp Greene west of town. The Red Cross asked for the "immediate assistance of every woman in the city." The challenge was laid down by a New York leader of the Navy League: "If a woman will get into the habit of knitting during the time that she is sitting in her home, at the club meeting, or even during the Wednesday prayer service, she will be able to accomplish wonders." *The Charlotte Observer* urged Charlotte women to "quickly acquire the knitting habit."

But not all women were accomplished or capable knitters. One well-to-do woman in Myers Park could not knit, nor could she learn, so she put Emma, her live-in cook, to knitting in the big rocking chair in the kitchen. "Emma would rock and knit socks for soldiers and Mother would bake cakes," her small daughter said, recalling the unusual scene. "Seeing them like this, I thought the world had turned upside down."

Out at Camp Greene off Tuckaseegee Road, silent movie stars such as Mary Pickford and Charlie Chaplin arrived to generate enthusiasm for the Liberty Bond Drive. Chaplin held a plate of dollar bills to call attention to the fact that it took money to feed soldiers. The Liberty war bonds were a challenge to all people of the United States to lend money to the government to finance the war effort in Europe. Citizens bought $25, $50, and $100 war bonds at the post office at a discount with the understanding that they could redeem the certificates in five years at a profit.

Chaplin's rousing speech in April 1918 in Charlotte raised almost $25,000 in war bond subscription. While he had the stage, Chaplin promised to kiss any woman in the audience who subscribed $5,000 worth of bonds. No woman did, and the several who pledged $1,000 didn't get kissed by the famous actor-director. The next month, Margaret Wilson, the daughter of President Woodrow Wilson, came to Camp Greene to entertain the troops.

The fortuitous United States alliance with Britain and France won the war, but an equally decisive result of World War I was the evident proficiency of women in the work force. Women had joined factory production lines and become medical volunteers and municipal workers. They proved they could shoulder public responsibility well. Rising to the challenges of World War I, the women's strength and work performance propelled the suffrage issue.

Within two years of the war's ending, the Nineteenth Amendment was passed by Congress in 1920 and sent for ratification by the States. It read:

The rights of citizens of the United States to vote shall not be denied or abridged by the United States or by any State on account of sex. Congress shall have the power to enforce this article by appropriate legislation.

While some young women marched for woman's suffrage, one enterprising young Charlotte woman had business on her mind. In 1914, Liz Conrad taught herself to use the machine that was revolutionizing the way people communicated and transacted business—the typewriter. After learning shorthand as well, she opened her one-woman business, Conrad Advertising and Letter Shop, producing ads and letter correspondence for customers. Few offices in uptown Charlotte had typewriters or trained typists, so she provided services to walk-in customers who dictated letters to be mailed that day or to be sent out to numerous customers.

Since she trained and employed typists and was a rare novelty herself, a self-employed businesswoman, girls new in town would come to her to ask advice or assistance in finding jobs. She gave free employment aid for many years, training young women and paying them while they learned.

When women finally got the right to vote in 1920, Conrad went to each precinct and asked permission to copy the registered voters' list. She then sold the lists to candidates. These were days when copies could only be made in handwriting or on a typewriter with carbon paper layered between white sheets of paper to create an extra copy. Using these skills, she waged a highly successful campaign to attract 1,000 new members for the YWCA. In 1924, she was again successful as campaign manager for Charlotte lawyer Julia Alexander, who won election to the N.C. House of Representatives. Not content to stay indoors and type, Conrad and her friends liked to camp out on weekends on land in Dilworth owned by E.D. Latta, property he later gave for Latta Park.

In 1934, Conrad worked toward starting the Charlotte chapter of the Business and Professional Women's Club, and she served as its president. To help women find jobs to match their skills, the club initiated a placement service. For more than 50 years, Conrad followed her career. She did not retire until the age of 82. Throughout her vigorous life, her concern and amazing drive continued to help women help themselves.

Two groups of stalwart women who organized in the 1920s began a century-long drive to make a great difference in Charlotte.

In 1920, the national organization that had ardently pushed for votes for women, the Equal Suffrage Association (ESA), had achieved its goal with the passage of the Nineteenth Amendment, but a wider vision remained. Gertrude Weil, the ESA chairman in North Carolina, called an organizational meeting for a state League of Women Voters (LWV) which would utilize the formidable organization, talents, and established network of seasoned suffragists.

Their goal was to "develop the woman citizen into an intelligent and self-directing voter and turn her vote toward constructive social ends" as stated in *The Charlotte Daily Observer* in 1922. The Mecklenburg league originally organized in February 1922 and was one of four operating in the state in 1930. Mrs. W.C. Shore was Mecklenburg LWV's first president and the second was Gladys Tillett.

Tillett reported the league's role in the passage of two bills, "one raising the age of consent in North Carolina from 14 to 16 years of age, and another increasing funds for the North Carolina College for Women" (known first as WC, later as UNC Greensboro) as explained in the LWV history *Eighty Years of Action, 1920–2000*. The League's 100 members in the 1920s studied education bonds, the League of Nations, disarmament and sanitation, and fought city and county commissioners for a new voter registration.

The state LWV president reported in *The Charlotte Daily Observer* in 1926, "we did work hard in the Get-Out-The-Vote Campaign, when hundreds of voters registered; and on election day we helped them get to the polls, and vote as they chose. . . . We helped to secure a policewoman for Charlotte, too. We have a splendid body of policemen here; but there are certain phases of work, especially among women prisoners that no man can do, and we feel that by having a woman in this position, Charlotte has made a great step forward. . . . We worked for the improvement of sanitary conditions in Charlotte, and used our influence in favor of modern garbage trucks and more frequent collection of garbage, which of course makes for better health everywhere." Another emphasis was participation in the national LVW effort for legislation to standardize the grading and labeling of canned goods.

But the Great Depression and World War II took their toll on league activities and the Mecklenburg league disbanded until 1947, when Isabel Peterson, a formidable, witty, no-nonsense leader was elected president of a provisional LWV. By 1948, they had 100 members, full status in the national organization, and were again in full swing. One of their first efforts employed the valuable league motto, "Study first, then action," which led to public determination that it was feasible and necessary to create a parks and recreation department in city government. One of the league's ongoing success stories and most valuable services to the community has been the informative, nonpartisan public forums for candidates, which they have sponsored for decades. Bea Wallas, when she moved to the South, followed a good friend's advice, "Join the LWV. You will meet the most interesting people." Wallas did. She became president of the league in 1957.

In the early 1920s, a group of 30 women who performed charity work and had previously called themselves "The Welfare League," was chartered as the Charlotte Junior League in 1926. The women had helped at hospitals, the Red Cross, and given out Christmas funds and dinners to needy families, but their focus shifted one night when the Cooperative Social Agencies met at city hall. At this meeting, the Alexander Home asked if someone would "undertake the establishment of a Baby Home in Charlotte to take in destitute babies from birth until the time they could enter the Thompson Orphanage here in the city at 18 months, so they would not have to be sent out of town. This was the work the Junior League wanted," reported league president Catherine Garrett Morehead. Since then the league has largely focused on the needs of children and youth.

David Ovens presented to the Goodfellows Club the women's idea and plan for the Baby Home, and Junior League members addressed other civic clubs to enlist support. Major ambitious league projects extended throughout the remainder of the twentieth century and on into 2001. These used the league's study, training, volunteer, and funding principles to help found and aid worthy projects such as the Nature Museum (1947), Charlotte Speech and Hearing Center (1967), Drug Education Center (1971), Berryhill Preservation (Fourth Ward, 1974), and others. The guiding tenet of the Junior League's mission has been, "when money is given, so are trained volunteers." During 1925–2000, the league gave $4.5 million to the city. While early members were consistently white, affluent, upper-class women who had time on their hands and servants at home, membership at century's end was biracial. Approximately 75% of the league's members worked either part- or full-time at careers.

While some women worked in groups to accomplish important goals, others forged their own single-minded paths. One of these was Ethel Lampley (1870–1970). She grew up loving stories. She was a farm girl in Anson County east of Charlotte who had writing on the brain, composing stories she wrote in pencil on paper bought with her butter and egg money. She married at 15 and became Ethel Thomas. When hail ruined their crops in Wadesboro, she and her husband found work in a cotton mill and she sold her first story for $10 to the *Wadesboro Messenger*. They found cotton mill work next in South Carolina and she earned 10 cents a day while learning her job, then 75 cents a day for 12-hour work. Without a child labor law, many children worked along with their entire families in cotton mills. When they moved to LeGrange, Georgia, again for mill work, Thomas began editing *The Shuttle,* the Callaway Mills textile employees' newspaper. She also wrote her first novels in LaGrange about textile mill life: *Truth Crushed To Earth, A Man Without A Friend, Driven from Home,* and *Bobbie's Bonus*. They were lively stories of romance, ambition, and adventure, up-from-the-bootstraps fiction of the Horatio Alger genre, akin to the wildly popular dime novels of an earlier era.

Ethel Thomas moved to Charlotte where she continued writing novels (by 1929 she had published 14). Her first novel written in Charlotte, a prospering textile mill town in that period, was *Only a Factory Boy,* published in 1912. In the novel, Orphan Jack is befriended by a kindly mill agent. Like most of her main characters he is an innocent, a young mill worker who defies the odds and achieves success through "pluck, luck, and virtue." Remarkable in Thomas's

In more than a dozen novels, Ethel Thomas painted a vivid,
sympathetic picture of early twentieth-century cotton mill life around
Charlotte and the southern Piedmont. Skilled in capturing authentic
dialect, she once loaded her truck with farm vegetables, put on her hat and
a long dress to infiltrate a union rally in Gastonia so she could write Alice
In Blunderland. Her books include The Way of a Woman and Only a
Factory Boy. As a popular columnist for the Southern Textile Bulletin,
she was known as "Aunt Becky," mixing millworkers' concerns with folksy
news, advice, and stories.

COURTESY OF THE ROBINSON-SPANGLER CAROLINA ROOM, PLCM

novels are her female protagonists, who are adventurous and romantic, and whose perils inevitably culminate in marriage.

One fictional mill village woman tells a newly arrived mountain wife: "Woman was made for something other than to be a servant." She shows the new arrival how to bathe, dress, clean house, talk, and how to value herself. The woman saves her butter and egg money, finds a librarian's job, and moves to town in order to educate her children. Her farmer husband had refused to let them go to school, so while he was plowing one day, she and the kids moved out and up. Thomas took her subjects from the people around her in the early 1900s mills of Charlotte and the Carolina Piedmont, people who were poor, proud, Protestant, Anglo-Saxon, and largely rural. Mill workers loved her books and passed the small, ragged hardbacks around reading them aloud.

In Charlotte, Thomas met David Clark, the publisher of the powerful weekly *Southern Textile Bulletin,* which beginning in 1911 came by mail to mill town subscribers with textile news of every variety. It also carried textile machinery ads, reports on legislation, and editorials opposing child labor laws, wage hikes, shorter hours for women workers, and attempts by unions to organize workers. Clark knew of Thomas's columns in the Georgia paper in which she was known as "Aunt Becky," giving out humor, sage advice, serialized parts of her novels, and folksy mill town stories of optimism and warmth. In 1927, Clark hired Thomas and gave her a regular section of the *Bulletin* known as "Mill Village Activities."

In it she praised improvements and mill town progress, adding in 1931, "Mill people who are crazy enough to think they have 'hard times' need a dose of the old days." Thomas called on the mills, solicited subscriptions, and communicated directly with workers and management. Through her, mill workers had a visible, audible voice, but her voice and her books consistently supported mill owners. When a young woman in 1929 sent verses to Thomas describing her cotton mill experience, "Here's to the man who's a factory hand/ As he toils amid the racket,/ Who pays a big price for grits and rice/With very small wages to back it," Thomas suggested the following alteration: "Here's to the man who's a factory hand, /And sings as he toils in this racket/ Who buys good clothes because he knows/ He has good wages to back it." The events of the Great Depression era greatly strained labor and management relations when some workers were pro-union and many others were not, and outside organizers arrived to rally workers in the mill encampments.

Thomas's last book, *Alice in Blunderland,* was a fictional account of events at the violent 1929 strike at the Loray Mill in Gastonia. To gather information, she dressed as a farm woman and attended mill worker meetings where protests were fomented. Another millworker in the area, Ella May Wiggins, who wrote folk songs protesting poor wages and treatment, was killed in events surrounding this strike and became a martyr in the workers' resistance.

With the 1920s' departure of Charlotte's young writer and reformer Forbes Liddell, the remaining, known female authors in the city were lawyer Julia Alexander, Ethel Thomas, and a newcomer, Adelia Kimball from Lowell, Massachusetts. Barely settled into her new rooms in the Addison Apartments on East Morehead Street, she wrote a newspaper notice which called for any interested short story writers to meet her at the chamber of commerce building one spring night in 1922.

"Two ladies from Gastonia" and a handful of fledgling writers came, according to an account printed by the Charlotte Writers Club. Kimball offered to teach a writing class in 10 sessions. She had taught in other cities, why not Charlotte? The group listened to each other's stories and exchanged ideas, and became the Charlotte Writers Club which has been meeting ever since. Kimball had published numerous stories, as many women writers did, under a beneficial, superficially masculine name, A.L. Kimball. Her long story, "The Girl from Pengarry" in the popular *Munsey Magazine,* was advertised as a "complete novelette: The adventures of a girl who had illusions and found them dangerous." One member of the class recalls that by September "we had some very encouraging letters from editors . . . and Miss Shelby sold a story!" Soon one writer sold a story to *McClure's Magazine,* which also published stories by Willa Cather.

Another newcomer with remarkable literary skill appeared one night at the folksy Writers Club meetings. In 1930, a 32-year-old Georgia teacher, Marian McCamy Sims, had moved to Charlotte with her new husband, lawyer

Frank Sims, who was also her brother-in-law. While teaching history and French in Georgia, she wrote for the Dalton, Georgia, newspaper and for *Atlanta Journal Magazine*. When she arrived in Charlotte, she had just begun writing fiction. Soon she accomplished an unusual feat. When her short story won first prize in the statewide fiction contest sponsored by the Charlotte Writers Club, she carried home the club's trophy. This was the start of a rush of short stories published in prime national magazines in the 1930s and 1940s such as *Collier's* in 1934, which published "A Diploma in Women." Her stories entertained readers of *The Saturday Evening Post, Ladies' Home Journal, McCall's, Pictorial Review, Good Housekeeping*, and *Woman's Home Companion*. Sims said, "These stories sold, once the ice was broken, as fast as I could write them."

Her best work, however, was yet to come. When she realized the form of the novel provided more "depth and latitude" than popular magazine fiction, she used her intimate knowledge of the middle- and upper-class urban South and wrote seven novels published in New York. In *Morningstar* (1934), she chronicles a woman's reaction to "small town conventions and stodginess." In her acclaimed novel published in America, Norway, and Sweden, *Call It Freedom* (1937), she dared to write about divorce, a forbidden topic at the time. Her acclaimed *City On A Hill* (1940), a social novel, exposed political skullduggery in Medbury, a town remarkably like Charlotte. Other novels were *Beyond Surrender, Memo to Timothy Sheldon,* and *Storm Before Daybreak*.

Critics praised her penetrating view of life in her region, her settings not in cotton fields and tobacco barns, but describing urban lawyers, businessmen, bridge players, and golfers whose quips, flaws, and flirtations she jotted in her dimestore spiral notebook for later use in her novels. She lived in Myers Park, was a member of the country-club set, an accomplished life master bridge player, an expert horsewoman, and gardener. Using this milieu in her novels, her forte was character and dialogue, revealing human glimpses written with "vigor and gusto . . . and that rarest of all feminine gifts," wrote novelist Struthers Burt, "a wry and rough and masculine sense of humor." When contemporary southern novelist Margaret Mitchell read Sims's *World Without A Fence*, she wrote Sims a letter: "I wanted to yell 'Hurray!' at a book about the South which dealt with normal people. And oh, how hard normal people are to write about!" This novel published by J.P. Lippincott in New York went into a second printing before it was published. Sims lived, wrote, and published in Charlotte until her death of cancer at age 61 in 1962.

Novelist Sims would not have known the world of the young working girls flocking to Charlotte, unless she had overheard them talking on an uptown street corner. Such a girl was Erma Mull, who was attracted to Charlotte for lively, good company and for the commercial jobs that were becoming more plentiful in the decades following the Great Depression. Charlotte was the place regional families came to shop. Mull came in the early 1940s to work as a salesperson at Ivey's department store on North Tryon Street. She sold silk gowns to soldiers for $25. Later she worked as a buyer for Virginia Frederick lingerie. She recalls what it was like to work as a clerk in the high-end store:

> To work there you had to wear a dress that was black, brown, navy blue. It had to be solid color. You had to wear pearls or a small pin and your earrings had to be button size. When you were hired, they asked, 'Do you go to church?' If you did not, you didn't get the job. Ivey's clerks were the best-looking women in Charlotte. One day I wore a print dress to work that I had sewed. It had small yellow flowers on a black background. Mr. Eichelberger, the personnel man, told me to go home and change my dress. 'Erma, you know you can't wear that here.' I said that I had a date tonight. He gave me 50 cents to go home in a taxi and change. At the door of the store, every day when I left, they looked in my purse. Mr. Courtney at the store would help you select the proper clothes. Later I was a buyer for Ed Mellon Company in better hats, coats, and evening wear.

> We girls lived in boarding houses uptown. We lived at Mrs. Lemons', then at Mrs. Charles Ray's, a widow at the Poplar Apartments. Five girls stayed in her five room apartment. I slept in the sun room and she fixed breakfast for us. On Church and Poplar Streets there were five or six boarding houses and everybody went there to eat. There were only two restaurants in town, the S&W and Thacker's. When the Selwyn Hotel opened, we went there. I saw "Birth of a Nation" and "Gone With The Wind" at the Broadway Theater. Since there were no apartments at the time, we had to live in a home. All these houses had beveled glass windows.

In the 1950s, two women named Elizabeth lived and gardened within a block of each other on the same shady side of Ridgewood Avenue near the outer edge of Charlotte's Myers Park neighborhood. They and their contributions were quite different, but equally lasting beyond their own lives. One founded Wing Haven Garden and Bird Sanctuary, which continues to attract thousands of visitors annually to her home and garden. The other Elizabeth wrote books that 15 years after her death are still popular, in print, and are considered by Allen Lacy of *The New York Times* to be classics of American garden literature.

Elizabeth Barnhill Clarkson arrived in Charlotte in 1927 as a bride and spent the next 50 years creating, with her husband Eddie, a remarkable garden and reputation for healing, teaching, and understanding the lives of small creatures—those birds and other wild animals who came to their door or were discovered within the three acres of their dense, welcoming oasis. By the 1950s, she had become a well-known authority on how to attract and care for birds of the Carolinas and any others migrating through.

Roger Tory Peterson visited and commented, "There is only one other place in America where wild birds are as tame as they are here." *National Geographic* writer and wildlife photographer Fred Truslow stayed overnight for the full show. Often there were particular birds who came and went inside the house: a wren and her offspring, and a foundling family of bluebirds. Such eccentric stories of rabbits, opossums, frogs, squirrels, often made the newspapers and occasionally *Audubon* magazine. One winter, Elizabeth Clarkson made a public appeal for anyone going to Florida to take an emaciated robin recovering from pneumonia. An airline ramp supervisor called and cleared the bird's passage on the next flight. No wonder the British ceramic designer for Royal Worcester Porcelain Company, creating a series of bone china reproductions of American birds, stayed at Wing Haven to study and model myrtle warblers and to study the Clarksons' Carolina wrens as models for Bewick's wren.

The Clarksons' garden became a largely formal, beautifully ordered maze of paths, pools, fountains, and verdant flowers as well as hospitable undergrowth in natural areas for wrens and for wood duck boxes. Docents opened the home and garden to the public on certain days and for tours of schoolchildren and groups, while Elizabeth dispensed Kool-aid, cookies, and creature stories. Often birds she knew and called by name alighted on her shoulders. She wrote articles in *Audubon*, and a book, *Birds of Charlotte and Mecklenburg County*, but became an enemy of her neighbors in the mid-1950s, when she opposed the wholesale nightly spraying of DDT by city trucks throughout her neighborhood.

Rachel Carson's book *Silent Spring* (1962) had not yet described how landowners all over America reported total loss of large populations of birds after local spraying. But in 1953, Elizabeth Clarkson saw the dismal effects on birds and animals (embryos shriveled in eggs and the disappearance of hummingbirds and bluebirds), so the Clarksons hired a lawyer to argue against the general fogging of their neighborhood.

People at the time held fresh memories of crippling polio epidemics of the 1940s and were eager to avoid potentially disease-bearing insects. In 1958, articles in *Audubon* and *Scientific American* would vividly describe the effects of general spraying, but in 1953, people gaily ran into the spray as the trucks passed, while Elizabeth in her peignoir blocked the approach of the spray truck in front of her house. Spraying was halted in the small area around Ridgewood Avenue, but continued in the rest of the city. In 1972 the U.S. Government restricted DDT use due to the clear evidence of dangerous concentrations of DDT in fish and birds. Russell Piethman, director of the Charlotte Nature Museum, described Elizabeth Clarkson as "among the first to recognize the dangers of DDT to the environment, in her housecoat and slippers standing guardian of nature in the middle of Ridgewood Avenue in the early morning hours."

Her neighbor, Elizabeth Lawrence (1904–85), led a quieter life in her very different garden down the street. Her garden bloomed as a changing, experimental laboratory for new plants about which Lawrence was curious. But her books connected her to a wide public beyond the southern region for she was "a gardener's gardener," sprinkling her books with quotations from her background in classical literature at Barnard College in New York City. When the Georgia native returned to live in Raleigh, she enrolled in the present-day North Carolina State University, where she was the first woman to receive a degree in landscape architecture. In their Raleigh garden, Lawrence and her mother, Bessie, kept daily garden records, which they compared to confirm their own observations. Lawrence had learned first hand "that a knowledge of plant material for the South could not be got in the library, most of the literature

Elizabeth Lawrence gardened for her own pleasure and exploration, but wrote to a wide audience of admirers in columns and acclaimed books: Gardens in Winter, A Southern Garden, Through the Garden Gate, *and* Gardening for Love. *She corresponded with Eudora Welty of Mississippi, Katharine White of Maine and New York, Rosa Hicks of Appalachia, and women throughout the South, comparing and swapping seeds and plants and telling their various glories.* The New York Times *praised her skill in describing the local and the particular with enormous artistry and universal appeal.*

of gardening being for a different climate, and that I would have to grow the plants in my garden and learn about them for myself."

From these observations came her first book, *A Southern Garden* (1942). She claimed as her garden terrain the states of Virginia, the Carolinas, Tennessee, Georgia, Alabama, and parts of the Southwest. Katharine White of *The New Yorker* reviewed a new edition in 1967, reporting that "*A Southern Garden* is far more than a regional book. It is civilized literature by a writer with a pure and lively style and deep sense of beauty."

When she moved to Charlotte in 1950 with her mother to live in a Ridgewood Avenue house beside her sister and her family, Lawrence brought plants from her mother's Georgia and Raleigh gardens as well as memories of generations of female family gardeners. Biographer Emily Herring Wilson describes Lawrence's great aunt's primrose jasmine, her grandmother's tea rose, and plantain lilies from her great-grandmother's garden that bound mother and daughter "to the past, to women in their family, and to one another."

Years of Lawrence's gardening columns for *The Charlotte Observer* and other books followed: *The Little Bulbs: A Tale of Two Gardens* (1957), *Gardens in Winter* (1961), and a posthumous book *Gardening for Love: The Market Bulletins* edited by *New York Times* garden columnist Allen Lacy (1987). This last book arrived at Lacy's door in the form of a large box filled with groups of letters received by Lawrence from 1944 to 1982 from "her farm ladies," letters Lawrence saved for the book she hoped to write. It is a fascinating book of personalities as well as plants, stories about women who advertised their seeds and plants in their state market bulletins, first recommended to Lawrence by her friend, Pulitzer Prize-winning author Eudora Welty. Welty introduced Lawrence to this grassroots farm wives' lifeline by putting Lawrence's name on the mailing list of the *Mississippi Market Bulletin*.

Lacy writes, "Some of Miss Lawrence's correspondents were highly educated, able to speak knowingly about chromosome counts or the poetry of Baudelaire. Others had only a grade-school education in a one-room country school, but were nevertheless able to write precisely and often poetically about the plants they raised and the lives they lived, both the griefs and the joys they knew."

One such farm friend was Rosa Violet Hicks, who lived near the Pisgah National Forest in western North Carolina. By mail through advertisements,

Hicks sold and swapped plants, more than 60 varieties, and gradually forged a friendship with Lawrence by letters. Lawrence also corresponded with author Katharine White (*The New Yorker* columnist and the wife of E.B. White) and Vita Sackville-West of England, all avid gardeners and widely published garden writers. In 1957, she wrote the introduction to an important reprinted anthology, *The Essential Gertrude Jekyll*, assessing the contributions of this remarkable British gardener. Jekyll (1843–1932) is credited with literally transforming English horticulture and garden design.

Lawrence's skill clearly extended beyond her plant knowledge. Her writing style was classic, warmly engaging, and anecdotal. Frequently visiting with her gardening neighbors, the Clarksons, she described their garden Wing Haven in 1961, "By night, the water-mirror reflects the stars, by day the clouds, in winter the green branches of pine trees, in spring the pale flower of the weeping cherry." Lawrence preferred one or two guests at a time rather than groups of visitors to her own home and garden. She called herself a "dirt gardener" whereas Elizabeth Clarkson looked elegant even when digging.

On clear, summer nights, Anne Bushnell Abbott spread a blanket in a meadow at the family's vacation home in Flat Rock. Lying on her back beside her children, she identified and named the stars. One of her children, Charlotte, was so fascinated that she took every astronomy course available by the time she graduated as a young woman from Wellesley College in 1919.

Charlotte Abbott returned to her hometown of Charlotte, but the whirl of parties and social doings made her miserable, so she wrote the University of Virginia seeking work in their Leander McCormick Observatory. She got the job. While there, she met and married medical student Luther Kelly and they moved to Charlotte. She had a Questar telescope in her backyard, which she and her children shared.

Charlotte Abbott Kelly also worked with the Junior League in its efforts to finance the new Nature Museum. In 1954, a planetarium was added at the museum and Kelly became its director. There she taught thousands of children and adults about the stars. They called her "the star lady." The facility was named the Kelly Planetarium in her honor.

CHAPTER FIVE

*A*s in World War I, wartime again brought out the ladies to buoy the spirits of soldiers training in the Charlotte area for service in World War II. In the early 1940s, church groups and families offered meals and fellowship for those who were completing advanced training as combat pilots and maintenance crews at Morris Field Air Base.

Knowing these young men were soon to be shipped out to the war zones, Charlotte women manned USO canteens and invited the soldiers into their homes. Sally Robinson, whose four older brothers served in the war, recalls soldiers from Morris Field in her parents' home and lively music on the family's old record player.

Women went to work in factories and mills, construction, and offices, taking jobs draftees left behind. Charlotte women joined the WACS (Women's Army Corps) the WAACS (Women's Auxiliary Corps Service), and WAVES (Women Accepted for Volunteer Emergency Service). They flocked to the navy and army nurse corps. For the first time in American history there were more married women than single women in the female work force. By 1945, more than half the women workers nationwide were 45 or older.

At home, women plunged seriously into the war effort. Shortages of sugar, gasoline, and rubber precipitated female skills in cooking, canning, saving, and conserving because of governmental rationing of products needed by the war effort. Metal was used for guns rather than zippers. Fashion in wartime showed pared down styles that used little fabric and subdued spartan colors. "Patriotic chic" they called it. Nylon stocking production for example shifted to parachute manufacture, leaving nylons in short supply. Rubber needed in war equipment was withdrawn from the usual manufacture of underwear, girdles especially.

The shortages were inconvenient—fewer cakes and cookies due to sugar rationing, fewer trips or Sunday joy rides due to gas shortages. Elizabeth Clarkson, who had always filled numerous hummingbird feeders with colored sugar water for the hundreds of summer hummingbirds who visited their garden "Wing Haven," gladly received sugar rationing stamps from friends who were not going to use theirs. These stamps allotted by the government to families and individuals were required for any purchase of sugar or gasoline.

Charlotte women in wartime read the comic strips such as "Wonder Woman." Mary Marvel was a positive powerhouse, a female equivalent to Superman. But there was also "Bringing Up Father," featuring a comedic married couple, husband Jiggs thoroughly dominated and henpecked by his wife Maggie. They also encouraged readers to conserve scarce foods and to buy savings war bonds to both save money and to finance the war effort.

Wonder Woman's wise and strong mission was to "save the world from the hatred and wars of men." Movies hyped patriotism, and movie stars Betty Grable and Rita Hayworth, and singer Lena Horne posed for "pin-up" posters for barracks or on shipboard, to be ogled and admired by soldiers far from home. Lucille Ball in 1941 played a wealthy woman who "did her part to speed victory in a defense plant." Heroines were brave, bold, self-sacrificing, lonely, and hardworking as they bore the trials of war at home without their men. Charlotte women stood in line to see these movies in the days before television when diversions were most welcome.

Some Charlotte women worked in the huge navy shell-loading plant on 2,200 acres on York Road. At one point 10,000 men and women were employed, some commuting 50 or 60 miles for these jobs producing ammunition to be sent to the war zones. A contingent of female nurses from Charlotte accompanied a group of Charlotte physicians and surgeons known as the 38th Evacuation Hospital. They went to battle areas in Italy and North Africa as a medical unit and performed with distinction under primitive and dangerous battle conditions.

Nurses Bea Johnson and Martha Peagram described life in the small tents, which nurses inhabited on the edge of the hospital camp. In muddy Italy, both nurses and doctors worked in combat boots, which the nurses called "L'il Abners." Forty nurses served the unit, which received litter bearers carrying the wounded soldiers on stretchers straight from battle. Often nurses wore helmets even while sleeping. And toilets were outhouse style. In North Africa water was rationed, and sometimes each person was allowed only one canteen a day for all her needs. Nurses often collected rain water for washing hair.

Bea Johnson recalled one Christmas at the front when someone in their unit summoned her, "Come over and see the Christmas tree." She thought they had somehow found balloons. But the doctors had blown up condoms and tied them with string, dipped them in methalate and epsom salts. "Nobody else had a tree like it," she said.

War correspondent Ernie Pyle visited Charlotte's 38th Evacuation Hospital Unit and reported, "One nurse was on duty in each tentful of twenty men. She had medical orderlies to help her. Most of the time the nurses wore army coveralls, but Colonel Bauchspies wanted them to put on dresses once in awhile, for he said the effect on the men was astounding. The more feminine she looked, the better."

Just as the war ended, Mrs. Ulysses S. Brooks was appointed to the draft board (Selective Service Boards of Mecklenburg County). The board's onerous job was to choose those most suitable for military service from draftees who by 1943 included all males ages 18–65. The rejection rate for both black and white draftees was about 37%. Mrs. Brooks may have been the first black woman to serve locally in this highly visible and unusual capacity.

Although women had entered the wartime workforce in record numbers, the general attitude of the population still insisted that "woman's place is in the home" in Charlotte and elsewhere.

Looking back on her career, Bonnie Cone told an interviewer, "I didn't set out to be a single woman."

Few women did in the 1940s. Cone was a working woman, a teacher who had no idea where her career path would lead as World War II progressed (1941–45).

Born in Lodge, South Carolina, she knew very early she wanted to be a teacher. She attended Coker College, rather than the state female teachers' college at the time (Winthrop College), because her parents felt Winthrop's student body (1500–2000) was "just too big a place for this timid little girl." In those days, the 1920s, Cone said "$400 would take you through college for a year." At Coker, a Baptist college, girls could be shipped home for smoking or playing bridge. Cone was given a scholarship to grade papers for two math professors. "If either one was absent, I had to teach the class."

She recalls that in her senior year the Dean of Women, who had never received a college degree, told Cone it was because she had been unable to pass plane geometry. She asked Cone to teach her. So with the permission of the math department chairman, Cone did and Miss Taylor graduated with Cone's class. This was one of her first experiences in mentoring others, helping them forward. After graduation in 1928, she taught in two small-town South Carolina public schools in Lakeview and McColl. In 1940, Dr. Elmer Garinger, superintendent of Charlotte's public schools, asked her to teach math at Central High School. She did until 1943, when the demands of World War II caused Duke University's math department chairman to ask her to help teach math to the navy V-12 officer candidates who were being educated at Duke. One of her students was Bill Styron, who would become a famous American novelist. Cone taught algebra, trigonometry, and analytical geometry with the agreement that at war's end, she would return to her job at Central High

High school math teacher Bonnie Ethel Cone, born in 1907 in Lodge, South Carolina, translated the academic needs of World War II soldiers returning to school on the G.I. Bill. Her postwar assignment by school superintendent Dr. Elmer Garinger put her in place to do something few thought possible. Her visionary perseverance and drive led efforts to create a new campus of the University of North Carolina, which opened as UNC Charlotte in 1965, with Cone as acting chancellor. She poses at the groundbreaking several years earlier for the Math and Science Building.

COURTESY OF THE UNIVERSITY OF NORTH CAROLINA AT CHARLOTTE, LIBRARY

School in Charlotte. "I had been recommended for the WAVES," the brand-new female corps of the Navy, but Cone felt that becoming an officer "would have killed my mother because women didn't do things like that in those days." Also, she recalls that she had a missing molar, and although the flaw would have been all right for a male officer candidate, "to come in as an officer in the WAVES in those days, you had to be perfect."

Before war's end, she did statistical work for the navy at the navy yard in southeast Washington, D.C., working in offices with classified materials and statistics on mine laying and sweeping. She developed a hungry "yearning to come back to teaching. . . . I could hardly wait to get there." Although offered teaching jobs at colleges, Cone came back to Charlotte and Central High in 1946, when the returning war veterans "needed a place to use their G.I. Bill." These former soldiers (nicknamed G.I.s) had their discharge papers in hand and were eager for preparatory courses for advanced degrees. The North Carolina director of extension in Chapel Hill decided to open centers to take care of these veterans. Cone recalls, "Dr. Garinger worked to get one here in Charlotte, and it was in the same building that I was teaching in at that time (Central High School), so he said, 'We want you to teach engineering mathematics, to test them in college.' " She was also testing high-school students, teaching high-school math, and supervising senior homeroom. Technical High School, as the center was called, drew many young men from the nearby mill villages and neighborhoods. Cone learned quickly that men from the industrial and lower economic areas of North Charlotte and Harding High School "had good minds and the ability to do the work. They just had parents who could not afford to send them to college.

"The first year we just offered freshman work . . . 274 freshmen students enrolled in night classes in classrooms that high school students filled by day." The G.I.s' courses prepared them for transfer to UNC Chapel Hill, N.C. State, Georgia Tech, USC, Clemson, Duke, Davidson, and other higher-level institutions. In the second year, Cone, who was at the center from early morning until the last class at 10:30 at night, described "long, hard days, but you had the feeling that you were doing something that really was important. . . . Many [G.I.s] were mature fellows who had no thought they would ever be able to get a college education."

However, Cone also said some "resented their [the G.I.s] presence very much. Some teachers would hide their chalk and erasers." Cone taught, recruited, and kept the books for the center. When the first director left, Cone says Garinger and the extension officials at UNC Chapel Hill told her that she "would have to be director of the college in charge of operations of our branch. . . . You had to do it. Dr. Garinger said so. He was my boss." So Cone directed the center (1947–49). From 1949–61, she was named director of Charlotte College, which was what the center became when the statewide locations were closed. From 1961–65, she was the college's president.

One of the teachers she hired in the early years was Edyth Winningham. She and her husband had just come to Charlotte, and Winningham had an M.A. from UNC Chapel Hill and had taught in Wilmington. In 1942, Winningham was the first woman to get an advanced political science degree in North Carolina. At Charlotte College, she taught history, political science, and French. She continued teaching these subjects when the college became UNC Charlotte. Winningham retired in 1967, after more than 30 years of teaching.

The late 1940s was a harrowing time because it looked as though Charlotte might lose a much-needed educational institution that had more than proved its need and worth. Of the four postwar college centers in the state, Charlotte's was larger than all the others combined. The university felt the centers had served their purpose. Cone recalls, "We were desperate when the University said it would be closed. In the spring of 1949 we were able to get legislation prepared, introduced, and passed to permit our local school board to operate two community colleges" continuing the one at Central High as Charlotte College and creating a black component as Carver College (at Second Ward High School) nearby. This was, of course, the era of entirely separate racial education, prior to the Supreme Court ruling in 1954 that mandated desegregation. Cone had perhaps unknowingly pioneered integration by admitting black girls to the nursing school at Charlotte College. "It never occurred to me that I couldn't. They didn't have a nursing school."

Studies showed Cone that the Charlotte area "was really a higher educational desert. There was no city in the U.S. of comparable size without a university either public or private." What was also clear was the insistence of industry, such as Douglas Aircraft in the mid-1950s, who needed Charlotte College to "give graduate engineering courses . . . and public schools were pleading for us to give teachers' courses for the master's degree." In 1963 legislation was passed to make Charlotte College a four-year senior college campus. And in 1965 under Cone's leadership it became, with much local celebration, the fourth campus of the University of North Carolina.

This sounds so simple and logical in retrospect, but it was a radical idea which took careful, persistent, and wise lobbying to effect this legislation. After many trips to Raleigh with influential Charlotteans including Liz Hair and others, Cone needed someone who was a strong supporter of Governor Dan Moore to speak to Moore in favor of the legislation. She called influential business leader George Broderick, who immediately went to Raleigh where he met with the governor to persuade him. Broderick called Cone at zero hour to tell her, "The governor is with us, Miss Bonnie."

The rest is history, as is the well-known character of Cone. Her talent for unrelenting persuasion, says former UNC system president C.D. Spangler, is like "water dripping on a rock." Another admirer described her "sweet, subtle witchcraft which turns strong, single-minded businessmen into sentimental philanthropists." One civic leader summed it up, "When Bonnie Cone gets you on the phone, you might as well just say, O.K., we'll do it, and then enjoy a pleasant conversation with her."

Such skills acquired donations of land for the university, funding, and countless other necessities. After such success as the "mother of the university," Cone served one year as acting chancellor. When a new chancellor was hired in 1966, she became vice chancellor for student affairs and community relations, finally retiring as fundraiser in 1977. Fruition for her was "seeing the institution come into its being and serve the people you knew it would be able to serve . . . that means the most to me."

One of the people who helped Bonnie Cone carry the Charlotte College ball through the state legislature for passage as the fourth campus of the University of North Carolina was Charlotte legislator Martha Evans. It was a team effort all around and state senator Martha Evans was a key player in the right place at the right time. A strong advocate for education, she served in the state house 1963–65 and in the state senate 1965–70, the first woman to serve in both. She was also the first winner of the WBT Woman of the Year Award in 1955.

In the senate, Evans chaired the education committee. A former physical therapist, she chose education and mental health legislation as special causes, working for a universal kindergarten system (in the days before there were public kindergartens), starting with pilot ones in Charlotte and other school systems. She worked for the licensing of day-care centers and meeting the educational needs of the retarded and emotionally disturbed. Her interest in preservation led to her advocacy in the restoration of the 1774 Hezekiah Alexander House in Charlotte.

Because Evans was the only woman in the legislature when she arrived in 1965, the media found a constant news angle in her femininity. Appearing in dress suits and sometimes a hat, she asked for and got a "modesty panel" in front of her desk on the floor of the Senate. *The Raleigh News and Observer* reported the event, which would "make it unnecessary for her to be continually tugging at her hemline." In the news report headlined "Only Lady Senator Is Hiding Her Gams," her deskmate, Sen. L.B Hollowell from Gaston County, protested that the front of his desk had also been boxed in when Mrs. Evans' was, and he wanted his desk panel removed. Evans, known for her lively wit, humor, and outspoken views, replied, "I think I should tell the senator from Gaston that he would look mighty good in shorts when the weather gets warm."

In the house, Evans had pushed through a bill to allow Mecklenburg County's mentally ill admittance into Charlotte's three hospitals, no longer requiring the long trip to Raleigh's Dorothea Dix state mental facility. She joined with other members of the Mecklenburg delegation in the effort to bring Charlotte College into the university system. She promoted legislation to revamp state mental health laws, to set up mental health centers, to prohibit the use of air rifles by children unless accompanied by an adult, and to institute auto inspection.

Evans was a tough campaigner and a fighter with a hot temper to match her red hair. As a freshman in the house, she fought against the speaker ban law of the 1963 session, which denied free speech on the university campus to Communists and others with radical views. She joined in writing the dissent to the speaker ban law, noting particularly its abridgement of academic freedom

74

and the possible resulting resignations of faculty professors, as well as the law's threat to future faculty recruitment. *The Charlotte Observer* described her: "In the infighting that is part of the legislative process, she was tough and outspoken. On the social side of political life, she was friendly and jovial."

A man was hoeing vegetables when Evans approached him as she campaigned door to door. He taunted her, "You ought to be canning these tomatoes instead of out trying to raise votes. And I bet you never hoed a row of tomatoes, did you?" Evans took the hoe and demonstrated with it until he stopped her, "Well, you've won yourself a vote even if you were doing it the wrong way."

Evans's years in Raleigh were the culmination of a lively political career that began in Charlotte in 1955 when she became the first woman to be elected to city council. She ran last behind six incumbents. But in the next election two years later, she ran second, only 400 votes from the lead. Her campaign for mayor in 1959 disappointed her; she lost by 926 votes to incumbent Jim Smith. She lost again in 1961. Her campaign flyer notes, "Progress is my purpose. . . . Consider the responsible jobs other women in government hold: Senators, Margaret Chase Smith, Maureen Neuberger; Congresswomen, Jessica Weis, Kathryn E. Granahan, Frances T. Bulton; U.N. Representatives Eleanor Roosevelt, Marietta Tree, Gladys Avery Tillett; Treasurer of the U.S., Elizabeth R. Smith; White House Physician, Dr. Janet G. Travell." But Evans lost again, and her Charlotte loss redirected her toward successes in Raleigh as a legislator. She was the first United States woman to be appointed delegate to the International Conference of Local Authorities held in Rome.

When she spoke to groups, newspaper articles often reported more details of her attire than her speeches, such as this *Winston-Salem Journal* report in 1964: "The lady senator wore a pale beige, knitted suit with matching toque of fur felt." The news item went on to quote Evans, "I'm not interested in clothes as such, but they serve my purpose the way packaging does for merchandise. I don't care for hats, but I love shoes. That's when I really feel dressed up—when I have on new shoes." When she attended the meeting in Rome, she recalled: "After becoming accustomed to [Eleanor Roosevelt's] tall figure, Europeans were surprised to see a dumpy woman like me."

Her perspective on politics was based on experience: "A woman usually has to come the long way up the political ladder . . . from City Council probably . . . unless she has lots of money. . . . There are no difficulties because I am a woman. I don't go to stag parties. . . . There are no real advantages except they all treat me kindly and gentlemanly and with respect."

Like numerous other notable Charlotteans, Evans was not a native of Charlotte or the South. She was born in Philadelphia, the daughter of an engineer, who took his wife and four children abroad every other year. She graduated from Boston University, became a physical therapist, did graduate study at Columbia University, Lafayette College, Duke University, Johns Hopkins University, and St. Louis University. She moved to Charlotte in 1946 with her husband whose job was here. Eleven years later she was Charlotte's first city councilwoman.

During the 1970s, another exceptional woman's presence in the area began to make a lasting difference. Dr. Mary Thomas Burke joined the faculty of UNC Charlotte in 1970 after a long and circuitous journey. She would stay at the university for more than 30 years, and her name would be synonymous with giving and teaching understanding, with creative mentoring, and extensive community assistance to hundreds of innovative humanitarian efforts.

Burke, a Catholic nun and a member of the Sisters of Mercy of North Carolina, was born in County Mayo, Ireland. She recalls, "I came to the States to become a Sister. I was really going to Africa. Two Sisters visited my home in Westport, County Mayo, and they said, 'We really need Sisters in North Carolina.' I was 17. I said, 'Well, North Carolina and Africa, they're all the same.' My life has been just one opening and blessing right after the other." She came to Sacred Heart College in Belmont, near Charlotte, and got her degree there while it was a junior college, then went to John Carroll University in Cleveland, then to Georgetown University.

She began as an elementary-school teacher, did graduate work in math to prepare to teach high school math, but the Mother Superior of the convent said, "We'd like for you to study for your Ph.D. in history" for that was what they needed at the convent. "So," says Burke, "off I went to Georgetown to get my Ph.D. in history. I was there about a year when they said, 'We really need you to come in as an academic dean here because we are looking for someone who is futuristic, to give us some leadership.' She wanted me to change to something that was personnel related and that is how I got into counseling. I finished one of my papers at Georgetown and did a few extra things. It became my thesis." She received her Ph.D. in counseling at UNC Chapel Hill. After serving as academic dean at Sacred Heart College, and being on an academic consortium for higher education with Dr. Hugh McEniry of UNC Charlotte, she was hired to come to the very new, very small, raw hilltop campus of the UNC Charlotte. McEniry invited Burke to begin the counseling department and graduate counseling program. In 2000, that program was one of the university's strongest, and had 17 graduate students. The university began a new Ph.D. program in counseling in 2001 to focus on the challenges of ethnic, multicultural, and bilingual diversity in counseling.

When Burke came to UNC Charlotte as a counselor in 1970, there was, as Burke described in the late '60s and early '70s, a lot of turmoil in the young population, people questioning their values.

> It was the beginning of the drug scene, the beginning of sexual revolution, the flower children, the Beatles, and children running away from home, so I was involved at the university and had a great deal of freedom. I taught four classes primarily in the evening because the university was going to evening students. So I had time during the day when I wasn't teaching. I saw a great need in Charlotte.

> In the fall of 1970 and spring of 1971, Dr. Jonnie McLeod and Dr. George Barrett started Open House, the Counseling Center drug program, and Jonnie was looking for someone to help. She asked if I would do volunteer training for these young people who wanted to help. I did the training for a number of years with all these hippie-type people in the basement of the YMCA on East Morehead Street, in two or three little rooms where water would come in under the door when it rained.

> I wore my long, black habit and veil, and they'd say, 'Ever done drugs?' and to Jonnie, 'Have you ever done drugs?' She was dressed in her nice, neat suits. We both said, 'No, but we know what it is to feel pain.' There was a great deal of unrest in the schools—not only drugs but other things. I had a graduate student who wanted to do something

for children who had no place to run when they ran away. I helped her write a grant, which helped start The Relatives. That was very successful. One young woman, Nicky Philmon, said, 'We need some sort of referral system since there was no place in Charlotte people could go to find information.' So she wrote a grant and I helped her. The students took the leadership and I stood behind the scenes. In 1973, the Junior League asked me to do some training for their women.

Junior League President Ann Thomas and education chairman Martha Alexander asked Burke to design and teach a year-long course for the professional women at night and during the day for those who didn't work. The women wanted specialized training to prepare them to do assistance work during the turmoil in the city. Burke says, "We called it the Live Course [live, to rhyme with give]. For some topics I didn't feel I had competence to do, I invited others to lead, persons from the university or the community. The B'nai B'rith women asked, 'Can't you do this for us?'" Burke did and an extension of this program continued for 20 years. University counseling students also assisted Planned Parenthood in working with the girls who had problem pregnancies and helped them deal with the issues.

Burke hesitates to claim credit, but agrees, when asked, that she mentored the next generation in a special way "because I was the constant who was there with them regardless of who came or went. They could come and talk with me. I was available. Being a Sister freed me to do the kinds of things I wanted to do because I didn't have to be home to take care of children or a home. I could take a whole weekend. I helped Kitty Huffman get many of the programs going for the National Conference of Christians and Jews. Many behind-the-scenes things."

For her work with the Junior League, Burke got a lot of criticism from persons who suggested she should spend her time on the other side of town rather than teaching and training the privileged. She said, "Listen, these women are powerful and they can get their husbands involved. When they came out at the end of the program to get their certificate and brought their husbands to campus and listened to what I had to say, that got them interested in supporting some of the things. If I just went out and worked someplace else by myself, I wouldn't have that. I was committed to make a difference wherever I felt the elements of compassion and mercy. I had a lot of energy. I could work long days and weekends."

Burke was also invited to get involved outside of Charlotte during the period of deep racial unrest and community division in Wilmington, North Carolina, in 1969–70 surrounding the actions of a group called "the Wilmington Ten." Burke's dean asked her and several others from UNC Charlotte to be on a team to commute several days each week to Wilmington to assist groups of citizens and educators there to talk and communicate about the severe problems in their city. For a whole year they commuted and taught (while still teaching several classes in Charlotte) and listened with small groups of Wilmington individuals. Burke recalls, "I presented concepts, some information about barriers to communication, what it means to be a whole person, the personal growth kind of thing. But we involved people in talking with one another about what it was about the other person that was difficult for them, dialoguing, explaining, so that the essence of each person's being touched the essence of the other person." She gives an example: "Share with your companion something you have found difficult in your relationship with persons of the other race. When was the first time you noticed that? Did you ever feel comfortable? What was it that made you feel comfortable? Our task there was to help build community and to help people experience community."

For Burke, this sort of personal contact is the key to her life and her vows. She told a *Charlotte Observer* interviewer in 1978, "The most important ingredient in our lives today is to have a close association with another human being. Time and again we see when someone loses their spouse, they die soon after. They die from loneliness." She adds, "I don't know what it is about me, but people aren't afraid to respond when I reach out to them. Being able to make contact with people like this gives me a sense of well-being, also courage, and the tenacity to reach out again and again to people who are hurting and feel that no one cares." Burke received the Counselor of the Year Award in 1998 from the American Counseling Association.

Burke says, "There are many threads to weave one's life." As with other women chronicled here, she had strong role models. "In Ireland our family knew a nun who came to visit. No pressure from anyone to be a nun. My mother was not interested in local gossip. She was interested in politics, listening

79

to news on the radio late at night." Civic and political events also shaped the issues which claimed Sister Mary Thomas Burke's attention. Some issues that Burke was counseling students and citizens about in Wilmington and in Charlotte would prove to be a major theme for decades to come. Historian Dr. Dan Morrill of UNC Charlotte states that "school desegregation was the defining moment of change in the latter half of the twentieth century."

Inez Moore Parker was a woman who "liked to take control of things" and she often did. Parker headed Johnson C. Smith University's English department, wrote a published history of that university, and created the archives in the university library.

On one particular occasion in 1957, she was directing the wedding of Aurelia Liston, the daughter of her good friend Estelle Hoskins Liston. Aurelia's father, Dr. Hardy Liston, had served nine years as president of Johnson C. Smith and his wife Estelle had grown up in Charlotte's First Ward neighborhood. So the bride's parents were prominent leaders in the black community.

In preparation for her wedding to James Roland Law, 29-year-old Aurelia Liston bought her wedding dress at Ivey's, Charlotte's high-end department store of the era. She posed for her wedding picture in her white, cathedral-length, princess-style gown at Ivey's Portrait Studio in the elegant North Tryon Street store.

Aurelia had no knowledge then or for years later what Parker did that Saturday morning several weeks before the April wedding. Parker tucked the elegant portrait under her arm, put on her hat, and went down to *The Charlotte Observer*. Few people were in the newsroom. The only person in the editorial department was Randolph Norton. He recalls that she walked up to his desk with the portrait in her hand.

> She asked me to run the wedding picture of Aurelia Liston. She was real gracious about it, more than I was, because I was on the spot. It takes a lot longer to say no than to say yes. I went over the fact that the *Observer* had never carried a picture of a black bride. The culture we were in at the time had signs everywhere, for 'colored' or for 'white,' and I said to myself, 'All hell would break loose if it got in

the paper.' At the paper the picture would go through a lot of hands.

At the time Mrs. Parker came, we had a whole section, 16 to 20 pages each Sunday full of brides. All white. The front page called the Society page was quite controversial—the choice of who got to be on the front. About six big pictures were enlarged on that front page. Who decided who got on the front was a committee of white women. Sometimes they consulted Mrs. Johnson, the publisher, who was also the widow of Rev. A.A. McGeachy, pastor of uptown's influential Second Presbyterian Church on North Tryon Street. Usually they chose Mrs. Got-Rock's daughter, debutantes, and the country club set.

We had a rule in the newsroom. You used a black person's picture when it was part of the news story. Usually that someone was in trouble.

No picture, however, of Dr. Liston appeared alongside the article when he was installed in 1947 as university president.

Norton recalled regretfully, "I succumbed to the culture. As managing editor, the only person I could have asked was Mrs. Johnson [the publisher], who was a great lady and ahead of her time, but the community wouldn't have gone along with it." This was before the lunch counter protests, desegregation of restaurants, buses, and schools that would follow in the civil rights era of the 1960s and 1970s. The Supreme Court had ruled in 1954, three years before Parker carried the photo to the *Observer*, that segregated schools were unconstitutional. But very little had changed in the South. Parker liked to "create firsts," says Aurelia Liston Law. Parker "decided she would have to step forward and get this thing through." Aurelia, the bride, didn't hear the story until many years later. But Parker and Aurelia's mother were good friends. "Mother was like Mrs. Parker, a go-getter."

Aurelia Liston Law was a 1948 graduate of J.C. Smith with a degree in mathematics. She didn't want to be a teacher. She wanted to be a tailor, but remembers that "father felt we all had to get teaching certificates, because the doors were open for us in the teaching and preaching fields." In 1993, former newspaper editor Norton, at age 87, interviewed Law in her home. Soon afterwards he invited her and her husband, Dr. James Roland Law, retired psychology professor at Smith, to talk to a class at Sardis Presbyterian Church on the subject of reconciliation and their views on race in Charlotte. They accepted.

While dramatic changes were taking place in the streets and schools, Betty Feezor reigned in the kitchens and homes of thousands of Carolinians. She single-handedly cheered the hearts and health of stay-at-home women. From 1953 to 1977, she created a warm and highly professional midday television show geared to practical advice and homemaking. For 30 minutes before the popular soap, "As the World Turns," she was a daily habit for women in the Carolinas and in Tennessee. *The Charlotte Observer's* food editor Kathleen Purvis wrote, "Women could finish feeding their children lunch and put them down for naps, set up ironing boards and tune in to Betty for practical advice, needlepoint and crafts, a sewing lesson and a recipe." She is still a cultural landmark, because anyone who does not remember Betty Feezor had to have arrived in Charlotte after 1977.

Feezor had a home economics degree from the University of Tennessee. But her gifts went far beyond ordinary household skills. She sewed her own clothes and taught viewers how she did it, talking without a script or rehearsal. She gave viewers confidence and appreciation for domestic arts. At her home, she made food to bring for television display during the recipe section of her show. Her son recalls, "I was 15 or 16 years old before I saw a refrigerator where you could eat anything you wanted." One shelf of their refrigerator always held dishes made for TV.

She was certainly the WBTV region's best-known female personality. Her advice was absolutely reliable and she was, as WBT's producer Loonis McGlohon remembers, "the most loved person on WBT, man or woman." Her out-of-print cookbooks are still so quickly bought in used bookstores that some bookstore owners keep a waiting list. Feezor's struggle with cancer became a public story also, as *The Charlotte Observer* ran parts of her journal in 1977, before her death in February 1978. She reigned in an era when many more women stayed at home with their families and few had opportunities for careers outside the home or church. With her warmth, enthusiasm, and talents, Feezor was a role model who lifted homemaking to a high art.

For African-American women in Charlotte from the 1930s to the 1960s, women's career options were still very limited. Thereasea Elder was born in 1927 in the Greenville neighborhood of Charlotte, one of six children, two of whom died very young. She chose nursing as a career for two reasons. She felt that if anyone in her home had been a nurse, these two siblings would have survived. And second, she had a role model. As a child, every day she watched a woman go by who looked like a nurse. "I thought her beautiful in her white uniform, her shoes and white stockings, and I wanted to be the same as she was."

Elder recalls that except for several teachers, all the working women in her neighborhood were domestics in the 1930s and 1940s. They did day work for several different employers or worked week in and week out for one family. The families in many cases practically adopted each other for a lifetime, their problems, successes, illnesses, and all. Elder's own father was head porter at the Myers Park Country Club.

Her most influential neighbor was a retired teacher, Jesse Bangum Robinson, who, according to Elder, taught in her home. Elder says:

> She had Biblical pamphlets she read to us. She also taught us how to sit, have tea, and cross your legs. She talked to us all the time, as my parents did, about getting an education, and what you owed to pay back to people in the community. It was a close knit community. Different people had different skills and they each taught what they knew. Some of the women kept others' children, and some who stayed home took in washing and ironing.

> There weren't any school buses then. We walked from Greenville [a neighborhood northwest of uptown] all the way to West Charlotte in all kinds of weather. Coming home from school, [we passed] people in the community out to see that the children got home. If their parents weren't home, they'd check on us. They'd ask us as we went by, 'What did you learn?' If somebody was sick, they'd bring food, wood, and coal, and build fires, helping each other out like Hospice does now. It was a close neighborhood on Hamilton Street near the Southern Railway where I-77 goes through now.

Sara Stevenson confirms Elder's experience. When Stevenson moved to Charlotte in 1941, she lived on Luther Street with her aunt, and after marriage, she lived on the same street in the Cherry neighborhood, an 1890s community close to town between Kings Drive and Queens Road. She doesn't recall many black women in her church who had major involvement in church activities. A few women were public school teachers, but "most of the women I met were doing domestic work." Hers was a comfortable, friendly neighborhood with some "older folk on the street and women sitting on porches watching out for the children. There were some women who looked out for the younger women. I admired Mrs. Hopie Slater very much. She was a retired educator, the first Sunday School superintendent at my church, very articulate. She dressed well."

Stevenson believes that, other than teachers and nurses, it was the PTA that first made it possible for black women to do public things. This was the avenue that led to Stevenson's becoming the first black PTA Council president in Mecklenburg County and the first black female on the board of education. She had served as PTA president at each of the all-black schools that her children attended in the 1950s and 1960s prior to school desegregation. She became president of the Mecklenburg Council of Colored PTA and worked closely with the Community Relations Committee in an effort to integrate the PTAs. "When we combined the PTA councils," she recalls, "a white woman became president, and I, as president of the black council, became vice president. It was assumed I would run for president at the end of her term."

Stevenson was asked to run for PTA council president. "When the votes were cast at a meeting, Phyllis Barach had organized a group to walk out if I did not win." Charlotte Watkins recalls that some others had readied a group to leave in protest if Stevenson won. She won. "A group of men walked out. They had come for that purpose."

The desegregation of Charlotte's public schools in the 1950s and 1960s led to great dissension and tumult, but also to unprecedented leadership opportunities for women.

The youngest and bravest of these was Dorothy Counts. At age 15, she was a tall, slim, dignified sophomore in high school who was among the first four students to integrate Charlotte schools in 1957. This was just three years after the landmark *Brown vs. Board of Education* decision by the U.S. Supreme Court.

And although times were calm generally, there continued to be a silent, dark undercurrent which could intrude abruptly, then withdraw into hiding like a wary predator. PTA activist Charlotte Watkins remembered an incident such as this. Having grown up in Kansas, she had neither fear of nor experience with such events. She had come to Charlotte in 1946 with her husband, a pediatrician. As a nurse, she immediately began work with the YWCA programs on East Trade Street and as camp nurse and adviser for Camp Allaha near Hendersonville. "We took the girls up there, it was an integrated group from Virginia, North and South Carolina. This was before the time of any integration at all. I was camp nurse for three or four years.

"On one trip to the camp we were followed all the way to a bridge between Charlotte and Belmont by members of the Ku Klux Klan, carloads of KKK people. They didn't bother us, didn't touch us, didn't approach us in any way, just let us know that we were being followed. This was about 1948, 1949, 1951. We were headed toward the mountains. We knew they were the Klan because they had their garbs on. That was my first experience with that."

Charlotte Watkins and Sara Stevenson became friends when they and others were working to integrate the two racially separate PTA councils into a single Charlotte-Mecklenburg PTA council made up of PTA representatives throughout the city and county. In the early 1960s, Watkins had been the first PTA council president when the county and city schools merged into a single entity. Watkins had run for board of education subsequently and lost partly due to the publicity that she was a Unitarian. Since the question of her religious affiliation had become a public issue, *The Charlotte News* asked her as a candidate to write a front-page piece in the newspaper that discussed her religious beliefs as a Unitarian.

Charlotte Watkins did not run again. Her husband Carlton, a pediatrician, subsequently ran for the board of education and served from 1966 to 1974 during the rocky period of bitter dissension and tension over desegregation. The Watkinses lost friends and contact with family members because of their pro-desegregation stance. At a physician friend's birthday party, Charlotte Watkins recalled that the women and men were talking in separate rooms, as often happened at Charlotte parties, when the men "reamed Carlton out" because of his desegregationist views. "It was terrible." The next day Dr. Watkins had a massive heart attack and Charlotte Watkins would soon abandon her role as the next president of the national PTA association. She chose to stay at home.

Charlotte Watkins, who had begun her school involvement in Charlotte as a nurse and chairman of the Charlotte PTA's city clothing closet in donated uptown space, was to serve on President Richard Nixon's Cabinet Committee on School Desegregation. She would arrange workshops throughout the Southeast to get parents, teachers, and communities ready for school integration. With funds from the Department of Health, Education, and Welfare, she hired people from the Department of Public Instruction to hold these workshops across the South. Twice she testified before congressional committees on integration. With the cooperation of public television station WTVI, she spearheaded the development of a television film called "Someone Has To Listen." The film appeared at a time of widespread disruption in both southern and northern public schools. It was shown to school groups nationwide and used to educate future teachers on the viewpoints of students actually involved in the process of school desegregation. Continuing her community service, Watkins became president of the Charlotte YWCA and a strong proponent of childcare programs in an era before the advent of public kindergartens in North Carolina.

In the 1970s, a small army of strong, articulate women emerged from the fray that surrounded the civil rights and desegregation issues in Charlotte. Acting separately and later in concert, each revealed in quite different ways, a startling creativity, courage, and uncommon wisdom.

When the appeal of the judicial decision in the landmark case, *Swann vs. Board of Education*, reached the U.S. Supreme Court, and federal judge James McMillan's verdict in the Charlotte case was affirmed, Charlotte stood at a racial and educational crossroads. Darius Swann, a black professor at Johnson C. Smith University, with his wife Vera, had sued to have their six-year-old son granted the right to be readmitted to Seviersville, an elementary school close to their home near J.C. Smith, rather than the all-black school to which they were assigned. Seviersville, writes journalist Frye Gaillard, "was one of only six in Charlotte where the level of integration was more than token." In 1964, "seven years after Dorothy Counts and Gus Roberts had broken the barrier, there were still 81 one-race schools in Charlotte, 57 all white and 31 all black. Only 21 schools were integrated," and those mostly with a handful of black students. The problem here was not just race, but another major inequity; the attendant supplies, equipment, building maintenance, and standards were to a shocking degree poorer in black schools than in white.

Judge McMillan, who trained at UNC Chapel Hill and Harvard Law School, was living in Charlotte but had been reared on a Piedmont Carolina farm. He heard the case and ordered the Charlotte-Mecklenburg School Board to eliminate all racially identifiable schools, and to use busing as a means to effect this. The board of education balked, delayed, appealed, and sent to McMillan a stubborn series of plans, all retaining some racially identifiable schools, and all generally protecting students in southeast Charlotte where many of the school board members lived.

In 1971, the U.S. Supreme Court upheld McMillan's ruling, which meant that the board of education and the Charlotte-Mecklenburg education staff were compelled to come up with an alternative. When they could not, Judge McMillan turned to an unlikely source, a diverse group of citizens led by a cheerful, white, 29-year-old lawyer's wife and mother of two who lived in affluent Myers Park. Maggie Whitton Ray grew up in Charlotte, had earned her master's degree from Brown University, and had lived and taught in Japan. She tells what brought this group together initially:

The Citizens Advisory Group evolved during a period of 30 to 60 days when the school board was required by the judge to hold a public hearing about the school desegregation plan. They invited people from all over the community, every geographical area, to speak at this hearing—real estate, ministerial, League of Women Voters, and other interested groups. The Quality Education Committee decided to try to bring some order to this hearing by feeding this group supper beforehand and see if there was some consensus among them. All these people came, so in a sense they weren't chosen. They were asked to speak and after the meeting we realized we had a lot in common, that we wanted fairness in the plan and stability for our families. Everyone agreed to form a group. It turned out to be a very socio-economically, racially, and politically diverse group. We sort of belonged together.

We saw the plan the school board was going to present to the court and we knew by then that it didn't solve the problems the judge wanted solved. They were not meeting the guidelines of totally integrated schools. The fascinating thing is that try as they might, the newspapers and the people who didn't like what we were doing tried to split us up. There was a tremendous loyalty. We had all compromised a lot to come up with this. The school board was willing to compromise with us for a joint plan.

The most difficult part was the time and effort it took to get to know the details of the process, the demographics of the community and how much each portion of the community was willing to give, and to pull all that together into something that would work. Getting the wisdom necessary to draw a good plan was hard, hard work. We had a mother who got into her car in the morning and would ride from the place where the children lived in the inner city out to the edge of the county where they were being assigned, and count the stop lights and measure the time it would take. This woman lived out beyond Park Road in Montibello. Her children weren't involved. She wanted to know how long it was going to take these five-year-olds to get out past Mint Hill on the bus.

Some said, 'I don't think our children would go that far,' or 'We really love this junior high. If we could keep that in our assignment plan, we would be willing to give this, that, and the other.' Trying to make it work and match took nightly meetings for about four months, four to five days a week, November and January through March. The women who had free time would meet during the day and do the scut work, the number crunching. The spirit of the group was so positive that it didn't feel hard. It was work. There were people who didn't like it and would try to distract us.

The plan this Citizens Advisory Group devised was presented and accepted by Judge McMillan, and put into effect, transporting thousands of children each morning and afternoon by buses throughout the city and county to achieve equitable racial balance as ordered by the court. It was an enormous upheaval with huge public controversy. And as demographics shifted, the plan was adjusted to maintain the required racial balance. A large part of the citizenry, including whites who could have fled to private schools, stayed. It seemed that

Fifteen-year-old high school sophomore Dorothy Counts was one of four students to begin integration of several Charlotte public schools on September 5, 1957. She is shown with a family friend behind her, entering Harding High School in uptown Charlotte among jeering students. Because of police barricades, they walked two blocks from her father's car to reach the crowded entrance. After four days of racial slurs, insults, and a thrown object, she withdrew. School superintendent Elmer Garinger had told his principals that summer, "Desegregation is not only the law, it is also right."
Photo courtesy of and by Don Sturkey

the words of former school superintendent Elmer Garinger were echoing throughout many of the county's churches and kitchens, words he told his principals in 1957 when Dorothy Counts had walked through the doors of Harding High School: "Desegregation is not only the law, it is also right."

Two members of Maggie Ray's Citizens Advisory Group who devised this desegregation plan were Sara Stevenson and Carrie Winter. Stevenson initially represented the PTA council and Winter had been invited to the initial meeting to represent the Charlotte branch of the American Association of University Women. Ray recalls that Stevenson had "come up through the ranks of being president of PTA and PTA council president. She was very forthright in making statements about how things were, but never angry or manipulative. Just the way it is and we need to fix that. Get busy."

One fixer, put on the front lines by a brilliant administrative decision, was "Kat" Crosby, who had begun teaching elementary school in Mecklenburg County in 1946 following her graduation from Johnson C. Smith University. In 1956, she became the school system's first in-service specialist for early childhood education. In 1972, when the desegregation order went into effect, she became principal of Billingsville Elementary School, even though she had no principal's certificate. Her boss said, "You got to make that school work." Quite a challenge, but Kat had exceptional talents.

When white elementary students from all-white high-income neighborhoods of Eastover and Myers Park were transferred as part of the desegregation plan to Billingsville Elementary School, a former all-black school in the midst of an old, settled black neighborhood just across the creek at the back of Eastover, it wasn't far at all to travel in terms of miles or blocks. But in terms of history and local culture, it was indeed the far country.

And the outstanding person, the new principal whom new students and parents found there was Kat Crosby, who "loved that job better than any job" because she recalls,

> those people were just hungry, thirsting for somebody to understand their concerns. They were so worried that their children would get mixed up with some black kids that didn't have the kind of home training their kids had. They were afraid they would take their habits on. They were worried some teachers weren't doing enough for their kids. I just listened to all of them.

> I am not a person who beats people up for having a concern. There were people who lived in Griertown [the neighborhood where Billingsville School was located] who may not have had as much money but they had as good homes. We had lots of children from apartments. We had all kinds. I started having 'Chats With Kat' saying 'Y'all can meet with me any Wednesday. Any parents who want to tell me something you 'shame to tell in PTA, just meet me and we'll talk about it.' So, I had my customers. Some three or four would come in. 'Well, Kat!' They'd be telling me all kind of stuff. Just me and them. I let 'em say anything they wanted to say. They'd say 'I'm worried about

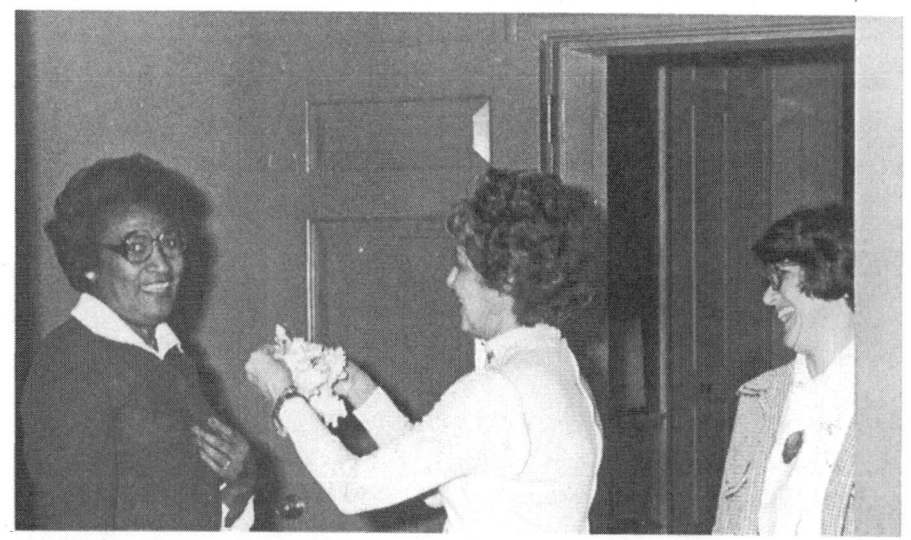

Charlotte Woman of the Year Award winner (1976) "Kat" Crosby (l.) is surprised by Sarah Bryant (center) and Maggie Ray (r.), who had won the award in 1972 and 1974 respectively. Crosby's skill as a community builder, outspoken educator, and as principal of an integrated school in the first year of school desegregation won high praise. Bryant's efforts as a founder and first director of Planned Parenthood and Maggie Ray's work as leader in sorting out the court-ordered pupil assignment stalemate in the early 1970s, led to their receiving the award.
COURTESY OF KATHLEEN CROSBY

my kids getting habits of black kids.' Or say 'I'm worried about my daughter getting habits from white kids that I think might influence her in a way I'd be nervous. Or suppose my child falls in love with some black boy? Or if my child fell in love with some white boy, I'd have feelings like you did because they wouldn't be accepted here.' I loved every bit of it.

We had both black and white teachers. Our biggest problem was to get teachers to realize they had to get ready for the children, have things ready the minute a child walks into the room. Be there early. Have things planned, have things out for them to do one on one, when they get there.

About supplies, I called down to the Ed Center. They said, 'What do you all need?' I needed extra books. Our library was so inadequate like back in slavery days. They worked on the kitchen. They enlarged the library, started giving us things.

Crosby's father, William Albert Ross, and her mother Beatrice Tucker Ross were educators in Winnsboro, South Carolina. They had six children, with Kat, the next to youngest. "I was the worst child he had," she says, remembering her father's creative discipline for her own troublesome ways. Crosby completed graduate school in New York while her brother and his wife kept her children in Winston-Salem. A neighbor down the street kept her children when her husband Joe, a manager of Mutual Life Insurance Company, had to go out of town.

Her accomplishments, her steady professional success, and the attendant publicity were a point of pride in her family. "You know how men get nervous? It never bothered him. He said, 'This is my wife. My wife is smart!'" When Crosby became the first black female area superintendent in 1976, Joe Crosby was not surprised, but others were. Her supervisory territory was all of Myers Park.

Maggie Ray praises Crosby's sense of humor as a key ingredient of her success. "Kat is a very funny person and had no shyness around white people. She could endear herself to the daddies, the suburban lawyers. She was very gregarious and almost outrageous. There is an attitude of fun and laughter around her. Humor goes a long way in tense situations and she used that adroitly. An intense loyalty developed between the parents there and her staff, the Cotswold students who were white and the Billingsville students who were black. There was a lot of commitment on the parents' side to make it work."

During the first months and years of Charlotte schools' integration, an amazing level of tension existed in the white community. To explore this, *Observer* columnist Kays Gary interviewed one parent, Peggy Culbertson, mother of four, who saw people in her neighborhood of Eastover leaving the public schools for the protection of private schools. "At one point," she says, "we were the only family on our street that had all our children in public school."

Culbertson recalls, "I staked myself out early." She worked to get a reading clinic at Eastover, worked at Irwin Avenue School and in the Boosters Club at West Charlotte High, and helped start a volunteer program at Villa Heights Elementary the first year of integration. She said that "the Kays Gary interview generated hostility to me, but I got good support and notes from across the state." One woman in Myers Park wrote Culbertson, "I can't give my name because my husband disagrees with me on this, but I support what you are doing."

Carrie Winter got involved, as most persons elected to the board of education do, by means of their own children in public schools and the PTA. Winter was a housewife and mother who was also an experimental bacteriologist. She had done pioneering work in fluorescent antibody research at Emory University in Atlanta and at the Center for Disease Control field station in Chapel Hill where her husband had specialized in pediatric dentistry. They moved to Charlotte in 1959 and he established his practice, and she was assigned to "set up a field station in Charlotte for the CDC, since Charlotte was sort of the gonorrhea capital of the Southeast at the time." In the meantime, the Winters adopted their first child, and she decided to become a full-time mother in 1960. She became president of the Starmount Elementary PTA and recalls that at Judge McMillan's desegregation ruling,

> the community went bonkers. The Concerned Parents group [who were against the desegregation strategies] tried to put parents on me to release our membership list to them so they could recruit, and I refused. It is not appropriate for the PTA to release it to anybody. I remember in order to be aware of what was going on, I went to the Friday night meeting where the Concerned Parents were getting organized. I wasn't liberal or anything, but it was obvious to me that they weren't doing right to get people geared up to fight the ruling.
>
> Either George Daly or Hugh Casey got up and tried to speak and get some reason inserted into the dialogue. He was hooted down by people I knew. The Foxcroft crew. Just like mob rule. It got me focused. As that went on, I started speaking out. I was on the PTA council and then became president. I was also a docent at the Nature Museum at the time busing was actually implemented and once kids got to school, the teachers weren't going to take them on a bus to any field trips. So Jane Harrison, the educational curator, and I visited at least one grade level in every elementary school in the county, taking programs to them. These school visits and other experiences were a crossroads for me. I realized that 'separate but equal' was not what it was out there.
>
> I saw disparity in facilities in addition to capital. Some schools did not even know how to utilize a resource person, or where a projector

93

was. You just came in cold to them. It showed we had not given program attention to all the schools, much less facilities. In representing the AAUW [American Association of University Women] on the Citizens Advisory Group, I was one of the few that didn't have a vested interest because of the group I represented. Working with Maggie Ray and Betsy Bennett on the CAG, was a wonderful opportunity to see the picture as a whole, to see how parents in different sections reacted. One of the most significant growing experiences I had as a community volunteer was being a member of the CAG in 1973–74. I met people all over the county and almost all of them supported me when I ran for school board in 1976. I became chairman and served until 1988. While on the board, I pushed for equity for women's salaries, and found the school board pretty unresponsive. We didn't have women principals [although there had been a few in the past].

During that period, superintendent Jay Robinson proposed two different assistant principals in the schools, one called API, assistant principal for instruction, and the other called APA, assistant principal for administration. Crosby recalls, "These APIs really contained some outstanding candidates for becoming principals. That's where a lot of women got into the job. We found that female coaches did not make what the men did. Coaches got an additional stipend. A friend's daughter was not getting the same thing a guy was getting. I called about it. I did things privately. I didn't think I could get anywhere making it a big issue. The public didn't care. And that was eventually corrected."

Winter lost her election and her seat on the board of education in 1988, she says, "because I had voted the right thing, pupil assignment. I really felt proud of losing for having voted for pupil assignment changes I to this day feel were right for those times. But that defeated me. It was very clear. My husband lost I don't know how many patients over actions the school board took in pupil assignment when I was on the board." In 1985, during Winter's tenure, the Charlotte-Mecklenburg Board of Education was honored for excellence by the U.S. Department of Education.

In contrast to Winter, Julia Maulden served only one board of education term. Elected in 1966, she rode the tempest of desegregation. Author and journalist Frye Gaillard in his chronicle of that era, *A Dream Long Deferred*, described her as a "middle-aged widow . . . who may have been the board's most respected member." Board chairman, lawyer, and Baptist deacon Bill Poe, who served with her, said of her years later, "I don't know anybody who wants to do right more than Julia Maulden." A woman of strong and stubborn principle, she urged more rapid desegregation by the board, but she didn't have the support for her position. The plans being sent to Judge McMillan by the board were being continually refused since they showed an unfairness and unwillingness to alter the segregated attendance patterns.

One story of Maulden's spirit lingers in Gaillard's account of board of education member Bill Booe. Booe, a lawyer, "brought to Charlotte politics a kind of viciousness and hostility that were not the city's style. . . . He grilled the superintendent, Bill Self, for nearly half an hour, treating him like a hostile witness in the courtroom. Finally Maulden felt compelled to intercede." Maulden, writes Gaillard, "was a formidable person on such occasions. She was gray-haired and faintly schoolmarmish, and for the first sentence or two her voice sounded meek. But she possessed also a gentle indignation firmly rooted in principle, and even Bill Booe was impressed by her wrath." She said, "Mr. Booe is accustomed to the atmosphere of the courtroom . . . and his manner of interrogation is offensive. Our superintendent is not on trial." The newspapers the next day agreed with her.

Maulden went on to join the Peace Corps as a teacher in Zaire. She coordinated an economic development project in Haiti, and in 1986 went to Nicaragua with a religious peace group hoping that their presence near the Honduran border would help deter guerrilla attacks in the area. But she believed her greatest accomplishment in Charlotte was "to remain sane and moderately winsome" while battling alongside Judge McMillan for the desegregation of the school system. She recalls, "As it turned out, I was engaged in what has become this century's overarching challenge: the battle for racial justice. I am glad to have played a part in inching us forward."

CHAPTER SIX

$\mathcal{T}$he decade of the 1960s rumbled with change. After the jolting assassinations of President John F. Kennedy, Dr. Martin Luther King, and Robert Kennedy, Americans would never be the same. These three along with President Lyndon Johnson had set in motion an agenda for justice toward African-Americans that played out in southern streets, jails, and university campuses. Congress passed the Civil Rights Act and women passed around copies of Helen Gurley Brown's *Sex and the Single Girl* and Betty Friedan's *The Feminine Mystique*. The National Organization for Women (NOW) was founded and urged that Mother's Day be celebrated with "Rights, Not Roses." While the smoke of protest filled the American air, the Viet Nam war boiled on.

In Charlotte in the 1960s, Ruth Wanzer showed the same energy she exhibited in the 1930s when she filled her Ford with her female sales crew and drove them to Carolina factories and plants to enroll workers in Blue Cross and Blue Shield hospital benefits. Born in Baltimore, she graduated from Goucher College in 1915 and came to Charlotte with her husband, an engineer who worked for the predecessor of Duke Energy. She was a founder and first president of the Charlotte Little Theater and state president of the American Association of University Women.

Wanzer displayed forthright executive skills and daring, which civil rights lawyer George Daly observed at organizing meetings of the Charlotte chapter of the American Civil Liberties Union. He recalls:

> When she helped found the Charlotte chapter in the late 1960s, she was probably 75 years old. She was a very dignified lady who lived in a very comfortable house and had no apparent reason to concern herself with civil liberties. Underneath her charming and hearty manner, however, there lurked a fiercely independent woman with a great sympathy for the underdog. She was the most fearless member of the board. The more controversial the case, the more she loved it, though of course she constantly protested that she was only on the board in order to rein in its young, aggressive members. For a number of years the local chapter's telephone rang in her home, and she fielded all the calls. I imagine some of her callers were a little surprised to have a maid politely answer the phone, and then summon a dignified elderly lady ('Miz Wanzer, you've got another one of them calls.') to speak with them, but you never know where you will find people with great hearts.

Wanzer was also for many years very active in the League of Women Voters. A friend told a story of one of Wanzer's LWV bus trips to Washington, D.C., which probably occurred during the 1950s. The bus made a stop in Virginia for a restaurant meal. One of the Charlotte LWV group was a black woman. When they entered the restaurant, the management refused to serve the woman. After everyone else had been seated, Wanzer stood up and in a loud voice ordered all 40 women out of the restaurant. They rose and left together without being served.

In chairing many civic groups, she inevitably ran tight meetings that started on time. Her friend Alys Honey recalls that the first time she met Wanzer was at a LWV meeting where Honey was five minutes late. Wanzer said, "You owe me $1 for every time you are late." Alys gave her $5 and replied that this would take care of the next few times. "That didn't go over well. I didn't know you weren't supposed to talk back to her."

Besides her civic habits, Wanzer was an expert bridge player and, as her son recalls, "cooked well and rapidly with lots of butter and high heat. She always set her table with good silver and china, and often used the silver goblets given her by the Charlotte Little Theater for all her work there. In spite of the formal nature of meals, the dogs were always fed scraps by her at the table with only slight attempts at being surreptitious." She consistently treated children as important persons, asking their opinions and conversing with them about wide-ranging affairs.

Two Charlotte women became so heavily invested in local groups that they rose to positions of state and national importance by mid-century. Helen Hunter's involvement and care for others led to four decades of her statewide leadership in mental health, PTA, social services, YWCA, and community charity efforts. May Lebby Rogers led fundraising efforts and planning in her presidency and board chairmanship of the YWCA during its push in the 1960s to build the Park Road facility at a cost of $2 million. The away-from-uptown site was highly controversial. In 1963, Rogers served on the national board of the YWCA.

One of the first things Ruth Easterling did when she moved to Charlotte in 1947 was to join the League of Women Voters. Born in Gaffney, South Carolina, she worked her way through Limestone College, monitored troop movements at Camp Shelby, Mississippi, in World War II, married, and then divorced in Mississippi. Her husband had taken over the family business there and, she said, "would make all these decisions without ever consulting me. He bought three farms without telling me about it, and then he'd expect me to help pay for it, and I did. I finally just got to the point where I could not submerge myself in the marriage."

She moved back to her home region, beginning as executive assistant to I.D. Blumenthal at Radiator Specialty Company from 1947 to 1978. While holding this job, she studied business law and personnel and business administration at Queens College, and was one of the first two women in Charlotte to pass the 12-hour certified executive secretary exam. In 1971 she was named Charlotte's Outstanding Career Woman of the Year. She accepted the award saying, "How proud I am to stand as a symbol of the 60,000 working women in Mecklenburg County. All of you should be standing up here with me. . . . We always stand together in the fight to make women persons before the Supreme Court of the United States."

Easterling had, in the two previous years as president-elect and president of the National Federation of Business and Professional Women's Clubs, concentrated her efforts in the 1970s and early 1980s toward passage of the Equal Rights Amendment. (It had first been introduced in 1923 to Congress as a proposed amendment to the United States Constitution.) As president, Easterling presented testimony before congressional committees in favor of the amendment. But the amendment, which passed in Congress but needed ratification by a specific number of states, bogged down in North Carolina and did not pass, even though Congess extended the deadline. In 1982, North Carolina was one of four states that determined whether the ERA would succeed or fail.

The 1982 deadline passed without securing enough states for ratification, dashing the hopes and many years' work of large numbers of American women. The ERA read: "Equality of rights under the law shall not be denied or abridged by the United States or any state on account of sex." But despite its failure to be ratified, the extensive decade-long effort united women into organized, effective activists, who fanned out in Charlotte and other communities to rise within the ranks of local and statewide government. Ruth Easterling was one of these.

In 1972 at age 61, she began her official political career. She was appointed to a vacant seat on the Charlotte City Council, lost a bid for state house in 1974, then ran again for public office in 1976, and won a seat as a Democrat in the North Carolina House of Representatives. She won every successive term, keeping that seat for 13 terms including the election 2000, when at age 89, she came early to the board of elections to file once again. Only four feet

10 inches tall, she sat on a phone book at the elections-office desk in order to give information at filing. In her years in the legislature, she has used to advantage her experience as a female in business, as a divorcee, and as a spokesperson for children, schools, and those who need health care.

Her opponents claimed she could not effectively serve due to her age. Republican N.C. House member Connie Wilson of Charlotte noted, "Every one of those younger opponents discovered they were wrong. I remember battling her on the House floor at three o'clock in the morning over Smart Start." Colleagues dubbed her "the Energizer Bunny" due to her lively endurance. In 1995 she worked to push through a major legislative reform in N.C. divorce laws, changing the way alimony was awarded. Its design was to end the consistent practice of "starving the wife," which had delayed, often for years, the division of property in divorce cases. To the legislator who called the proposed bill "a piece of trash," she replied "marriage is more than a sacred covenant, more than a loving relationship. It is also an economic relationship, a contract between two people."

Not long after this, she pushed for a state Office of Women's Health, which a Wake County Republican called "the most discriminatory bill I've seen." Easterling countered, "Think for a minute about some of the diseases we think are women's diseases. I have osteoporosis. Those of you who have been here for 10 years know I am three inches shorter than I was 10 years ago. For years, the National Institutes of Health conducted no surveys. No attention was paid to osteoporosis because they didn't consider it a general disease among the citizens." A Banner Elk legislator credits Easterling with securing desperately needed funds to finish building a child-care center in her mountain district. "She went to bat for us and got it, a state-of-the art facility serving 95 children." Her legislative colleague, Senator Fountain Odom describes Easterling: "She tried to arrive at consensus. . . . She is graceful when she is victorious and she's gracious when she does not prevail."

When lawmakers considered a bill approving a 24-hour waiting period before abortions, they were inattentive during debate. Her ire rose, "If this House had been this quiet during the substantial debate on this very important bill, I wouldn't be standing here right now," she began. Referring to the preceding debate, "We called women girls," she said. "We inferred by our inattention and by some of our remarks that adult women don't have the capacity and don't have the sense to consider an important issue like abortion. I would like to discuss this bill and debate it when this House is in a mood to pay attention."

In Charlotte she starts her day with a prayer and a one-mile walk. In Raleigh it's stretching exercises at six a.m. and her standard breakfast of cereal and bananas. In a Charlotte store, former city councilperson Cyndee Patterson bumped into Easterling at age 89 buying makeup. Easterling has won North Carolina's prestigious Order of the Long Leaf Pine twice, once from Governor James B. Hunt (1999) and from Governor Terry Sanford (1964). She was a founding member of the Charlotte Women's Political Caucus. In 1996 she won the Mecklenburg County Women's Commission Award for sticking her neck out in advocacy for others.

In 1970, after Martha Evans lost the legislative seat in the North Carolina House of Representatives, which she had held for four two-year terms, there was a brief hiatus in which women's highest elected offices in Charlotte were to the board of education or as county treasurer. (Jessie Caldwell Smith was elected to county treasurer 1940–60 and Jaunita Cadieu, 1964–70). Education was perceived to be an area of female expertise and concern, so a handful of women were occasionally elected to the board of education as far back as women's gaining the right to vote, beginning with Mrs. Jane Renwick Smedburg Wilkes, Maude Turner Finger, and Sonora Robinson Purser, all three elected to the Charlotte School Commission in 1921. In 1948, two Charlotte women served one two-year term each in the N.C. House—Jennie Erwin Craven and Susan Erwin Helms.

Something happened in the 1970s to change things radically. Was it the massive, "shaking loose" unrest and protest created by the civil rights movement and the Vietnam War? Was it the rolling wave of consciousness-raising precipitated by Betty Friedan's startling national best-selling book, *The Feminine Mystique* first published in 1963? Was it the birth control pill, first available in 1961 and widely used by the 1970s, which gave women a control of their lives with choices such as fewer children, careers, postgraduate study, or elective office? Was it Helen Reddy's 1973 Grammy-winning song, "I Am Woman"? Or that the Equal Rights Amendment passed both houses of Congress in 1972, giving hopes for ratification by the states as required by the

Constitution of the U.S.? Or Gloria Steinem's *Ms Magazine,* launched that same year? Or Billie Jean King's efforts to get the U.S. Open to award equal prize money to women and men? Or when First Lady Betty Ford and "Happy" Rockefeller, wife of the governor of New York, talked openly about their mastectomies?

Women were talking, telling each other things they'd never voiced before. They were meeting and organizing in groups to get things done, things political. Neighborhoods became cauldrons of political activity.

What better place to begin a Charlotte movement than in a Myers Park woman's backyard?

Liz Hair came to Charlotte from St. Louis via Wellesley College and marriage, motherhood, divorce, then remarriage. Her lawyer father had run for Congress in Missouri and lost despite the efforts of eight-year-old Liz who handed out campaign cards on a St. Louis street corner for her father's candidacy. Dinner table talk at her parents' table was wide-ranging, argumentative, and political. In Charlotte, she worked in precinct organizations and in support of Spencer Bell's election to legislature and to the U.S. Senate. She soon got to know Gladys Tillett. In 1960, Hair was appointed to the Mecklenburg County Board of Elections. When the board's full-time chairperson resigned, Hair had seniority, making her elections chairperson. She worked with the League of Women Voters to get voting machines, and held the first mobile voter registrations when John F. Kennedy ran for president in 1960. Many people came out to vote that year, people who hadn't voted since casting their ballots for Franklin D. Roosevelt. Hair served on the elections board until 1970, and in 1972 decided to run for office.

Hair recalls that she first tried to get her friend Betty Chafin to run. Chafin said, "You have the name recognition. You should run." As chair of the board of elections, Hair's photo had often been in the newspapers, and as a rare and prominent female official, she was well known. About that time, the Democratic party chairman called Hair from down at the county elections office saying, as she recalls, "'Liz, you gotta help me think of another man for our ticket. We only have four men.' I said, 'Oh sure.' I'd always noticed in the newspaper, when the city council is seeking applicants, they always referred to men. I decided to run. I just surprised myself and everybody. Others encouraged me. And when I went down to file, I was scared to death. I had watched television and thought, what would happen if there were some women there, maybe smarter in their decisions, maybe not so very macho? I like men and like my husband, but as a race, men seem awfully insecure in decision-making and behavior. Women bring a sensitivity and another kind of intelligence and information system to politics than men, and it is quite valid."

She recalls, "It was 1971, before my run for office, which I never considered doing." She invited a group of about 25 diverse women to gather in her backyard guest house to raise consciousness about electing women and about women's issues. Her friend Martha McKay told Hair, "We need a women's political caucus in North Carolina." McKay had been involved in the origins of the caucus in Washington. About the same time, Hair's daughter Cam, who was married to a law student studying on the G.I. Bill at Chapel Hill and had a three-year-old son, cornered her mother. Cam said, "I want to talk to you. I sit at a desk next to a guy who does the same job that I do, and he hasn't worked there any longer, and he makes $800 a year more than I do! You could do something!" Hair says, "I began to gather statistics about how the zoo keeper makes more than a day-care worker, and how we had only three women on boards at that time. I really got revved up. We called a meeting in the basement of an auditorium at Queens College in Charlotte." Hair became temporary chairman and the search began for women candidates who could file for office in February.

"That was January 1972, and we were very enthused, all psyched up about who we could get to run." Few women at the time held office throughout North Carolina. Only one woman had been elected to Charlotte City Council (Martha Evans). No women had served as county commissioner. According to *The Charlotte Observer*, "In 1971 . . . women held only two of the 188 posts on city commissions—and one of those was on the inactive cemetery commission."

When 225 women attended the caucus's first public meeting in January 1972, the bipartisan group quickly grew into a formidable political force. "We were basically a third political party," said Colleen Spencer, an organizing member. When a seat became vacant on city council in 1972, the noise made by the caucus helped pressure the appointment of Ruth Easterling to fill the vacant seat. Easterling was a Women's Political Caucus leader. Charlottean

Since Elisabeth (Liz) Hair grew up in a political family in St. Louis, Missouri, she got involved in politics soon after moving to Charlotte in 1952. She pushed her daughter in a stroller while campaigning for a local Democratic candidate. Hair was the first woman appointed to the county board of elections, which she later chaired. Following the organizational meeting for the Charlotte Women's Political Caucus held in her backyard, she was the first woman elected to the county board of commissioners (1972), which she chaired during part of her four terms. During her tenure, the Women's Commission was begun.
CAMPAIGN POSTCARD COURTESY OF LIZ HAIR

Deena Culp had made an impassioned speech before City Council urging that a woman be selected to succeed council member Patrick Calhoun. In this fashion, Easterling's remarkable decades-long career in politics had begun.

The organizing caucus women, "the Caucus Ten," comprised the original 1971 steering committee of the Charlotte Women's Political Caucus. They were Marilyn Bissell, who became a Mecklenburg district judge, county commissioner, and state representative; Betty Chafin Rash; Deena Culp; Ruth Easterling; Liz Hair (these latter four are described above); Micki Riddick, former executive director of the Charlotte YWCA, who worked with the state in the mid-1970s to establish a halfway house for women released from prison; Marie Rowe, former vice chair of the Mecklenburg Republican Party; Colleen Spencer, who chaired the task force that established the Shelter for Battered Women; Hila Stratton, who ran for the House in 1968, and served as president for the N.C. Federation of Republican Women; and Pat Locke Williamson, city council member.

And in November 1972, Liz Hair was elected county commissioner. Headlines reported, "Liz Hair floats to election on a tide of coffee." Many more women were full-time homemakers at that time and dozens of morning coffee gatherings were held in neighborhoods where Hair could meet and talk informally with women. The women voted. When asked much later who voted for her, Hair responded, "I got more votes than any other from the blacks. I think blacks trust white women more than they trust white men. I had good rapport with them and good experience on the whole. I'd come to sword points with some of them on the election board. But I'd earned their respect and affection."

The slogan for the national Women's Political Caucus was "Let's Make Policy, Not Coffee." Hair was to learn at the early meetings of the board of county commissioners, where she was the first female commissioner in Charlotte history, what her role might be. Charlie Lowe said to her in a gathering of the commissioners, "You can be like a hostess to make people feel at home when they come up here." Hair recalls saying okay. She felt that "it was not important. He was very worried about my coming on the commission. He had someone else in mind." Hair served four terms as commissioner on the board, which makes financial decisions for the county. She was top vote-getter, but was not asked to be chairperson when that first happened, as was customary. She did serve as chair from 1974 to 1977. During her tenure, she pushed for food stamps, riling board chair Bill Harris, who later became her good friend. She also pushed for creation of the Women's Commission, which succeeded remarkably. She had worked on the Carlisle Commission, created by Governor Terry Sanford, on whose campaign she had worked. This commission drew up the blueprint for the community college system and worked on changes in the governance of the university system, which included admitting Charlotte College, at first as a two-year, then as the four-year institution that became UNC Charlotte. She also recalls approaching the then-chairman of the county commission and saying, " 'You say you're going to appoint five more men to another committee. Don't you ever think about women?' He said, 'Sure I do, honey, all the time,' and gave me a little pat."

When the Women's Commission was begun in 1974, responding to pressure and publicity from Betty Chafin and the Women's Political Caucus, and endorsed by numerous local women's organizations, Hair recalls, "The commissioners and critics said, 'Well, all right, you can have the Women's Commission, but they won't have any staff. They have to do all their own work. They won't have any funds.'"

Originally named the Commission on the Status of Women, the first Women's Commission consisted of nine board of county commissioners appointees. Nancy Klein presided as chair and Sarah Stevenson as vice chair. Other charter members included James G. Babb, Jr., Marilyn Bradbury, Flo Bryant, Carrie Graves, Eddie Hodgson, Betty Maxwell, and William P. Mullis. Hair remembers, "We had a women's commission that just would not quit. Just dynamite, highly professional people." The Women's Commission grew into a highly trained resource for Mecklenburg women's identified needs. In its first decade it sponsored or cosponsored hundreds of seminars, workshops, and conferences, offered job counseling and a job bank, and provided key leadership in establishing the first Shelter for Battered Women, Charlotte's Council for Children, and Charlotte Emergency Housing to provide temporary shelter for women and families.

The decade of the 1970s bubbled with female political activity. Nationally, the women's movement was in full stride, lending focused energy to local efforts by the Women's Commission and the caucus for passage by the North Carolina legislature of the Equal Rights Amendment. Betty Chafin won election to the city council in 1975 and became mayor pro tem in 1977. Her seasoned political contemporary was Louise Brennan, a longtime Democratic worker and a chairman of the Mecklenburg County Democratic Party, who was elected to the North Carolina House of Representatives in 1976 and served four terms. Brennan's effective focus on legislation enabled positive changes for day care, arts funding, health care, domestic violence, mediation for custody, and equitable distribution for marital property.

Chafin understood about teamwork and mentoring among women. She remembers a time in Charlotte when it was absent in politics. She came to Charlotte in the mid-60s, almost immediately after college. She was single and got involved in Democratic politics at the precinct level. "I became a precinct vice chair. You just get your friends to come to a precinct meeting and get yourself elected." Party involvement led her to meet Liz Hair, who invited her to a meeting in 1971 in Chapel Hill where a group of women convened to talk about organizing a North Carolina women's political caucus. "We went, got excited, and decided to organize a Charlotte WPC. At that first meeting Polly Paddock nominated me for the board because she said we need somebody younger. I got elected and became one of the first presidents of the caucus.

"Out of that caucus we started recruiting candidates for political office. This and getting the ERA ratified were the major objectives." At a meeting Liz Hair said, "You are trying so hard to get me to run [for county commissioner], will you chair my campaign?" Chafin did and Hair won in an election where most Democrats lost to a Republican sweep that even put a rare Republican governor in office.

Chafin Rash, sitting in her office in 2000, recalls the women's strategy: "We organized every precinct in Mecklenburg County. We had a veritable army, five or six hundred volunteers at least. Mostly women. Men played a role primarily in fundraising. This was not an area that women had much experience in." Most importantly it seems that the "huge team of women had the caucus behind us. The community was ready to elect a woman . . . someone like Liz who would take an interest in their issues and be concerned. We had no Big Daddy thing [such as a political boss to give his blessing], but Hair had IOUs from the party because she had been involved so long. Many of those men were willing to step in and help. But most of the strategizing and organizing was done by women . . . and a far more grassroots campaign than others had run at the time. . . . We were pioneers, Liz and I."

Chafin worked in several more campaigns before she was recruited for city council. Again women helped, as did a horde of UNC Charlotte students. Chafin was associate dean of students at UNC Charlotte at the time. She had earned a Master's of Public Administration from UNC Chapel Hill, which is often the career training ground for city managers, county managers, budget directors, and planners.

Subsequently Queens College's Joe Martin hired Chafin (who since marriage, is Betty Chafin Rash) to develop a women's leadership program at Queens. She also taught two courses, and later became director of corporate relations through the development office at Queens, also serving on the city council (1975–81).

"When I went on council and became mayor pro-tem, a high-powered board like the university park research board needed a council member and needed a woman. Jackpot! When I first was elected to city council, the style of the current incumbent council members [all men except for Pat Locke], was to go into the back room and decide what was going to happen. I stepped into that. We really had a rough time when Harvey Gantt and I became the only members of council to actively support district representation. A lot of men in Charlotte, particularly from the business community, told me that that was the end of my political career. It would tear up city government . . . but I was re-elected the following term and led the ticket. . . . The referendum for district representation passed by 88 votes." Subsequently district representation was also adopted in the county commission and board of education to assure equal representation geographically.

Chafin Rash credits the strong support of the Women's Political Caucus with her early success. When she was campaigning, she recalls running into Martha Evans, the first female city council member and first female state senator from Charlotte, at one precinct where Evans, who was no longer in public office, was on her way to vote. Evans said, "I didn't have the help of all these when I ran. I ran on my own." And Chafin Rash adds, "I never saw her really support other women. Many of the original founders of the caucus were very supportive of each other. Later many of us did mentor younger women and encourage them in their campaigns."

Chafin Rash worked closely with Leslie Winner and co-chaired two of her campaigns for N.C. State Senate, which she won. "I think I was mentor to women who came after me like Minette Trosch, Laura Frech, and Pam Patterson." Chafin Rash comments on the wise influence and advice of Gladys Tillett whose background, like Evans's, was more of working alone as an individual with grit, dogged intellect, grace, and gutsy tact in men's terrain. But Chafin Rash says "Tillett worked continually through the League of Women Voters and attended meetings in Raleigh long before any 'the time has come days' of the caucus." Chafin Rash's career led to operating her own consulting firm and serving as executive director of Central Carolinas Choices, a 14-county regional collaborative working to facilitate planning and visionary cooperation among regional interests for the future.

Kate Gordon, former president of the Mecklenburg County Women's Commission and the Charlotte Women's Political Caucus, remembers the energy of the women's movement in 1976. Women joined forces, led by the Women's Political Caucus and the local NOW chapter, and successfully defeated N.C. State Senator Jim McDuffie of Mecklenburg. In McDuffie's campaign for election, he had promised to vote for the ERA and then in a remarkable "in-your-face" action, had reneged on his promise. The state legislature did not ratify the ERA, but the network created by the women in support of it continued to work for candidates and key issues of concern for women.

When asked how she reacts to having political power, Liz Hair demurred, "You never see yourself as powerful. I have always felt power is something that—like people say about love—if you give it away, you have more back. Spread power around and get people really involved, not just try to tell them what to do." Hair encouraged other women to run. One was Ann Thomas, a Republican and former Junior League president, a Texas native who had worked for the CIA in Washington in the 1950s. Thomas ran at Hair's urging, was elected, and became chair of the county commissioners. She recalls that she had been chairing both the Department of Social Services Board and the Social Planning Council of the United Way. The Junior League was beginning to take public stands. "My residential campaign was a very positive experience."

Thomas continues, "When I ran for county commission in 1978, I went every weekend with my then nine-year-old daughter, and we walked in a different neighborhood from August until the election. She would go on the other side of the street and we had literature, and I would say, 'I am Ann Thomas, running for county commission and I would appreciate your thinking about voting for me.' And Carol would say, 'My mother is over there, and she is running for county commission.' Every now and then, she would have somebody say, 'Little girl, your mother should be staying at home with you!'" Thomas won, and was subsequently hired by First Union where she worked 15 years, retiring as director of the First Union Foundation and head of the bank's community involvement efforts. Thomas credits as mentors her parents, particularly her father who was head of the chamber of commerce in their Texas town, but "he did not teach me about business like I wish he had. I always felt equal even though maybe I shouldn't have." She recalls a college pre-law honors program teacher who "urged me to go to graduate school, and when I didn't, he got me a job with the CIA instead. . . . If I had been a boy, I am sure I would have gone right on and never thought twice about it."

Thomas's closer-to-home mentors were Charlotteans Alex McMillan, Frances and Don Bryant, Sally Van Allen, and Mary Montague, all of whom were strong community leaders. "In those days young women did not present themselves and say, 'I would like to do so and so.' You waited to be asked. The first thing I was asked to do was to be involved with the Charlotte Symphony." Thomas became the first woman to serve on the Civic Center Authority which had to increase the size of the board in order to get a woman appointed in 1974. "It seems a long time ago," she says, "but it was relatively recent. Liz Hair was the first woman on the Auditorium/Coliseum Authority."

Liz Hair credits Gladys Tillett as being a remarkable role model and mentor to her in the pivotal years around 1960. Tillett lived about four blocks from the Hair family home in the Myers Park neighborhood of Charlotte. Tillett had been a vice chairman of the Democratic National Committee in 1943, the first woman so elected. In that role at the Chicago convention, she was the first woman to ever address the national Democratic Convention. She was very active in Senator John F. Kennedy's campaign for president in 1960. Hair recalls going over to Tillett's house:

"Often on a summer evening, Sam and the kids and I would be finishing dinner, and she would call. . . . We worked on speeches and how she handled Kennedy's Catholicism in the eastern part of the state, how she would confront something that was a big problem for the candidate. . . . She would go to eastern North Carolina with its very Baptist constituency" where Catholicism was rare and at that time politically suspect. She would, continued Hair, "present Kennedy's candidacy in such a way that a lot of times it made a difference. She was a model of graciousness and tact. She helped me when I ran for office and gave me advice."

Tillett was a role model for many younger women, even those whom she did not know personally. Tillett's gracious-lady demeanor belied a tough mind and eloquence evident in a formal speech made in 1960 to a group of

Democratic women in Huntersville. Arguing for religious freedom, she made many speeches defending Kennedy from attacks about his Catholicism in his presidential race against Vice President Richard Nixon, who was a Quaker. In the Huntersville speech, she said:

> Do you think that because the Quakers wait for the spirit to move them in the Meeting House, that Mr. Nixon will be slow to speak up at cabinet meetings? Of course he will not.
>
> Do you think that the fact that some Quakers are pacifists should be examined in this campaign or that voters should begin to fear that the vice president, a Quaker, might not be willing to go to the mat with the enemies of our country?
>
> Your answer, and mine is, of course, a resounding 'No.' Then why in the name of justice and freedom can't you and I and all the rest of us, grant the same right to Senator John Kennedy—namely, the right to render unto Caesar the things that are Caesar's, and to God the things that are God's?
>
> When the Kennedy sons were called to fight for their country in the front lines, they were not asked whether they were Protestants or Catholics or Jews. . . . Supporters of Kennedy are not voting for or against the Catholic Church. They are voting for Kennedy as a free American worthy to be President of the United States.

Tillett, as U.S. Representative on the United Nations Commission on the Status of Women, made equally arresting arguments in 1963 for the enfranchisement and human rights of women in countries around the world: "Woman power is the unused resource of many nations." Citing the fact that some countries still held women in slavery, she criticized the United States: "We have not put our full force behind equal rights for others because we have not been willing to support our ideals through binding agreements. I do not think we should continue to follow a course of speaking for our ideals while being unwilling to make them binding." Tillett continued as an ally and ambassador of Eleanor Roosevelt's own articulate advocacy for human rights worldwide.

The Women's Political Caucus in Charlotte was just what Tillett had in mind in fostering women's leadership and talents. "I think the caucus was critical in my even thinking about running," said Mecklenburg district judge Jane Harper

    Thereasea Elder, a Charlotte native, knew at age five that she wanted to be a nurse like the woman in white who passed her house every day. Elder earned her R.N. and worked as operating room nurse at Good Samaritan Hospital, then trained to be a certified public health nurse and became one of two black nurses who were assigned to integrate public health nursing by visiting white families for the Mecklenburg County Health Department. In retirement, her work continues with teenage pregnancy prevention, health care, education, the Black Women's Caucus, and community history groups.

              PHOTO BY LARRY HOWARD, COURTESY OF THEREASEA ELDER

in 1989. Harper joined the caucus in 1975 and served on many committees and as president. The caucus taught her how the city and county worked and how to run a campaign. "When I decided to run for office in late 1989," recalls Harper, "I got tremendous support from members of the caucus ... broad-based support from both Democrats and Republicans."

One woman who knows what it is to have support and to pioneer professionally and politically in the black community is Thereasea Elder, R.N. She left hospital nursing work at Good Samaritan Hospital in 1962 to join public health nursing with the county health department after she was certified in the public health program at UNC Chapel Hill. In Charlotte's public health department, she was chosen as one of two black nurses to integrate public health nursing by visiting white families. She was given responsibility for working with a whole section of Charlotte in the northwest area. "You had to take care of everything in that area . . . clinics, teaching, home visits, school visits, talking with parents . . . one year we had so many hearing and attention problems, we washed every child's ear in Bethune School. You were the social worker and you were the nurse. I always wore my hat and carried my nursing bag.

"We had a maternity clinic. Everything was segregated at the time. We talked to them before they left about planning and pregnancies. The only thing we had at the time was the condom, and the women had no control over that. The women had no controls over their own lives at that time. We just accepted that. Some women, after so many pregnancies, would have tubal ligations with the permission of their husband. He didn't have to sign, but they had to have their husband's permission."

Elder's influence during her career and after retirement included becoming a charter member of the Black Women's Caucus, a non-partisan group she sees as trying to "enhance mental health as well as emotional health. I look at it as a growth of the medical field." Elder personally mentors junior-high-age girls and works with cancer prevention, the Community Relations Committee, and the Red Cross. She was a founder of the African-American Historical Society and chairman of the Greenville Historical Society, named for the northwest Charlotte neighborhood where she was born and raised on Hamilton Street.

The Black Women's Caucus' annual event is the Blackberry Brunch, where awards—the Crown Jewel and the Community Service Awards—are given for trailblazers in the community. The caucus focus has been to bring together a strong, united band of black women from a cross-section of the black population, who are dedicated "to the uplifting of disadvantaged minorities in the struggle for equality of social and economic opportunity." One black woman Elder credits with having a large early influence in Charlotte was Marie G. Davis, who served as principal for many years at Fairview School, which was an elementary school for blacks. Davis fostered a summer training program to support and further train young black teachers. Her husband Dr. George E. Davis was the first black educator to teach at the school that would come to be named Johnson C. Smith University. Together, Marie and George Davis raised matching money across the state to enable the Rosenwald Fund to build schools in rural areas for black students between 1917 and 1932.

Fearless, outspoken Doris Cromartie worked on the front lines to obtain rights denied to blacks and women. She was an investigator for the Equal Opportunity Commission's southern office in 1964, just after the Civil Rights Act passed. She visited homes of black workers to investigate their complaints. When she looked into a female bank employee's complaint that women could not rise above clerical or teller work, Cromartie was told by bank officials that women's small fingers were better suited to adding-machine work. Cromartie retorted, "I'll remember that in case I need a brain surgeon." Cromartie went on to form Employment Practices, Inc., a consulting firm to aid employers in understanding employment laws.

CHAPTER SEVEN

$\mathcal{W}$hen Elizabeth Conrad Corkey received Charlotte's prestigious Outstanding Career Woman of the Year Award in 1966, she was in the midst of an amazing, radical medical and service career.

Native Philadelphian Elizabeth Conrad had her college Phi Beta Kappa key when she entered, then graduated cum laude from the University of Michigan medical school. Her medical specialty in obstetrics and gynecology led to her choice to practice where there was a great need for doctors. In 1932, when she went to teach at China's Shanghai Medical School, she met the Rev. Harold Corkey at the language school in Peking. She married Corkey, a Presbyterian minister from Ireland. They moved to Manchuria, where he was a minister, and where their two children were born.

Because Dr. Corkey was skilled in handling difficult births, many Chinese women sought her help. Among these was the pregnant sister of Henry Pu Yi,

China's storied "Last Emperor." Subsequently the Corkey family was placed under house arrest by the imperial Japanese army. After Pearl Harbor in World War II, the Japanese army held the Corkeys at the Weisheim Internment Camp from 1942 to 1945. In this camp, Corkey tended many of the 1,700 fellow prisoners.

While the Corkeys lived in Goldsboro, North Carolina, after the war, the Rev. Corkey had several churches, and Dr. Corkey earned her Master's in Public Health at UNC Chapel Hill. This degree brought her to Charlotte in 1955 as assistant director of Mecklenburg County Public Health. She taught at Charlotte College and at its successor, UNC Charlotte.

Dr. Corkey's outstanding and rather daring contribution to the Charlotte community in the sedate, conservative 1950s includes her early advocacy for birth control and well-baby clinics. She worked on in the 1980s when she herself approached her 80s, continuing in clinics serving the elderly, the retarded, and the mentally ill long after she had retired.

A Quaker, she helped found the Charlotte Friends Committee and exerted strong leadership (like many other outstanding women included here), as president of the Business and Professional Women and of the Charlotte YWCA.

Through their mutual interest in public health, Dr. Corkey came to know and work with Sarah Bryant, a young Charlotte native who was a Myers Park housewife in the 1950s. Bryant suspects her own interest in helping young girls began when she worked as a teenage counselor at a camp on Lake Wiley for underprivileged girls. In the 1950s, she had served on the YWCA Board and was asked to be on the Florence Crittenton Board. At first Bryant tutored in the school that the Crittenton Home for pregnant, unwed girls conducted near Memorial Hospital. Then she served on the local and national Crittenton Home Board of Directors.

As she got more involved, Bryant and others realized that Charlotte needed something like a planned parenthood service to offer skilled counseling and education about contraception. They saw that wealthy women could get care from their doctors, although contraceptive devices were against the law until

1941 in many states. The poor could go to the Crittenton Home, but, says Bryant,

> middle-class people with low income were having trouble. A mother of three who could not afford to have any more children didn't have anywhere to get help. Or a young married couple not ready or unable to start a family had no options.

> Maybe I was naïve or just bold, but I called together leaders from churches, businesses, the health department, from medical and political fields . . . and everybody would say, 'Sarah honey, I'm just too busy.' I'd say, 'Would you give me six weeks? Let's talk about it.' So we met at the United Way. After three months, the group decided to go for it because there was a need. In New York at the headquarters of Planned Parenthood, I looked at their map and it looked like Charlotte was in the Third World. Planned Parenthood was very well known and much respected in the northeast, California, Michigan, and Missouri. They had a place in Atlanta and Miami. The map was pretty blank. We needed help here.

At a regional meeting in Columbia, South Carolina, Bryant says her group's leaders were advised, "'If you raise $10,000, you can open a clinic.' We did that and were given the equipment of a former OB-GYN doctor. We had many volunteers. A retired Marine general was our financial person. We were told by the head of the health department that we had no idea what we were getting into, the running of a clinic. But we found out pretty fast." Bryant was the director for two years, and the clinic operated on grants from the Reynolds Foundation, the Duke Endowment, and a small grant from the United Way. The organizing group became their first board of directors.

With expert assistance, they set up a counseling room and a training program for counselors, Bryant recalls. "Later the doctors in Charlotte urged us to open an abortion clinic, since there was one in town which was operating pretty badly." For several years in those early days, Bryant says,

> OB-GYN doctors gave their time to come to the clinic and do examinations and prescribe contraceptives. In about 1971, we opened the clinic and in 1974–75, doctors at the clinic were doing abortions. Our main concern was care. We believed young women have the right to

make this choice. The difficult part was when the public protested, not understanding that the purpose of Planned Parenthood was to help women so they would never have to choose abortion.

The clinic was down on McDowell Street in a large building with a parking lot. Since it was a multi-purpose building and we were on the fourth floor, protesters could not come on the premises. They had to stay on the street to demonstrate. The director at that time was Neal Leach. He would go out and serve them coffee and talk to them on the street. We had lots of threats.

[Bryant picked up a red telephone she keeps on a shelf in her home.] This is the red telephone I used that first year to answer calls from people who asked where they could go to get help from Planned Parenthood. At first, I had to send them other places. I had calls like the one from a boy at a pay phone who asked, 'How do you know if your girlfriend is pregnant?' Or once two college students on spring break drove from Nashville, Tennessee. All I could do was send her to Washington, D.C. or Atlanta.

And then there was the morning about nine o'clock. I still had on my robe when the front doorbell rang. At the door a young couple stood and looked astonished. They asked, 'This is Planned Parenthood?' I laughed and said, 'Yes, what there is of it. Come in and sit down.'

I ran upstairs, put on my clothes and came down and said, 'Now what can I do for you?' They were married. She had a job to help him through graduate school. She thought she was pregnant. It would be a terrible hardship if they were going to have a child right then. So I took them to the Planned Parenthood clinic to the doctor. She was not pregnant, but it further emphasized our need to help. Fathers would call on this phone worried about their daughters. Parents from Wilmington called. There needed to be someplace, not just me on the telephone. I kept a record so we could see what the trend was, what the needs were. We had to do more.

And they did.

Joan Zimmerman didn't set out to be a showgirl. Or a major civic force. But she did and hers is quite a story.

Zimmerman left her native Chicago as a toddler when her Irish father and English mother moved to England. There in Lancashire County she spent her childhood and finished an executive secretary course at an English business school. When she took a civilian job with the U.S. forces in Germany, she met Greensboro native Robert Zimmerman, an army corporal. They married in 1956, and Joan, between the birth of two sons, held part-time jobs. She and her husband were living in Raleigh when the general manager of the state fair came by the public relations office where Joan worked. The manager suggested a show in the new Raleigh arena. He had seen a flower and garden show in New York that was a great success. He wanted to suggest one for Raleigh. Her employer didn't buy it, but Joan did.

"It was a really good idea," she recalls. Her husband was tired of traveling seven states for his family's firm selling electrical equipment to farm suppliers, so they tried the show in Raleigh. People loved it, but the Zimmermans decided to look for another city where it would be even more successful. Demographic studies pointed them to Charlotte, where they moved the show in 1962 to the new Charlotte Merchandise Mart. It was a hard sell at first, because Charlotte wasn't used to large public events, so the couple kept their day jobs. He sold insurance. She did bookkeeping and even sold encyclopedias.

Renamed the Southern Living Show, and later the Southern Spring Show, the event drew the sponsorship of *The Charlotte Observer,* which Joan credits as giving them "instant credibility." Then they devised another show at Christmas, similar to the show they had staged at the High Point Furniture Mart. Joan thought, why not put all those church bazaars and small events together? In 1967 they put together the Southern Christmas Show and subsequently the Southern Woman's Show, later to creatively expand this "show business" to other cities as the International Women's Show.

In the year 2000, the company Southern Shows, Inc. produced 21 shows a year in 14 cities, shows which attract 500,000 people. To do this, they work with major national corporations and media concerns who seek face-to-face contact with a captive audience and also provide a ready-made hungry market for the wares of hundreds of artisans, craftspeople, and small businesses. Each vendor pays a straight fee for exhibition space, ranging up from the smallest

10-by-10-foot area at about $400. The 40-person company experienced 12% growth in revenue in the 1990s.

At the Christmas Show, women are 80% of the crowd. Joan Zimmerman jokes about the man who said, "I paid six bucks to get in, but I'd pay 10 to get out." The average visitor spends $146 on food, gifts, gee-gaws, fancy decorations, Moravian cookies, ornamental decorated gourds, which include gourds resembling pigs, panthers, and hornets by the Gourd Lady, carvings, clocks, toffee, fudge, dulcimers, aprons, quilts, and more food. If the women are on a bus from Chester, for example, they can't leave until the bus leaves, so there are plenty of benches inside to sit on, plenty to eat, and plenty more time and access to more sights and shopping while waiting.

Joan had noticed that women who came to the women's shows in 1985 attended the financial planning and estate-advice sessions, but also flocked to the fashion shows and gourmet-cooking exhibits. So Southern Shows began including these events and also booking author talks and self-help sessions.

The Charlotte Christmas Show which draws busloads of shoppers from as far as Raleigh and Charleston, began as a three-day event, but in 2000 the show ran 12 days in November; it attracted 145,000 people and 600 exhibitors in 1999. "It's hard to imagine that this region only 40 years ago didn't know what a consumer show was. They didn't exist in our region, so explaining was a challenge," says Joan. "We couldn't get money from the banks. We didn't have wealthy families, so how did we fund it? We came up with a plan or as they call it in England, a 'scheme.' But we can't call it a scheme here, it doesn't sound quite right. We came up with a plan that would require all exhibitors, anyone involved with our shows, to pay 50 percent of their fees up front." That was 40 years ago. They had to establish credibility and Joan's boss, North Carolina public relations ace John Harden, "provided all our publicity hoping we would succeed, and he would get paid back. He taught us the need for trust and the need for friendships if you're going to succeed in business. It took us a long time to make any money on shows . . . so neither of us gave up our day jobs. We kept producing the shows on the side."

What else Joan Zimmerman has produced is a long career of astonishing civic involvement in Charlotte. In 1988, *The Charlotte Observer* called her "one of Charlotte's top civic leaders" after she chaired the Charlotte Convention

& Visitors Bureau, the Women's Political Caucus, the Charlotte chapter of the American Cancer Society, served as vice chairman of WTVI, and held prominent roles at the Charlotte Chamber of Commerce, Queens College, Covenant Church, and the Airport Advisory Committee. In 1987, she was the first recipient of the Business Woman of the Year Award and in 1999 was awarded *The Business Journal's* Business Woman of the Year Award. Along with other awards and honors, she was a rare female on NationsBank's Charlotte Board of Directors. Name almost any public or civic business or educational organization and she has worked for it, either at or near the top level during her 40 years in Charlotte business.

Joan says that part of her success has been in the partnership with her husband. "People ask how we're able to work together and stay married and happy so long. I'm going to tell you the secret. We know how to compromise. When we first went into business together, we decided that my husband would make all the big decisions and I would make all the small decisions. And he says, 'You know, it's interesting. In 37 years we've never had to make a big decision.'"

The best-known black woman in Charlotte in the 1950s and 1960s was "Chatty Hatty." Hatty Leeper also shone as the first black, female radio announcer in North Carolina.

As a teenager in the 1950s, Leeper and other youths were recruited by Charlotte radio station WGIV to work at the hugely popular rhythm, blues, and gospel music station. Leeper began as a "girl Friday" but soon was invited to talk on the air. She wasn't nervous: "Just give me a microphone and let me go," she said.

Leeper became a disc jockey who picked out and played tunes on the air and later booked national acts for local concerts. At WGIV, many performers and her colleagues were black, and she found herself questioned as to why she wanted a job in broadcasting, which was considered a man's world. People told her, "You should be home washing dishes and clothes." But she capitalized professionally on one of her best assets, "I love to talk. I could talk non-stop all the time."

Young women who have succeeded in broadcasting, such as Sheila Stewart, news and public affairs director at WGIV-AM and WPEG-FM, give her credit: "Because of her, so many doors opened for women in radio." Leeper is a member of the National Black Radio Hall of Fame and was inducted into the North Carolina Association of Broadcasters' Hall of Fame in 2000. WBTV reporter Steve Crump reports, "Even decades after WGIV's heyday, she is still one of the most recognized [radio] names."

Leeper left WGIV, moved to WRPL, and later to WAYS as announcer and sales executive. After earning bachelor's and master's degrees, she worked at Gaston College as broadcast department chairman. In 2000, she created Chatty's School of Comunication, a radio-TV-computer graphics school. Charlotte leader Willie Stratford says of Leeper, "She has a contagious personality, is aggressive in terms of business, and a good role model for other women. She has innate ability and charm that radiates. It attracts people." Leeper admits, "I have that extra whatever-it-is. That wheel that turns."

When Sis Kaplan and her husband Stan came from Chicago in 1965 to work and settle in Charlotte, they moved into a new and quite foreign time zone socially and culturally. Blacks still sat in the back of Charlotte buses. Schools and restaurants were segregated. Jews and Catholics were present, but distinct minorities. They, like blacks, knew their expected place was the background, sidelines, seldom foreground.

Sis Atlass Kaplan was Jewish, from a Chicago radio family. She learned the business early from her father and became a producer of shows and creator of programming for WBBM-TV (CBS) in Chicago. She won national and local awards for programs and reportage from 1956 to 1960. In 1960–64 she became a radio and television director for a Chicago agency and in that capacity produced and supervised sports programming for the Chicago White Sox, supervised media time buying, and produced documentary films, commercials, and programs about baseball clinics and sports.

In 1965 she became co-owner, with husband Stan, and general manager of WAYS Radio, and subsequently WROQ-FM in Charlotte, and also owned and operated a Jacksonville, Florida station. It came as quite a surprise to her that neighbors were offended when she and her husband bought a house in the center of prestigious, old Myers Park, across from the former Duke Mansion on Edgehill Road. Also, her neighbors did not know what to think about a mother who got her child off to school, and went to work every day at an office. A woman who ran things, who ran businesses. She sensed clear disapproval within the community of women.

"I had always worked," she recalled. "There was so much difference in Charlotte and Chicago. In Chicago you could live, work, and socialize with diverse people. Diversity did not exist here. It was WASPs and blacks. We saw a great opportunity." She recalls the 1960s when district attorney Elliot Schwartz got the first conviction for a cross burning in North Carolina. She got involved with the Community Relations Committee, which worked to smooth public antagonism to civil rights issues and events and to act as a change agent and problem solver for the community. She chaired this key group and numerous others that focus on human justice and community service. For this, she received the National Conference of Christians and Jews' Humanitarian of the Year Award in 1994, the same year she received both the award as Charlotte Woman of the Year and the Mecklenburg County Bar Association's coveted Liberty Bell Award.

While serving in the 1970s and 1980s as president of the National Radio Broadcasting Association, with its several-thousand-member radio stations, she worked with the Criminal Justice Commission to secure legislation for additional district attorneys and judges. The commission also forged ahead to secure a bond election for a new courthouse, and studied how blacks' and whites' legal cases were dealt with, and how quickly they were handled in the criminal justice system. They secured considerable funding for the community in terms of grants. Kaplan followed Jack Tate as chairperson of this high-profile and remarkably effective citizen group, whose efforts were not always appreciated by the criminal justice system.

Kaplan was a member of the Board of Visitors of Davidson College when it came out publicly that the Presbyterian school founded in 1835 was operating under a policy in which non-Christian faculty members could not get tenure. Kaplan recalls, "It was in their constitution. I was going to resign. It was a really interesting time." She didn't have to resign since public attention and reassessment led to a change in Davidson's policy.

In 1975, the Kaplans started a group of weekly newspapers, which were later formatted to become *The Charlotte Leader*. In 1988, they sold *The Leader* and repurchased it in 1994 with Sis Kaplan as president of Leader Newspaper, Inc. The local in-depth focus of this newspaper "is our strength, our one and only emphasis," she says. When asked who her mentors or best teachers have been in her career, Kaplan quickly cites Charlottean Jack Tate and Bill Veeck, with whom she worked in the early 1960s in Chicago.

Kaplan warns today's young women not to take for granted "what people before me and people in my generation have done to open the doors. They need to be ever vigilant not to lose but to gain momentum and opportunities for women. Choice is something you better get vigilant about."

Ann Cook wore it. The Charlotte Museum of History displayed her smart, blue, burgundy-trimmed uniform worn by early female letter carriers for the United States Postal Department in Charlotte. Essie Swearngan was the first female letter carrier in town and petite Ann Cook, the second. In 1909, shiny brass buttons on each burgundy-trimmed breast pocket have the design of a person walking above the initials P.O.D. (Post Office Department). At the neck, Cook's pale blouse had a burgundy tie knotted men's style. Wearing this along neighborhood sidewalks to deliver mail in the early part of the twentieth century, Cook must have been a proud and welcome sight. She was one of the women who gradually held civil-service positions. The rationing board during World War II included a black woman, but Charlotte waited past the middle of the twentieth century to hire women on the police force and was slower still to put them in uniform in the field of police protection.

Eloise Brown was hired in 1925 in the detective division of the Charlotte Police Department, where she developed a systematic record-filing technique. Two years later she was put in charge of a license bureau and became assistant clerk. The League of Women Voters in Charlotte claimed credit for pressure to put a woman in the police department in 1925. Attrition caused by World War II created two rare openings as dispatcher and desk sergeant, which Brown filled until war's end when she became chief secretary in the traffic division until she retired in 1959. Two other female colleagues held similar responsible jobs of a clerical and record-keeping nature during the latter period.

Not until a new police chief from out of town arrived in Charlotte was the absence of female police officers seriously questioned. John Ingersoll, the new police chief who was from Washington, D.C., decided the police department needed sworn female officers within the police station. In 1967, he and his staff set out requirements for female candidates. They insisted on the completion of a four-year college degree, although male police officers were only required to have a high school diploma at the time.

Gail Sloan, the first sworn female officer, had graduated from East Carolina University with a bachelor's degree in psychology in 1966. She was 23, married, and back in Charlotte when she noticed a newspaper article about Chief Ingersoll's decision to hire policewomen. She later recalled, "I went down to apply. They said they had to do a background check. They sent Sergeant Killman, who told me later on, they had told him to go down there [to Greenville, N.C., her college town] and find every roommate I had, any kind of demerits for four years. I came back clean. They said we had to be 5' 8" tall and weigh at least 160 pounds. I am about 5'8" so that was no problem. But I did weigh less than 160. About 152. They told me I could eat bananas and all that. But they said, since I was close enough, they'd waive that. . . . They were showing me things, trying maybe to discourage me, seeing if I was going to be okay, this was in the crime lab in the old building, showing me pictures, horrible death scenes, mutilations, to see if I was really interested. They hired me." *The Charlotte Observer* noted in front page headlines: "Woman Recruit, 22, Blonde, 5-8, Cute, She Doesn't Look Like A Cop!"

Then they hired Mickey Casey, the second female recruit, three weeks later. When recruit school started, Sloan recalls that since she and Casey would be full-fledged officers, "We had to do everything physically and mentally that men had to do. We were really watched in recruit school." The department soon hired two more women, Sallie Keene and Jeannette Houser. When three of these four graduated from the police academy, they became investigators in the Youth Bureau. The next year, Cheryl Williams and Annie Gillespie were hired. Gillespie was the department's first black female officer. For five years, the five women were the female police-force contingent. The fact that the women were placed directly in the Youth Bureau, a plum appointment, was

In 1966, Gail Sloan (r.) was the first sworn female police officer in the Charlotte Police Department and Mickey Casey (l.) was the second. Chasing suspects was difficult in the high-heel shoes and skirts they were required to wear. J.C. "Jake" Goodman was chief of police when female officers were finally allowed to wear slacks.
COURTESY OF CHARLOTTE POLICE DEPARTMENT

considered unfair, since some male officers had been trying to get in the Youth Bureau for years. Sloan said, "We knew that, so we bent over backwards not to flaunt the fact we could go right in and into plainclothes. We had no choice." If somebody said anything about it to Sloan, she and the other women would say, "Well, I would go into patrol. But they wouldn't let me go in patrol."

In the Youth Bureau, "the ivory tower," as police officers called it, Casey remembers that they were loaned out within the department and to outside agencies for law-enforcement-related work. "The public did not suspect a thing when one of us would go into an undercover situation. We were initially assigned what I call dead-end cases, just to see if we could do anything with them. We tried to make the best of what we had. We had to hustle because we were the first female officers. It was almost a make or break situation.

"Some of the male officers wanted to make us secretaries. They wanted to drive, and we would take notes. And back at the station when it came time to do the dictation on the case as you would normally do, they looked to us to do the paper work. . . . In some situations we did that to keep everybody happy." Casey recalls that they were tested by sexual overtures. "We were prime targets. Perhaps me less so than the other girls because my father was on the force. If you turned down somebody, you could reap repercussions, definitely.

"There were guys, to use the analogy of the female on a ship, who felt we were just bad luck. But we were there, and we just had to make the best of it. We ended up honestly enjoying our work. Anyone who is in law enforcement will tell you that police work is 95% social work. It was right up my alley. I was with the department 30 years and retired in 1996," says Casey. "To think you could make a difference in someone's life, that's immeasurable, a positive difference." The women were sent to speak to community groups and to teach female security classes. They led babysitting security classes for women who brought their teenage daughters to class. Employers often sponsored classes for their employees to attend. The female officers also represented the police department on numerous community boards.

Cheryl Williams had also graduated in sociology and wanted to be a social worker. In late 1967, a friend told her about the police department openings for female officers. "It appealed to me. It sounded like a social worker with a gun. Really neat. My mother hit the roof. She said, 'I didn't send you to college to be a police officer. I'm worried about you.' But in the end it was, 'This is my daughter, the police officer. Isn't that cool?'"

Williams was 22 when she began her job. She found there was no such thing as a clothing allowance for the women. They worked in plainclothes several years before getting a clothing allowance like their male counterparts. "The men who worked in plainclothes got it because they wore suits, but we got nothing, and we were required to wear dresses and heels. And to get it the women worked together to lobby for it. This was typical of us. We got the allowance finally."

Sloan said that since they were hired in the late '60s, when long hair was definitely the fashion for men and women, "we had to have hair not down to the collar." Williams was proud of her long hair, but she was told to cut it, wear it up, or wear a wig. She bought a wig to wear to rookie school, which proved mighty sweaty during mid-summer on the practice firing range.

J.C "Jake" Goodman was police chief when the women were finally allowed to wear slacks. This was a major event, because in the Youth Bureau "we were assigned cases where we would be chasing kids and wearing heels and dresses and that just didn't cut it," says Cheryl Williams Horner, "or if you are filing and having to bend over. When we could wear slacks and pantsuits, we had to be careful they were proper." And when they were allowed to wear uniforms in the 1980s, they were men's, with men's ties and men's shoes. The uniforms helped, even though they may have been ill-fitting, because after 1973, women who joined the police force were required to go straight into patrol and could also work in fraud, sex crimes, the detective division, and in the Police Attorney's Office. Jean Larson was the first hired to work in the Patrol Bureau and was also made the first female sergeant in the late 1970s, followed by Piper Charles, Andrea Huff, and Gail Sloan in the early 1980s.

Horner worked as a hostage negotiator for 15 years. She recalls one situation when the case involved what police described as

a 1073, a mental subject. This girl was tearing up an apartment. We got there before the patrol unit arrived and could hear her inside smashing things, screaming. A crowd gathered. She had a razor. We told her to quit and tried to calm her down. She went into the bathroom with the knife. My partner said, 'Go in there and get her,' so I went in and she had her back to me at the sink, still cutting on herself, but superficial cuts, not real bad. She turned around. When I told her 'Drop the knife,' she did and then she picked me up. I am about 5'9" and a pretty good size. She threw me up against the wall in the living room and it about knocked me out. The last thing I remember is that my partner and two patrol officers went in to get her. You don't think about being afraid. You've got a job and you just do it. Like on a homicide scene, you do it and then you go home and throw up. Or you go home and cry. Many a night I have cried all the way home, especially working juvenile. Something takes over on the job. There are certain steps any officer needs to follow at any crime scene.

Advancement was another issue. Sloan took the sergeant exam in 1981, but never did make sergeant although her scores were as high or higher than some men who made sergeant. "It was kind of the same thing as the other minority. Even though they made good on the test, they weren't promoted because they didn't think they were capable. I'd say, 'How come I didn't make sergeant?' They said, 'Because you have never been patrol.' But they wouldn't at the time let me be in patrol, no women in patrol until 1973."

Sloan heard these statements often: "'Men aren't going to take orders from women. Why would a police officer take an order from you?' They said actually they were protecting us by not putting us in that position. So I went and got a lawyer outside the department, Arthur Goodman. They researched it. I guess the police department didn't want the publicity, so they opened it up, and I made sergeant in 1980 or 1981."

Sloan felt that egos had a lot to do with some of the attitudes toward the female officers. "They hired pretty good-sized men who could handle themselves. Then here come these women, soft talking. It really hurt some of their egos. 'What are you going to do when you are beat up' they asked. Well, we got beat up. We just did like the men. We'd cry later. I don't think any of us cried in front of the men. But we cried later. I don't doubt some of the men cried later, too. Also some of the policemen's wives felt intimidated by us. I can understand that to a degree. Here is their man out riding with another police officer, which is us. And that's all I ever considered myself, just a police officer, not like a woman that's trying to get somebody's man. Some of the women made it hard on their guys. But we were just good friends. That caused problems."

Sloan became a mentor for female officers who followed her. Horner recalls that Sloan "sort of trained me when I first came on the department. I rode with her and watched her for a couple of days. We were talking in the car and the radio all of a sudden called her number. Everything excited me back then. I'd hear a siren and be ready to go."

One of the early policewomen on the force described how two officers had called needing assistance of a juvenile officer. The two officers got her in a room alone in an abandoned house and tried to pull her clothes off. She fought them, and they were unsuccessful. She did not report it at the time of the incident in the late 1960s, knowing "if I had reported it, I would not have been believed." In the months and years afterward, she saw these officers in the course of her job and did not speak to them, nor did she ever report her experience. The women agreed that their time as the first women officers was like being in the trenches together.

The three women, Horner, Sloan, and Casey, followed three long-term career tracks and retired in the 1990s with about 30 years apiece as police officers. Sloan was the first female captain and kept breaking barriers no female officer had done. She went into patrol and up the ladder into administration. Casey went into crime prevention, enjoying media relations. Horner was on the first rape unit for 14 years, was one of the first two sex crime investigators in Charlotte, and continued in the district attorney's office. Horner reflected how interesting it was that all three "had such different career tracks, all three in police work, officers carrying guns, but in whole different kinds of jobs." Sitting in a room together recalling their decades as police officers, they laughed about the first times they got beat up, or chafed with wearing skirts and heels while chasing fugitives, or struggled with some who fought, or feared the suspects would get their guns, which the policewomen had to carry in their pocketbooks.

At the turn of the century, female police officers are a familiar sight all around Charlotte. One 31-year-old police rookie, Sue O'Donaghue, said, "Police work takes a strong person, not only physically, but mentally and emotionally. You have to be a fast decision-maker and confident in yourself and your abilities." She finds it hard to gain initial respect from her colleagues as a female, "When you first come out, some of the guys will look at you like, 'Is she going to be there if I get in a fight? Is she going to stand her ground?' I hope everyone on my shift knows I will be."

Hilda Gurdian doesn't take no for an answer. Even when her bank turned her down for a small-business expansion loan, she kept on.

Gurdian and her family are part of a huge surge of Latino or Hispanic immigrants to the Charlotte area in the 1990s, increasing nearly sevenfold in the decade ending in 2000. Latinos have been in the area for decades, as Olga Parra can attest. Parra came to Charlotte from her native Ecuador in 1964 with her husband and soon got involved with helping other Latinos who were, like herself, also learning English. Parra is described in *The Charlotte Observer* as "a longtime Hispanic activist and founding member of the Latin American Women's Association." The group was begun in 1992 by a group of women who felt committed to promoting excellence in Hispanic women and their children, particularly in the areas of education of human services. They give many scholarships annually. Parra is credited with being "a consistent and persistent voice of support." The *Observer* recognized her, along with Maria Soler, executive director of the Hispanic-Latino Community Resource Center, as two of Charlotte's recent "Heroes of Democracy."

Newcomer Hilda Gurdian has made the news in more ways than one. She has been featured in numerous interviews as an articulate and successful spokeswoman for Latinos, as well as a businesswoman. She makes news as the publisher of *La Noticia*, which is not the only Spanish-language newspaper in Charlotte, but is recognized as the one "with the most extensive local coverage and the most useful information about how to adjust to Charlotte." Gurdian and her family know firsthand the difficulties of assimilating into a southern city, which has been largely unchanged ethnically until recent years. Historically Charlotte has been about two-thirds white Anglo-Saxon Protestants and about one-third southern African-Americans.

But in the 1990s, the Hispanic population of Charlotte increased by 129%. Only Arkansas and Nevada's Hispanic population grew at a greater rate. Mecklenburg County's Hispanic population grew in the 1990s by 157% with a 112% Asian increase. Adjacent Union County's Hispanic population grew a whopping 192%.

Gurdian remembers when she first heard about Charlotte. She was sitting in her bedroom in Caracas, Venezuela, reading English language magazines to which she subscribed in order to keep up her fluency in English. She read *Entrepreneur, Good Housekeeping,* and *Fortune*. An article in *Fortune* described the "10 best cities in the U.S. for small business" citing Charlotte, Jacksonville, Florida, and Athens, Georgia. She recalls, "It captured my attention. I wanted to be north of Miami, so I went to the American Embassy to get every bit of information about Charlotte: weather, growth, southern hospitality and so on."

Gurdian's family owns four newspapers and one radio station in Los Teques, a suburb of Caracas. She says she and her husband Alvaro brought their two young sons to America to seek a place that offered better opportunity. They felt that Venezuela was not offering opportunities for their future. She had started an advertising agency there in 1986.

When she was a girl, Gurdian dreamed of being an interpreter at the United Nations. She could at one time speak French, Italian, Spanish, and English. When she arrived in Charlotte, she realized she would have to relearn English, finding it so different to speak than to read. She recalls, "It took me three years. I listened to tapes in the car, in bed with headphones. I'd repeat what people spoke. I'd repeat in a mirror, 'This is going to work.' I listened to tapes of Stephen Caufield's *Ten Habits of Successful People* and Dr. Ken Blanchard's *One Minute Manager*. I had to study American culture, how to behave in ways that would not offend anyone. How to dress. How to talk and gesture. In my country people touch people too much, get too close. I feel after these eight long years of hard work, I have overcome these obstacles."

Gurdian's newspaper gives annual *Excelente* awards to four recipients: Hispanic businessman of the year, Hispanic businesswoman of the year, a Hispanic community service person, and a non-Latino most supportive of the Latino community interested in promoting unity among those in the community. "We want to work against stereotypes, that Latinos are in construction or landscaping. We have a work ethic, are family people, religious people. We want to show the community who we really are. Many people coming here today come with four years of a college degree. Some come without any English. Some doctors or accountants have to work in construction, landscaping, or at hotels waiting on tables to learn English."

Gurdian found Charlotte very open to women and Latinos. She says, however, "I had many challenges. I had to find money to expand the business. As a businesswoman, I couldn't get a loan from the bank where I had an account. I was turned down because I had no credit history. I had a wise and thorough business plan. I had an account with that bank for a number of years. I had good references. They said come back only if you have collateral."

So she put $15,000 of savings into the business, leased equipment, and for two years paid herself very little. When their business grew and had some money, their credit history enabled them to get the loan they needed. They hired communication consultants, and she took courses in corporate training at CPCC. Gurdian knows from experience how difficult life is for people from different countries, because it took her years to make the adjustment, to get established, and to lose enough of her accent that she could be understood and accepted as a businesswoman in a southern city.

Many people told Gurdian that she would not be successful in Charlotte because it was a "good old boys' city." So she worked harder and has been accepted as a successful businessperson. Eight years since her arrival in Charlotte in 1992, she feels "like a student who is very happy to have done my homework." Her feelings about and description of Charlotte are very positive, which shows she has indeed learned how to succeed in this place.

CHAPTER EIGHT

*I*n the late 1960s and early 1970s, Minette Trosch tended her three small boys while her husband Lou taught business administration at UNC Charlotte and also practiced law in Charlotte. She recalls that when they first came to Charlotte in 1965, Lou couldn't practice law because he was from out of state and could not take the North Carolina bar exam for a year. He became a law clerk on a very low salary, and Minette planned to teach to help support them. With a degree from DePauw University she completed her course work for her M.A. in political science from West Virginia University. She completed her thesis while pregnant with their first child. "Back then, you went for a Mrs. degree. If you wanted well-educated children, you got well-educated your-self," she recalls. "They didn't let you teach once you got pregnant, so by February I was out of a job. I worked nights for my dad's accounting firm.

Later, I had children and side jobs. I showed and managed duplexes with a baby on one hip."

But when her youngest of three sons was three years old, she recalls, "I was going stir crazy and wanted to go back to school. Lou said, 'What do you want to do?' I had done the volunteer route until I couldn't do it anymore. I didn't like coffee klatches or gossip." So in 1977, when she was "bemoaning the loss of my wonderful talents to the world," she remembers how an odd opportunity arose in her own living room.

District representation began that year, allowing geographic electoral districts instead of all candidates running at-large for city office. Lou and Minette lived in the new District Five, which Ken Harris had filed for. Near election time, Harris switched to run for mayor instead (an election which he won), which left District Five with no Republican candidate. A neighbor came to the Trosch house to ask Lou if he would run. He declined, but suggested they consider Minette instead. "My mother said, 'I'll keep the baby.' So I said, I can't whine anymore. I can walk out that door. I did. I filed.

"I knew nothing. I had lots of education and am very outgoing, although timid inside. I had never spoken in public. Knew nothing about zoning. So I locked myself in a room. I studied and read issues. Studied zoning. I promised myself if I got elected, I'd know planning better than anyone else.

"I had to go up to *The Charlotte Observer* office to be interviewed as a candidate. Before I did, I found out where the *Observer* staff lived and went to nearby thoroughfares they had to drive to get to work. I asked homeowners along these roads if I could put up my sign in their yards." After Trosch's *Observer* interview, a staff member said to her, "You've got such a good campaign. Your signs have sprung up all over!"

"Nobody," says Trosch laughing, "will ever say I go unprepared."

Trosch won election to city council along with Laura Frech. Two other female council members, Pat Locke and Betty Chafin Rash, were already on the council. Trosch served five consecutive terms. In 1983, she switched from her district seat to run at-large and she won handily, garnering the most votes among council candidates, therefore becoming mayor pro tem. She recalls, "I was burned out by then. My teenagers and my parents walked the streets campaigning for me. Other women supported me. We had no money, but we won. I found out that this can happen if you really learn your issues and give it your all. Part of the reason I switched was that I didn't feel the belt road was a good thing. This put me at odds with the 'good old boys.' My priorities were for road spending by technical and federal standards, not to build roads as a political payoff."

She had become so knowledgeable about planning issues, she was asked to be on the National Board of Directors of the League of Cities and received a national award because of her experience in planning and belt-road issues. Nevertheless she and Frech were called "the Bobbsey Twins." Looking back, Trosch says "I loved the job. I hated the campaigns and asking people to pay or to vote." She resented opponents or critics saying, as they did about many of the early female council members, "She's nothing but a housewife with nothing else to do all day."

When Trosch chose not to run in 1987, the idea of going to law school began to appeal to her. "I had been involved in state laws and wanted to know more about how to make laws. In law you can do something about it." But first she entered the master's program in counseling at UNC Charlotte, chaired by Dr. Mary Thomas Burke. She took most of the courses toward the degree, but decided instead to take the LSAT, a preliminary to entering law school. She was also running a family business in uptown Charlotte for a year, turning it from a financial nightmare into a very profitable venture, which they then successfully sold. The whole family got into "avid small business training," reminding Trosch of a frequent male complaint against female council members, "These women don't understand business!"

When Trosch was 49, she entered law school at UNC Chapel Hill. One son was in law school there already and another was just entering the freshman class. When she went to interview for law school, a group of her sons' campus friends cheered her off. "Go, Miz Trosch!" they said.

Law school was "the hardest thing I ever did. I lived up there during the week and did very well. Law school was a gift to me. Doors opened for me. I finally have the gift to do what I wanted to do." In the early days of her marriage and role as parent, "I didn't know I could create my own choices. . . . I should have always been a professional person. I have people whom I mentor and who mentor me, and they are not male."

After her graduation from law school in 1995 at the age of 52, Trosch's law practice in family law fell into place as she used her counseling skills learned in UNC Charlotte graduate courses and her experiences on council and with women. She practices in a small law firm, which includes her husband, her son, and four other lawyers. She describes her work as "anything involving the beginning of marriage (prenuptial agreements) to the dissolution of marriage, as well as adoption, custody, child support, domestic violence, separation support, and division of property." She counsels and works for many female clients and says of herself, "I've shed the stereotypes I felt the female should be. I have done stay-at-home mom and now I can do in my life what I wanted and be excited about it. This phase is the best of all."

Trosch credits her tenacity in part to her mother, who said, "You can always do it." Her mother Mary Gilby Conrad had six children. "Mother took three of us several summers to Western Carolina, so she could renew her teaching certificate. She was a graduate of Carlton College and had a graduate certificate to teach mentally disadvantaged kids. This is where I learned that life is about always growing."

Ann Hammond learned in the midst of her four terms as city councilwoman that she "wasn't a very good Republican." So she switched parties in 1988 and continued for two additional terms. The story of how she was first elected typifies a circa 1980s trend in which a suburban neighbor takes leadership in a neighborhood concern and brings it to action within the city's political process. Often in Charlotte in the late 1900s, this leader was a woman.

Hammond lived on Sardis Road, an old farm-to-market road in eastern Charlotte, a road which connects the Matthews area with Providence Road. A native of Virginia with a degree in French from Duke University, she had been invited to join the Junior League in Charlotte and chose to work with the league's study and action Planning and Growth Management Committee. She read anything she could find on the subject and developed contacts with city staff and planners in the league study process. When the Sardis Road thoroughfare construction plan arose, "I drew on some contacts with the Planning

Commission and council. Minette Trosch was my council representative and she put me in touch.

"I knew we couldn't stop the expansion, but we got constructive input on the engineering plan." The road was residential, and they got the five-lane crossing section with a left-turn lane changed so there would be turn lanes only at significant intersections. She recalls, "It helped minimize the width of the median. You can refine a road to maximize tree preservation.

"I got to meet people in the neighborhood, put my name in to get appointed to the planning commission, but was unsuccessful. I got the advice that planning commission appointments were so political, I'd do better to run for council."

When Trosch was scheduled to run for her fourth term on the council in District Five in 1983, she dreaded the forthcoming election battle. She recalled Hammond's smart success in neighborhood issues. Trosch and Hammond went to the elections office minutes before the midnight deadline where Trosch switched to run at large and Hammond filed for Trosch's District Five council seat. It turned out to be a very savvy political move for both women. Both were elected as Republicans, and six women sat on the 10-member council that year.

Hammond recalls, "I made planning my strong interest in my eight years on council. My experience there was wonderful, especially the first four years. Democratic Mayor Gantt's leadership style was very reinforcing to me, coming out of the neighborhood movement. He cared about planning aspects. My final two terms were with a more polarizing council. . . . It was a great joy my first term to sit next to councilwoman Laura Frech, one of the smartest people I have ever known. She had wonderful historical memory and had been on council since the 1970s. She, Pam Patterson, and Trosch were mentors." Hammond recalls that Trosch "had a keen sense of process, how you go about getting something done. We had sons the same age and became good friends. She and I went over agendas before meetings, and it was good to have informational/process gaps filled in. . . . At the time it was less likely that a woman on council would be engaged in business interests, such as Carla DuPuy, Lynn Wheeler, and Cyndee Patterson are now."

Hammond was on the council four years, was defeated in the 1987 primary, and in the gap was looking for something to do. "Someone told me that Huntersville was looking for a part-time planner." Although she had no professional training, they told her, "Your experience is great." At the end of 1988 she was hired. Later she asked if she could keep her job and run again for Charlotte City Council. The Huntersville officials agreed. She served one term beginning in 1989, ran in 1991 as a Democrat, won, and became mayor pro tem, since she led with the most votes. She later ran unsuccessfully for mayor. In all, she served four terms on the city council.

"As soon as I lost, I signed on full-time in planning in Huntersville," which had long been a sleepy village among rolling countryside but was rapidly becoming a burgeoning bedroom community for Charlotte and for people desiring to live near Lake Norman and near the I-77 artery. In 1977, Hammond earned her Master's of Science degree in Architecture in Town Planning and Urban Design from the Architecture School at UNC Charlotte. It was the first year of the program. One of her professors, architect David Walters, became her professional mentor.

Hammond explains her compelling interest in planning: "I grew up in Albemarle County, Virginia, outside Charlottesville. That does something to people. Your concept of what is right and good for the environment is the University of Virginia and the wonderful area there. This marks you to maintain that high standard. In most southern cities you see these strips and wonder, why are we doing this to ourselves? The rules are actually sanctioning what is happening. Why can't we do it better? You see examples of ways it was done well in the past and you say, let's try to do it again. My passion is taking what my mentors have given me and pointing others to that."

"You do this by taking a planning commission on a walkabout in Dilworth or Fourth Ward or in Boston to see the three-dimensional space, compared to a two-dimensional city space, and give people the chance to experience the city in a new way. When given the choice, they may choose the environment that makes them feel better. Look for quirky things that are great."

Hammond's work as planning director of Huntersville required that she and her staff propose and maintain the ordinances that regulate zoning and to administer these. "We guide people through the ordinance requirements, so they can develop a plan that complies with the ordinance. Huntersville standards are different," she says, with parking lots to the side and behind. Working with car dealerships and fast-food enterprises, which are not used to such standards, requires patience on both parts, but "they are getting it. If you make national franchises do it and they want to be there, they will comply."

At the age of 55 in the passionate light of a new career, Hammond was lured away from Huntersville to a large opportunity beginning in 2001 as director of planning for Nashville and Davidson County, Tennessee. She sold her Sardis Road farmhouse (a local historic landmark built in 1869) and she moved, like many early nineteenth-century Carolinians did, to the new prospects of Tennessee. She says, "I stayed home with my children and wouldn't trade it for anything. Consequently we [she and Trosch] are of an age when you might think we are winding down, but we are very fresh in our careers, unlike how I would be if I had been doing it since I was 23. I can't recover the financial reward, but the joys of seeing children grow are irreplaceable rewards."

Neighborhood residents alarmed by the prospects of sudden change have proved a fertile garden to raise vigorous, new female leaders, particularly since the late 1970s and 1980s in Charlotte. At public meetings, an organized, energized, articulate woman armed with facts was once a rarity, even in the early 1970s. One who could rouse and round up a creative neighborhood group rose remarkably in this ripe field—Susan Green.

She grew up in the Rock Hill and Charlotte area. After college and graduate studies, she worked for the Equal Employment Opportunity Commission as an investigator and conciliator in eastern North Carolina, then moved back to Charlotte to work for CPCC and as business manager of the Charlotte Opera. In 1977, she and her husband had just bought rural acreage and built a house in southern Mecklenburg County in the sparsely settled, wooded section of pastures and fields known as Lower Providence. Six months after they moved in, a neighbor called to say, "The county is going to vote in the morning to build a belt road next door to your house."

Susan said, "They can't do that. There's not been anything on television or in the newspapers. America doesn't work that way." Susan learned there would be a meeting at nine the very next morning. She drove 18 miles into Charlotte and spoke before the county commissioners, although she had never been to a public meeting or spoken before elected officials. They voted, she recalls, "three to two in favor of a line that several commissioners had drawn with a blue marker that swung across Carmel Road, crossed McAlpine Creek next to me, south of Highway 51 and through properties that their friends and other officials owned. I got mad."

Green spent the next 48 hours getting 450 people to come to a North Carolina Board of Transportation meeting two nights later. This group formed the Southern Mecklenburg Association. They elected Green president, and she began calling on officials, lobbying, and making statements at public hearings and rowdy debates. One debate pitted Green against developer John Crosland. Green recalls that on the strength of these experiences, the city and county were pushed to adopt a conflict-of-interest policy that subsequently affected city council, county commission, and the planning commission. The neighborhood group's efforts resulted in the creation of the Metropolitan Planning Organization which brought "a planning process for land use and transportation decisions to the six small towns in the county. Green watched I-485 "developed in the area where state engineers, planners, the city council, and the Southern Mecklenburg Association agreed it should not go."

The notoriety gave Green high visibility, and she began working with leaders of other neighborhood concerns in the Elizabeth and westside groups. In 1978, she was selected to be in the first Leadership Charlotte class, which was designed to train and educate future leaders. Green's choice of study was the lack of equitable ambulance service for Charlotte's westside. Green soon realized that her research and investigations gave her at least as much or more knowledge about certain issues as city council members had. She got together a campaign team, paid the filing fee, and called Virginia Bowser, whom she had met in the Women's Political Caucus, to get advice on how to raise money. Bowser, who raised funds for the American Red Cross, told Green, "For clinking money, shake the can. For folding money, shake the hand."

Green asked Oliver Rowe, whom she knew from her work with the Charlotte Opera, to help. He became her mentor and contributed when she called on him for $500. She went to see Hugh McColl, president of NCNB, now Bank of America. Green remembers saying, "'You don't know me, but I am going to run for county commissioner, and I know you are going to give money to support others who are running. I want you to give money to support me, too. I want 20 minutes of your time. Would Tuesday or Thursday of next week suit you better?' And he saw me! He wrote me a check and convened his key executives next Monday and said, 'All right, tell them what you told me.' So I did.

"McColl said, 'I am going to support her. I have already given her $500, and I want you to support her too.' That was how I got started. I was the youngest person, as far as I know, ever to run for county commissioner and get elected. I came within 800 votes of being the top vote-getter, the first time I ran." Green was 30 when she was elected.

She worked at the job as though it was a full-time job during her four years in office. At the end of that time, she wanted to do something else. She filed to run for Congress in the Ninth District. She got 42% of the vote in the primary and lost to D.G. Martin in the primary runoff. When the numbers came in and he was declared winner, she stood on a chair and endorsed him at the election gathering and drove with him the next morning to the other counties in the district to campaign for him against his Republican opponent Alex McMillan.

When Green had finished her second county commission term, she recalls, "I gave away all my bow ties and suits. I have not worn green since or put a necktie near my face." Both were trademarks of her campaigns. Since that time in various fields, she has exercised her skill in connecting people, "to take the gleam in somebody's eye and find the resources to make it come true. That's what I've done in one field or another." She says one of the things she learned coming along is "you don't step on the fingers of somebody who is coming up the ladder behind you."

Ella Scarborough says she has always been political. The five-term city councilwoman, who is the daughter of a Baptist minister, has been involved in protests since the 1960s. As a Charlotte public official, she took her protests into the official arena in terms of housing and crime prevention for her District Three constituents in Charlotte's west and southwest neighborhoods.

In Sumter, South Carolina, where she grew up, Scarborough was involved in civil rights sit-ins when she was 13. She says, "Three hundred of us were jailed. We were protesting because we couldn't walk in the front door of the Sumter Theater. We could only go in the back door to see movies. We wanted to be treated like first-class citizens. The first time I was able to go in the front door, my mother and I and my best girlfriend and her mother went to see 'Who's Afraid of Virginia Woolf?'"

In 1968 she protested at South Carolina State University at Orangeburg when four people were killed in the "Orangeburg Massacre." She recalls, "I was on the front line. We crawled back on our bellies to the university infirmary to see our friend who had been shot. The next day they dismissed the whole school."

As city councilwoman, she served for 10 years (1987–97) and tried "to ensure people were not discriminated against in housing—to get local money, pushing it into housing mainly in the neighborhoods of Druid Hills, Reid, Park, and Amay James. We made a checklist for absentee landlords before renters moved in, and the state of the house when they moved out. We got a city ordinance against absentee landlords' allowing drug dealers to rent houses in the neighborhood. I got three death threats while on the council. A 70-year-old woman called me up, 'Miz Scarborough, we slept on the floor because drug dealers were shooting between houses!' I got to know the police officers. They blow their horns at me today."

In 1997 Scarborough ran unsuccessfully for the U.S. Senate; in 1999 she lost her bid for mayor. She had come to Charlotte in 1971 to work with the Charlotte-Mecklenburg Schools as a librarian. "I was married and barely pregnant. When they learned I was pregnant, they made me quit. Took back their contract. They said, 'When the baby is born, call us back.' I subbed as librarian and worked at Quail Hollow Junior High from 1970 to 1975, then went to Duke Power as technical librarian and was there for 22 years, as supervisor of the library information center, then the information technology library, then as corporate communications specialist." She became the national president of the Nuclear Librarians Association and served as president of Metrolina Librarians.

When Scarborough's second child was nine months old, she took the baby with her to colleges and universities as she recruited for Duke Power. She recalls the 1980s when she and other councilwomen went on trips and to meetings into what had been a male bastion of activity. On the management retreat, Scarborough recalls that the men said, "'We're going golfing. What are we going to do with Ella?' 'She'll go shopping,' they said. I played golf," Ella recalls. "The boss said, 'If she wants to play golf, we'll teach her.' He put me in his cart and showed me how to tee off and all that. I've been playing ever since."

On a trip to view other cities with the city council, board of education and members of the county commission, the men would go to a baseball game. "The women can go shopping," she remembers hearing them say. "But Gloria Fenning and about three other women went with me to the baseball game. I enjoyed those ladies. We could caucus in reference to issues." Her succinct advice to other women who balance a full-time job with family and elective office is "Focus. Organize."

Councilwomen Scarborough and Minette Trosch compared notes on their frustrating experience in the early days of fundraising for their political campaigns. They raised money in $15 and $25 amounts while watching male colleagues pull in thousands of dollars from an evening's phone calls. Betty Chafin Rash, who served on the council from 1975 to 1981 says, "It's no fun being the token," recalling the days when she and Pat Locke were often the lone women on council or when Chafin Rash was the solitary female on boards of directors or advisory groups. She sees women gaining in politics as they gain in business, the professions, and involvement in the Charlotte Chamber of Commerce, historically a strong power-broking base of civic approval. In 1990, four women served on the board of directors of the chamber. In 1995, Sharon Decker was elected the first female president of the chamber, a major breakthrough.

Carla DuPuy became a successful businesswoman and three-term county commissioner who served as chair (terms beginning 1984, 1986, 1988). She led a series of successful bond campaigns and gave strong leadership as board chair of the Public Library of Charlotte and Mecklenburg County (1982–84) in a difficult period following the departure of the longterm library director in 1982. As a business leader subsequent to her elected service, she has watched the remarkable progress of women since the 1980s. She sees more women rising to strong leadership in business, industry, and politics because they've learned how to play the game. "One of my boys was playing soccer last year, and I went to one of the games, and I asked one of the little girls, 'Where are the cheerleaders?' They had no cheerleaders. They were all playing field hockey."

Kate Gordon, former president of the Mecklenburg County Women's Commission and the Charlotte Women's Political Caucus, was excited by her talks with young women participating in a Young Women's Leadership Conference. "They take it for granted that, of course, they can be anything they want to be."

Minette Trosch and DuPuy agreed that the skills they learned as young girls to negotiate and to compromise, have served them well in public life. Velva Woollen, three-term city councilwoman, learned skills in her tenure with the Junior League as member and as president. League work taught her how to read a budget, run a meeting, raise money, and study issues. She has so often appealed for large amounts of money for the community, she says that she "heard somebody say one night, 'If I see another fundraising letter with Velva Woollen's name on it, I'm not going to send any.'"

Woollen's concern for the economically disadvantaged led her to six terms as chair of the Charlotte Housing Authority, along with service as chair of the board of Discovery Place and chair of the Salem College Board of Trustees.

Two popular four-term city councilwomen have been Cyndee Patterson (terms beginning 1985, 1987, 1989, 1991) and Sara Spencer (terms beginning 1993, 1995, 1997, 1999). Both proved to be formidable campaigners and opponents whose careful and intelligent attentions to issues and to their constituents created a solid base of support for their service. Even changes in Spencer's district boundaries beyond her home territory of Dilworth did not deter loyal voters from re-electing her.

Patterson grew up in Miami and arrived in Charlotte in 1979 with a background in finance to work for NationsBank. While working for the bank in 1982, she and a colleague, Koni Kirschman, originated an uptown street festival, SpringFest, which was quite successful. Since 1985, she has held parallel careers as a public servant and as an ace organizer of special events for corporations and cultural groups with her company Patterson Blake, Inc., a corporate meeting, planning, and special events consulting firm.

Also in 1985, she was elected to city council, where she served until 1993 with a term as mayor pro tem. In the 1990s, she became president of Lynnwood Foundation in Charlotte, which as a non-profit, preserves the historic Duke Mansion in Myers Park and operates the Lee Institute at that location, which focuses on collaborative, boundary-crossing community leadership.

Martha Alexander married a Charlottean and knew from the outset that they would live in Charlotte, where he began his medical practice. Alexander's father was an attorney and a city councilman in Duval County, Florida. Her parents were active in the Democratic party and Martha was elected vice president of the student body at Florida State her senior year, 1960–61. "At that time," she says, "women could not run for president of student government."

In the interim before she first ran for the North Carolina Senate in 1990, she had two children, was an active volunteer, president of the Junior League, and held several jobs. She was the chaplain's assistant at Presbyterian Hospital for several years. When Alexander took the job at Presbyterian, she recalls, "They wanted someone with a master's degree. So I went back to school and back to work at the same time. I took nine hours of classes and worked part-time at the hospital. The professors at the university let me take the counseling courses first, reversing what a curriculum would look like, so I could get those skills and use them at the hospital."

For 11 years, her subsequent job was executive director of the Council for Alcoholism and Chemical Dependency, begun in the 1950s, later known as the Chemical Dependency Center. It provided education and outpatient treatment. Earlier, it had been a referral agency, referring people to Open House, a drug treatment center started by Dr. Jonnie McLeod in the basement of a house.

When Alexander ran for office, a constituent told her, "You are going to bring a whole new perspective to the legislative process. With your background in counseling and listening, you are going to listen to people, and they are going to be surprised." One lobbyist came by her office one day at the legislature and when he left he said, "You listened to me. I don't think you agree with me, but you listened." Alexander feels that "people need to be listened to . . . and I need to know what I am voting against as well as what I am voting for."

Alexander lost her first race for the legislature. "I received over 41% of the vote, so I knew if I was running in the right place at the right time, I had an opportunity. So I went out again, this time to the House of Representatives. I won in 1992 by 50 votes. Ever since I got there, I have worked on mental-health issues and those concerning addiction and developmental disabilities. People are not aware how many issues are state issues that relate to every facet of their life, particularly in education and health."

Alexander regards her father and Dr. Mary Thomas Burke as powerful mentoring influences in her life. "I met her [Burke] in the early 1970s when I was developing a course for the Junior League and wanted someone to help me. It was a time when we were all going back to work or going back to school, unless you were like Jonnie McLeod, a physician. For the rest of us, we raised our children and did volunteer work and that was fine, but I saw a need for women to have a resume and some specific skills. Dr. Burke came to the league and did a Christmas program. I followed her out the door, saying I want UNC Charlotte to do this, and I want you to help."

Alexander was elected to Jo Graham Foster's seat, which former school-teacher Foster had held for 10 terms (terms beginning 1972–90). Alexander sees Foster as "a role model for many women, as was Liz Hair, and Ruth Easterling, a real champion of women. She has given me specific bills she knew I would be interested in. When I got to the legislature there were three women I spent a lot of time with my freshman year. I would just sit and listen to them, 'B' Holt of Burlington, Ruth Easterling, and Marie Colton Waters of Asheville. We'd go over to Darryl's at 11:30 at night for dinner. They talked about the past and about current legislation. A lot of legislation is going back and fixing things or bringing things up to date. Child care issues, for instance. Things change, so I just listened to why they were going to vote or not vote on something. They'd say, 'Remember how we tried to do that.' They have a good sense of the body as a whole, the people there." Alexander felt that Mecklenburg state senator Leslie Winner was really good at new ideas and getting a bill through legislation immediately, which was very unusual.

Since Alexander had, prior to her election, traveled to Raleigh several times to do advocacy work on behalf of an issue, she agrees, "I knew a little bit how it felt to be on the other side. I also knew how to work it on the other side. I was told you could not go into a certain area, but the minute they took a break, boy, I was on that floor and right there. What I went after was accomplished. They had told me it was too late. Because of my persistence, they finally gave me that microphone and let me speak to this committee, and they finally took care of what it was. But I knew how to work the system."

In the 1990s, she recalls that there were about 25 females out of the 120 legislators, with seven women in the Senate. Alexander was minority whip under minority leader Jim Black, also of Mecklenburg. One committee she was on had no other women, so she drove consistently to Raleigh just for the meeting. "Because there are so few women, it really behooves us when we are put on something, to be there. It is not to our advantage at all to scream and yell and holler. We just need to keep being there. I did speak to the majority leader. One day when something occurred, I said to him, 'I can't believe you would do that to us women.' He said, 'Don't get that sexist thing with me.' I said, 'It might not have been your intent, but you need to understand something. I will get into it. I worked on that bill. We needed to have been included.'"

Alexander returned in 2001 for her fifth term, joining other female colleagues from Mecklenburg County including Easterling and Connie Wilson, 41, a Republican banker with Charlotte-based Bank of America, who has served five terms. In 2001, Alexander was named "Advocate of the Year" by the National Association of Alcoholism and Drug Abuse Counselors.

In the 1970s through the year 2000, women increasingly won elections and served multiple terms for public office. Once they are in office and achieve a good record of cooperation and accomplishment, it is hard to unseat them. These women consequently have the occasional reward of running unopposed.

In addition to these are numerous females elected to equally important terms on the board of education, the boards of commissioners of Pineville, Davidson, Huntersville, Matthews, Mint Hill, and Cornelius. Women have been elected Register of Deeds; mayors of various town; county treasurer; judge; and township justice of the peace.

Charlotte women who have served
in some of the major city, county,
and state elective offices
(terms of office are listed by beginning dates)

Martha Alexander	state house	1992-2000
Marilyn Bissell	state house	1972, 1978
	county commission	1980-82
	district court judge	1984-92
Louise Brennan	state house	1976-82
Becky Carney	county commission	1996-2000
Sue Carter	city council	1999
Carla DuPuy	county commission	1984-88
Beverly M. Earle	state house	1996-2000
Ruth Easterling	state house	1976-2000
Gloria Fenning	city council	1985-87
Laura Frech	city council	1977-83
Susan Green	county commission	1980-82
Ann Hammond	city council	1983-91
Pat Locke	city council	1973-79
Maggie Markey	county commission	1998
Carolyn Mathis	state house	1972, 1974
	state senate	1976-80
Sue Myrick	city council	1983
	mayor	1987-89
	U.S. House	1994-2000
Cyndee Patterson	city council	1985-91
Pam Patterson	city council	1981-85
Betty Chafin Rash	city council	1975-79
Ruth Samuelson	county commission	2000
Ella Scarborough	city council	1987-95
Ann Schrader	county commission	1992-94
Sara Spencer	city council	1993-2001
Ann Thomas	county commission	1978
Minette Trosch	city council	1977-85
Lynn Wheeler	city council	1989-2001
Connie Wilson	state house	1992-2000
Leslie Winner	state senate	1992-96
Velva Woollen	city council	1983-87

In the year 2000, *Charlotte Observer* staff writer Jim Morrill reports that in North Carolina, female voters outnumber male voters 2.6 million to 2.2 million, although women remain under-represented in the state's congressional and legislative delegations. If this seems odd, it is helpful to remember that it took North Carolina until 1971 to ratify the Nineteenth Amendment, passed in Congress in 1920, which gave women the right to vote:

The right of citizens of the United States to vote shall not be denied or abridged by the United States or by any State on account of sex. Congress shall have power to enforce this article by appropriate legislation.

And North Carolina has yet to ratify the Equal Rights Amendment passed by Congress in 1972. For it to pass, ratification was necessary by 1979.

Women have so rapidly taken to elective office in Mecklenburg since the 1950s that nothing should be surprising. But Sue Myrick's rapid rise from city council member to Congress would be astounding in any era. She amazed even those who knew her best.

Few would dispute that Sue Myrick is a loner and a workaholic, a passionate maverick, a religious woman, and most often a fiscal conservative. Her remarkable rise from small-business owner to city councilwoman (1983–87), mayor of Charlotte (1987–91), and Republican United States Congresswoman from North Carolina in 1994 at the age of 53 is astonishing. Nor is it without losses and odd career zig-zags.

In the early 1980s, Myrick was president and CEO of Myrick Advertising and Myrick Enterprises with her husband, Ed. She ran as a city council candidate from the Citizens For Effective Government, a vocal, well-organized, conservative group who criticized and challenged the school bond referendum, the new convention center, the NFL stadium (Ericsson Stadium), garbage pickup arrangements, and other matters of city council concern. She was elected to the council and to mayor, unseating popular mayor Harvey Gantt with the help of the CFEG. The CFEG steadfastly opposed Gantt, who saw the convention center and Ericsson Stadium as opportunities for economic growth for the city.

Myrick lost her first attempt as mayoral nominee in 1985 by 58 votes, when she underspent her opponent by a third. In her mayoral race in 1991,

Using her background as a savvy advertising executive, city councilwoman Sue Myrick placed herself in the hectic rush-hour median of Independence Boulevard at Pecan Avenue to promote her candidacy for Charlotte mayor in 1987. Myrick, a Republican born in 1941 in Ohio, amazed skeptics by winning against popular Democratic mayor Harvey Gantt. She went on to win election as a U.S. congressional representative (R-N.C.), winning her fourth term to that office in 2000.
REPRINTED BY PERMISSION OF THE CHARLOTTE OBSERVER

however, she spent $280,369 and won, with over half of what she spent going to Myrick Advertising without profit for signs, buttons, brochures, and newspaper ads. She recognized what Gantt did not, that the city road situation was critical to the thousands of newcomers to Charlotte, who were distraught with inadequate roads on the edge of the city. Gantt lived in the center city and his popularity as mayor left him unprepared for Myrick's innovative advertising skills (once she stood in the median of Independence Boulevard with her sign) and with perimeter residents' backlash. Also, a Republican electoral tide helped sweep Myrick into office.

She chose not to run for a third term as mayor and in 1992 sought the nomination for U.S. Senate for the seat held by Democrat Terry Sanford. She lost the nomination and became a distributor for Amway, a company that sells detergents, cosmetics, and air fresheners. She sold distributorships. "It's not selling like you think of selling. I'm building a network of distributors who own their own businesses," she said.

And soon, in 1992, *The Charlotte Observer* reported, "Amway helped sell Myrick. Distributors from around the country contributed to her Senate campaign (an election she lost) and no doubt to the campaign that followed." Through Amway, Myrick had made speeches to conventions in Charlotte and around the South. Myrick considered a career as a motivational speaker while she and Ed turned back to advertising and to their nonprofit group called the Charitable Outreach Society. "This is just another period of our life. We're survivors," said Myrick in 1993.

When she filed later that year for the long-held Republican seat in Congress in the Ninth District (encompassing parts of Mecklenburg, Cleveland, and Gaston Counties), she faced stiff competition, particularly from fellow Republicans, who had long waited for Congressman Alex McMillan of Charlotte to vacate the seat held by Republicans since Eisenhower days. Myrick won with 66% of the vote on a Republican surge that resulted in Republicans controlling congressional delegations in both Carolinas. She walked into the Charlotte Convention Center on election night holding the hand of her two-year-old granddaughter.

The media swept her up in reportage. She appeared in a "Good Morning, America" election feature and was featured in squibs in journals such as *Congressional Quarterly*, which called her a "Republican true believer." In Washington, she continued her forceful presence, characteristically wearing bright, solid-color suits, large button earrings, a gamin-like haircut, a wide smile. She worked for constituents and legislation for the homeless, for rail transportation, and drug and crime prevention, causes she had long pursued while in local office. One of her most ardent local efforts had been pushing for creation of a homeless shelter in Charlotte.

Her survival instinct surged again when she was diagnosed with breast cancer and had a lumpectomy in December 1999. She chose three months of chemotherapy, the nausea and effects of which she described as "pure hell." After she lost her hair, she wore a wig. During treatment she missed about a third of

House roll call votes, but cast others in person on the floor of Congress wearing a large pink surgical mask to ward off germs. Chemotherapy leaves a patient very susceptible to germs, so most patients obediently avoid public contact. Not Sue.

One important vote was to eliminate the so-called "marriage penalty" tax. This vote brought her in her mask to the House floor. Charlotte newspapers did not carry photos of this, but months later *The Charlotte Observer* published an extensive feature story on Myrick's operation and its aftermath, focusing on educating women to discover and examine their own bodies and learn their options for treatment and recovery. The *Observer* quoted Myrick, who was embarrassed at first, "Wearing a mask bothered me because you feel like everybody's looking at you. 'Why are you wearing a mask?' After I got used to it, it didn't bother me at all." She accepted the invitation by producers of the television program "Good Morning, America" to take hours of film footage during her chemotherapy for use in a possible piece about her experience. Myrick co-sponsored a bill to expand Medicaid coverage to women with breast and cervical cancer.

Myrick said, "I've always found it's easier to hit things head-on and just go through it and move on, no matter what it is." Part of her spring and summer of the year of her recovery were spent on her successful re-election campaign in 2000 for her fourth term in Congress.

Depending on your point of view, Betty Seizinger has, since her arrival in Charlotte from Michigan in 1976, been an educator, political force, organizer, and fly in the ointment all the way to Raleigh and points beyond. Her forceful, articulate drive to educate the public about candidates and issues, and to organize forces in 1995 to repeal the statewide food tax had Democrats thinking she was a Republican and Republicans sure she was a Democrat.

Partisan politics is not in her blood. She studies the issues and gets others to join her with action, just as she did with her students when she taught world history in Charlotte's public schools at Northwest Junior High and at West Charlotte High School. At the latter, she began the debate team and coached the first Charlotte debater to win a national championship. As president of

Charlotte's League of Women Voters (1993–97), she and others brought the league loudly before the public as a dynamic, visible force to be reckoned with politically. She formed coalitions with other community groups on issues such as a referendum for an uptown arena and for national health care reform. Televised candidates' forums suddenly became the order of the day thanks to her leadership. She and her supporters persuaded the city council to participate in a primary debate or forum for the first time with the city paying for filming and logistics. They then held forums for the county commission, board of education, legislature, Senate and House races also.

But the food tax campaign was her most far-reaching success. Mobilizing the league and many more organizations throughout the state, Seizenger and others began a campaign to repeal the 4% state food tax "because it was just plain unfair—you shouldn't tax what you need to live." She recalls that they began "brow-beating legislators and getting thousands of people across the state involved, encouraging them to have a voice in their own government. We got 100 organizations to line up behind the repeal."

The legislature had rarely seen anything like it. Seizinger became "that woman." And before it was over, the public pressure caused legislation to be passed that eliminated the first 1% of the food sales tax in January 1997, the second 1% in January 1998, and the final 2% in May 1999. For her efforts, Seizinger received the state's highest civilian award, the Order of the Long Leaf Pine, awarded by Governor James B. Hunt, who during the effort, as Seizinger recalls, "had not been real happy about the way we were pushing it."

Ever since she arrived in Charlotte in the 1970s, Seizinger has been intrigued with the city, its people, particularly its women, and the Charlotte way to "get things done." She saw that men made the decisions about who got on important committees. At meetings of a women's group, she often heard a committeewoman say, "Just wait 'til I get Thomas tonight. We'll get the money for you." At social occasions, she saw "the power these little women had over men. I even joined a sewing circle. I was told it was a big compliment to be invited. It's a good thing I knew how to sew." She learned during the fight to pass the Equal Rights Amendment in the 1970s that "some women didn't want to be flat out equal, because they'd be losing their power. They could do more this way."

Standing in a grocery line, she was fascinated to learn "you could ask any question there and get any answer. But women didn't speak out in public. But I speak out. And now a lot more speak out." In 1999, Queens College celebrated Seizinger as a "modern-day suffragist," awarding her an honorary doctorate "for inspiring those around her, never giving in, not being afraid to voice her opinion on crucial issues, and for belief in the dignity and potential for greatness in all people."

CHAPTER NINE

$\mathcal{A}$lthough early twentieth-century Charlotte women had enjoyed various local forays into the world of art, more typical was Bloss Lucas, who as an unmarried daughter living in her parents' household, taught china painting for young ladies in the parlor on certain afternoons. Others left town to study art or find careers in New York or Philadelphia. The serious pursuit of art by daughters of the town was seldom applauded. "Serious pursuit of art" means choosing to paint instead of hosting or attending social functions, or choosing sculpture instead of marriage and childbearing.

In the predominantly Scots-Irish, no-nonsense town that had long valued frugal practicality, art was generally considered a frivolous occupation except for the stitching of fanciful, intricate quilts, flower arranging, or the creation of fashionable dresses.

Art had, however, been taught since the mid-1800s at Charlotte's female academies, those predecessors of the uptown Presbyterian Female College

(1896–1910) which continued as Queens College (beginning in 1914 in Myers Park). Art courses such as drawing and painting were taught at Queens and the college's merging forebears since before 1862, at the beginning of the Civil War. Latin, music (voice and piano) and the classics were staples in the curriculum there and also at Elizabeth College (1896–1915). Such early studies generally fostered an appreciation for art and potential pursuit of art as a hobby rather than a career.

One female career artist may have provided inspiration. A female icon central to the Queens campus is the elegant, often-costumed sculpture (on campus since 1940) of Diana, the huntress, her bow poised from shooting an arrow. The piece was created and donated by the noted Anna Hyatt Huntington, well known for building with her husband, Archer Huntington, the famous Brookgreen Gardens in South Carolina.

Since most young, unmarried women had the limited option in the first half of the twentieth century to become a nurse, missionary, teacher, shop girl, librarian, seamstress, governess, waitress, maid, or to live with and to care long-term for elderly parents or relatives, a local professional artist was rare indeed.

When Katheryn Woods Kortheuer came to town in 1937, Charlotte was intrigued. The city gained a gifted female artist and teacher who would have significant influence through her work as curator, acting director, registrar, and board member at the Mint Museum of Art. The Mint had just opened the previous year in Charlotte as North Carolina's first art museum. Charlotteans had never seen anything like the brilliant color and style of Katheryn and Dayrell Kortheuer's home. Neighbors were fascinated by its novelty and gracious, lively sophistication, and also, they were no doubt skeptical of the out-of-the-ordinary residence where the couple "took life lightly and painting seriously."

Katheryn Woods Kortheuer, who was born in Long Island, New York, had graduated from the New York School of Applied Design and did two years of graduate work in New York City at the Ecole De Beaux Arts and at Nincolaides-Furlong Atelier. At age 20, she received a Tiffany Foundation Fellowship for summer school at the Tiffany Estate on Long Island, where she met fellow artist Dayrell Kortheuer, whom she married. They visited Charlotte in 1928 on an arts assignment and moved here permanently in 1937. She soon was directing mural painting in the Charlotte city schools, "believing mural painting was the most direct expression of art for everyone, everywhere." One of her murals enlivened her son's school, Elizabeth Elementary.

As volunteers, the couple began teaching art in 1938 to adults and children at the Mint Museum. She was considered one of the best American muralists, and he was nationally known as a prominent portraitist and landscape artist. Katheryn's mixed media methods, using glazes and polymers, gave brilliant Persian/Oriental aspects to her floral landscapes. In 1948, she and her husband with five other artists founded the Guild of Charlotte Artists, which continues into the twenty-first century. In her work with the Mint, she served as acting director 1955–58, established the Mint's sales and rental gallery, began cataloging its large collection of art, and retired as curator in 1973. Her primary legacy, apart from her paintings, was to form the "foundation that made the Mint an educational institution accessible to all ages," enabling local people to view and learn to appreciate art, and to acquire the skills to create art.

Two artistic colleagues of the Kortheuers in the 1940s in Charlotte were watercolorist and mixed-media visionary Alice Steadman and Sara Everett Toy. After graduating from Sweet Briar College, Sara Everett in her early 20s studied painting at the Art Students League in New York and at the Pennsylvania Academy of Fine Arts. She exhibited her paintings at the Mint Museum in the 1930s and began studying sculpture at Cranbrook Academy in Massachusetts and at Black Mountain College. She became acting director at the Mint in the mid-1940s and taught sculpture at Queens College, specializing in sculptured heads and busts of living persons. Toy's good friend was Charlottean Rosalie Hook Gwathmey, the daughter of C.C. Hook and the brother of Walter Hook, premier architects of early twentieth-century Charlotte.

Rosalie Hook was an art student at the Pennsylvania Academy when she met fellow student and painter Robert Gwathmey. Both were social activists. Hook vigorously supported racial tolerance and voting rights for women. When Hook and Gwathmey married in 1935, Hook decided two painters in one family wouldn't do, so she began classes in Pittsburgh with a professional photographer. In New York, she studied with Paul Strand. On trips she took photographs in the South and in Charlotte of black neighbors and workers, including the Second Ward neighborhood which backed up to her family's home at

423 East Morehead Street. Her photographs often became the departure point for many of her husband's noted paintings. Often when he saw something he wanted to paint, he asked her to photograph it.

Rosalie and Robert Gwathmey had a joint exhibition in Richmond in 1946 at the Virginia Museum of Fine Arts. She exhibited her work at the Museum of Modern Art saying, "I am particularly interested in photographing the Negro in my native South because of the problems that face him—housing, jobs, discrimination. These things I would like to see bettered."

Her childhood home in Charlotte was located between the white neighborhood of Dilworth with many homes of the wealthy on one side, and behind them, a street of black families' homes in Second Ward where Sara, the family cook, lived. Rosalie noted, "Two streets back were the real slums." Rosalie's photos of these neighbors and their homes and scenes were given to the New York Public Library and remain an important, articulate social commentary on Charlotte's black neighborhoods and their residents in the 1940s.

In the 1960s, work at the Mint Museum attracted another young newcomer who had just arrived in Charlotte, one whose expertise in ceramics would make a major imprint on the city and region.

Daisy Wade Bridges was born in Bluefield, West Virginia, and graduated from UNC Chapel Hill in art history. When she went to New York University to get an a master's degree in retailing, she walked with friends to the Wedgewood Showroom at 24 East 4th Street, where the old Guggenheim was located. There they had the good fortune to meet Annie Reese Wedgewood, who showed them Wedgewood antiques and explained the history of some early pieces. When Daisy graduated, she asked Mrs. Wedgewood for a job. She got it, earning about $25 a week in 1955 and 1956.

Daisy became a collector of Wedgewood. "Mrs. Wedgewood showed me those eighteenth-century pieces and," Daisy says smiling, "it was the beginning of my craze. I was always a collector. In World War II, my brother was in the Air Force, and I collected war memorabilia. When I was seven, I went to the New York World's Fair and began collecting anything art-deco style. I kept scrapbooks on the style. It caught my eye." Daisy's father was the president of Bluefield College. Her mother was a Colonial Dame with Charlotte and Greensboro connections, who graduated from Greensboro College around the 1870s.

Her grandfather was with the Norfolk and Western Railway, a large company that leased coal lands in western Virginia and West Virginia for coal mines. Her grandfather and grandmother, Ernestine Barger Caldwell, had homes in Salem, Virginia; Bluefield, West Virginia; and in the coal fields. Her grandmother traveled widely, to South America, the Orient, or to Europe every spring and to Florida in winter, leaving the children with servants and with her husband who stayed close to the coal business. "The social world of my grandmother's era allowed most anything if you had the money." So Daisy had grown up in southern West Virginia in a family with world-wide interests, travels, and acquisitions.

While working in New York for Wedgewood, Daisy began collecting right away. "Mrs. Wedgewood had a library in their home. I could borrow any book and read it, then take it back. She told me a most valuable thing. 'Buy two books on Wedgewood for every piece you collect.' I got totally absorbed in the subject of eighteenth-century Wedgewood, which is my particular field and interest." At the Wedgewood Showroom in New York, Daisy was part of the important distribution point for Wedgewood in America. All orders for American buyers came through that location, buyers such as those for Van Ness in Charlotte, or Macy's or others who came to see and buy in the New York showroom since there was little transatlantic travel at the time.

After her New York job, Daisy went with her husband Henry Bridges to Paris so he could study music. He was a Davidson College graduate, a native of Tennessee, and he and Daisy returned in 1960 to live in Charlotte after their Paris years and after he got an M.A. in sacred music at Union Seminary in New York.

Newcomer Daisy was introduced to Mary Myers Dwelle by Daisy's realtor, who had learned of her interest in art and ceramics. Daisy recalls Dwelle as "an imaginative, wonderful, generous lady. I started working at the Mint full-time helping Katheryn Kortheuer and Mint Director Bob Schlageter put on an exhibit of ceramics. Milton Bloch [subsequent director of the Mint] gave me the title of guest curator of ceramics." As a member of the International Wedgewood Seminar, Daisy met Melanie Delhom in 1962 in Chicago, when the Seminar met at the Art Institute. Delhom invited a group to a party at her house, where she showed her fantastic collection of Wedgewood. She had bought an entire collection from a famous English collector. Daisy recalls, "I told the Mint people when I returned about this great collection in Chicago, that we ought to try to get it. We got it. And she brought so many other pieces. Meissen, Persian pieces, French faience, and others." Daisy made the contact and educated Mint officials and board members as to Delhom's expertise and the value of her collection.

Delhom and her collection were being courted by a wealthy Texan, by the Arkansas Rockefeller family, and by Charlotte's Mint officials, each of whom sought to acquire and house Delhom's collection and her own expertise and presence. Tempie Franklin, a tiny, persuasive Mint auxiliary spokesman, and later board chair, lobbied city officials and wealthy patrons to expand the Mint [which had become a department of the city of Charlotte in 1978] in order to house the Delhom Collection. The Delhom connection with the Mint was made by Daisy Bridges in 1964, and Delhom came in 1966 to supervise the ceramics facility's construction. The reoriented and expanded Mint opened in 1968 with great fanfare on the Delhom Collection. Quietly, the collection put Charlotte on the museum and ceramics map because Delhom's collection is one of the most significant historic ceramics collections in America.

Melanie Delhom believes that selected ceramic pieces, their art and process of creation, can relate the history of mankind. Her amazing collection is that of a passionate lifelong educator whose expertise in world cultures and ceramics is vast and widely respected. Born in 1908 in Fort Worth, Texas, Delhom questioned local evangelists about religion. After being dismissed by them, she embarked on a spiritual quest through the Ft. Worth public library, explored Buddhism, Hinduism, and in the process became interested in Oriental ceramics. "The earliest, unbroken line in how mankind recorded his story and expressed his thoughts are in clay," said Delhom. Her extensive travels and business ventures led to her retirement in 1964 to devote all of her time to teaching, study, travel, and collecting. Her collection of books complements her collection of ceramic pieces. Hers is a teaching collection, which according to Margery Adams, art history professor at Queens College, includes "numerous documented pieces of fabulous quality and rarity. And with each culture, she knows the people, rulers, geography, religion, their way of living, and how ceramics were used. Many museums have ceramic collections as inclusive as hers, but nowhere can you find it all displayed at once, as in Charlotte."

Delhom's "roving classroom" of ceramics enthusiasts was the first group of Americans permitted to visit China following President Nixon's historic 1976 visit to the formerly "closed" country. Phil Busher of the Mint describes arrangements for the visit: Virginia Burkhead, a travel specialist, "went through the mayor's office, then the governor's in beseeching the Chinese Embassy with little hope of receiving permission to enter China. Seven days later, Burkhead received a letter saying that China would be honored to welcome Miss Delhom and her students to watch the making of porcelain and to visit the porcelain museums! They offered to let her purchase an object of her choice from the palace display. Her choice demonstrated her connoisseur's eye, much to the dismay of the palace curators.

"Miss Delhom selected an enamel-painted, porcelain miniature vase, slightly over three inches tall. The brushstrokes, color, shape and intricate detail (nine dragons depicted) could come from any of ancient China's great ceramic periods. . . . The miniature vase is only one of five made, on orders of Mao Tse-tung, to demonstrate to the world that China's great artistic secrets were still alive."

On the 30th anniversary of the Delhom Gallery in 1998, Delhom, at the age of 90, was still driving her Chevrolet Caprice to work each day at the Mint. She was awarded the North Carolina Award in Fine Arts by Governor James B. Hunt, Jr. She is a founder of the American Ceramic Circle. Her view is that the most impressive potter she has met in her lifetime of touring the world's ceramics sites and processes, is Dorothy Auman of Seagrove, North Carolina, who "had such expression in her hands and in her face while working the clay."

Daisy Bridges worked and traveled with Delhom, increasing her own expertise by visiting 73 countries. Bridges' interest widened to explore American ceramics when she saw two pieces from the Rookwood, Ohio, pottery, a pitcher and small bowl she has in her living room. While Bridges was working as a volunteer with Charlotte's Crisis Assistance Ministry, that organization's board member M.E. Weibler asked if Daisy could help with temporary housing for battered women. "I sold my collection of English Whieldon, salt glaze, and Wedgewood jasper" for this purpose. Later, "I gave my creamware to the Mint. Melanie's and mine put together came out to be just about the finest collection in the world. Hundreds of pieces, fine and very rare."

In order to buy ceramics pieces, Daisy Bridges says, "I made the money on the stock market." She used the income from money she had inherited to continue investments to fund ceramics purchases and her travels for collecting purposes. Her husband Henry, she says, "is a wonderful man, but he wouldn't pay $2,500 for a teapot."

Her travels and knowledge of ceramics led her and museum curator Stewart Schwartz to explore the riches of Catawba Valley pottery in North Carolina. They sought out potters and collected for an exhibit at the Mint, which, Bridges recalls, "turned out to be a sensation. Ceramics experts had never seen this glaze before. The Catawba pottery ash glaze is like that from the Han dynasty (300–400 B.C.) in southern China. It turns up in the American South in the early nineteenth century. Southern China and the southern United States have a poor, rural society in common. They didn't have money for salt glaze. Ash glaze costs nothing but is labor intensive. All you need is clay and fire, ashes from oak logs. You put ashes in the slip and the flames have ashes in them as well. The chemical reaction between the potash and flames firing at 2,200 degrees changes its whole nature." The catalog became a best seller with collectors buying all the Mint could print and reprint. Later, at an auction, one of those catalogs went for $150. Bridges went to China to watch the glaze made there as well as in the Catawba Valley of Piedmont North Carolina. Bridges sold pieces to Sotheby's, whose catalog gave Catawba Valley pottery national publicity. The Smithsonian bought a whole kiln load from Burlon Craig, a Lincolnton potter.

One most remarkable Charlotte artist who was always pushing ahead of the times was Mary Todd Shaw. During the '60s and '70s, she taught painting at the Mint, but her work was sculptural in nature. She exhibited her postage-stamp prints and her unusual open-sided boxes incorporating collected items with strange and marvelous juxtaposition. In the 1960s, she was one of the city's most visible artists and an unusual voice in conservative Charlotte. Once when her work was not being shown locally in exhibits, she created a tail-gate exhibit in the parking lot of Spirit Square. She sent out invitations and served refreshments to drifters and guests in tuxedoes until the police arrived and shut down the party.

In 1983, painter Ruth Ava Lyons and her husband, sculptor Paul Sires, arrived in Charlotte, where they lived and worked in their home in Dilworth. They were in their 20s, fresh out of graduate school, and Ava had just completed a Fullbright Fellowship in Bolivia, Peru, and Ecuador. After several years in Dilworth, they were awarded a three-month out-of-town residency where they worked in large, loft studio spaces. Looking at their work space on their return, they decided, "we had to do something. So we drove around Charlotte looking. We drove all over. Out on North Davidson Street, we came upon this sleepy area, all boarded up, desolate. We drove past a man who was a snake handler. He had a boa constructor. Interesting, we thought!" Seeing the derelict mill village and the huge, abandoned mill along the multiple railroad tracks in North Charlotte, "we were stunned. It looked like a place time forgot, the little town area and houses. I saw a little 'For Sale' sign on a burned-out house. And it became ours. We bought it about 1985 to use as studio space for both of us.

"We did so much work on it, we realized we needed to rent space out in order to pay for the renovation. The vision for the several-block area developed of necessity. We didn't rent to plumbers or for storage, but held out for arts-related tenants. We did no advertising. We feel it is a miracle that things evolved the way they did into an unpretentious, nice community."

In the revitalized North Charlotte village, just north of the city and its high-end condos, banks, and hotels, the small-scale street gradually became, by the turn of the century, a hot spot for art. Several galleries, art spaces, coffee houses, cafes, condos in rehabbed industrial buildings, a theater, and shops are there with lively events which include frequent musical performances, poetry readings, and a monthly gallery crawl which reaches out from uptown to this funky NoDa neighborhood (short for North Davidson). As artists and activists, Ruth Ava Lyons and Paul Sires with their Center of the Earth and their Blue Pony Galleries, were the catalyst for this down-and-out neighborhood's major transformation. Just as remarkable, the area has become a magnet for artists. Lyons doesn't have statistics on the residents, but "we probably have the largest percentage of literary, film, dance, and visual arts persons who live and work here as you'll find anywhere else around. Not just the mill houses, but the mill itself has been renovated for affordable housing."

Lyons, talking from her NoDa gallery where her painting space is in back, says, "We sell and show works by artists across the country. We represent 50 artists from all over."

In a city where women own the majority of the art galleries in 2001, gallery owner Dot Hodges can recall when art galleries were rare. In 1980, she and Christie Taylor opened what is the oldest art gallery in town, the Hodges-Taylor gallery. Erudite Leon Guttmann, who from mid-century onward owned Guttmann's Galleries in Myers Park, sold prints and elegant gifts, often of art quality, but he knew what Charlotteans didn't, that Charlotte in the mid-twentieth century was not quite ready to support a true art gallery. By 1980, it was ready, but Hodges and Taylor had some educating to do.

Uptown was their focus from the beginning, first a storefront at the bustling, renovated Latta Arcade, followed by an expanding series of moves into high-profile street-level sites until their elegant digs in modern Transamerica Square. Across the foyer is Noel Gallery, owned by B.E. Noel, who features African-American and Latin-American art. Noel is one of the very few female African-American fine art gallery owners in the country.

Taylor had managed galleries in Winston-Salem before coming to Charlotte and had attended Queens College and the prestigious Pennsylvania Academy of Fine Arts. She recalls that art students at Queens were not permitted to draw from nude models. Dot Hodges majored in French at Sweet Briar College and enrolled in art classes at UNC Charlotte. There she met university professor and remarkable painter Maud Gatewood. Using her own art knowledge and contacts, she became, as arts writer Jane Grau describes Hodges, "a cultural beacon, assisting then North Carolina National Bank in making purchases, and holding exhibitions in her home to educate people about the value of art in the community."

Together, Hodges and Taylor show and sell fine prints, photography, paintings, and sculpture. They have from the outset of their partnership, chosen to work with regional artists who have national reputations.

In 1989, Christie Taylor curated a traveling exhibit called "Nine From North Carolina: An Exhibition of Women Artists" which included four women who lived in or had close Charlotte connections: sculptor Clara Couch, jeweler Paula Garrett, painter Maud Gatewood, photographer Carolyn DeMeritt, and

165

painter Gina Gilmour. Each had exhibited widely and one, Gatewood, was listed in *Who's Who in American Art* and *Who's Who in American Women*. The exhibit was initiated as part of the outreach and educational extension of the new National Museum of Women in the Arts (NMWA) near the White House in Washington, D.C. The Museum's purpose from its opening in 1981 is "to highlight the outstanding contributions of women to culture through the ages and to promote appreciation for women's creative accomplishments today."

Wealthy art collector Billie Holladay, founder of the museum, recalled the early days, the 1960s, of collecting art, when she and her husband saw a painting by Clara Peeters in Austria. Coming home, Holladay tried to find out about Peeters, and searched through the bible of art students, H.W. Janson's *History of Art.* "I was surprised to not find a thing about this wonderful painter, but astonished to suddenly realize that no woman was mentioned. Not even Mary Cassatt. It was difficult to believe." This revelation set the Holladays on their quest to find support for and build a national museum to show and give researchers sources to see and study the history of women artists.

In 1989 Taylor's exhibit celebrating living North Carolina female artists carried out this premise in the third NMWA State Exhibition. Printmaker, arts activist, and freelance curator Jane Kessler wrote catalog notes about women artists for the exhibition, saying, "More often than not, woman has sought and found her voice without the sanctions or rewards of her own society or has garnered support by denying her own femaleness. . . . In the 1970s as female artists began to experience the authority of their own voices and to act out of their 'inner strength,' an interest in female imagery surfaces. Writer Lucy Lippard noted, 'There is a lot of sexual imagery in woman's art—circles, domes, eggs, spheres, boxes, biomorphic shapes, maybe a certain striation or layering . . . fragments, which imply a certain antilogical, antilinear approach also common to many women's work.' Also women's work is often more autobiographical than men's."

The nine women chosen to represent North Carolina in the exhibition were strong evidence against the old theory that women were not considered capable of creating art of comparable quality to men's. This theory had dismissed Mary Cassatt, who was esteemed in France for her paintings of women and children, and Anna Hyatt Huntington, whose most stunning sculptures were of animals. The four Charlotte women artists chosen for the NMWA exhibit brought a wide range of talent: Clara Couch's large, mysterious clay vessels; Garrett's strongly Japanese-influenced jewelry with extraordinary linear quality; Maud Gatewood's arresting, pared-down visual passages, which suggest a haunting, lonely narrative; and Gina Gilmour's paintings of compelling human figures of calm and struggle within a landscape of oasis.

Photographer Martha Strawn, who is art professor at UNC Charlotte and a co-founder of Charlotte's Light Factory, has been thoroughly preoccupied by alligators in recent years. She has taken them as a vehicle for art, leading to appearances on NPR and a book, *Alligators: Prehistoric Presence in the American Landscape.* Another book containing extensive photographs of ancient Indian art is a recent area of focus. Photographer Susan Page also exhibits her work in one-person exhibits throughout the United States. One of these was "Working Women," showing women at work on their jobs. It toured extensively.

Showcasing the range of her creativity, Carolyn DeMeritt's remarkable photographs of Native Americans for the book by Frye Gaillard, *As Long As The Waters Flow,* contrast with the startling portraits of adolescent girls, just at the age of abandoning innocence. At this precarious age, the girls in some of these portraits appear "spooky, uncomfortable, unsettling." As she shoots pictures of the girls during six years of their budding adolescence, DeMeritt says, "I don't direct them. I'm a comfortable presence, sort of a weird aunt. As I shoot, the girls become less the picture of girls inhibited. This is definitely a collaborative effort." DeMeritt exhibited at the United National World Conference on Women in Nairobi in 1985. Her video of women AIDS victims and their words was the subject of her widely shown video "Give Me My Flowers."

Mildred Packman, at age 88, lives in a retirement center in Charlotte, where some of her vivid paintings and photographs keep her company. At age 75, she enrolled in her first watercolor class and took classes led by prominent watercolorists. When she was young, she pursued her interest in photography. Her husband told her not to touch his Leica camera, but eventually they compromised and she got her own camera, a Rolleicord, and did her own darkroom work. She was allowed to join her husband's all-male camera club and won one of the monthly contests sponsored by the club. One award-winning photograph in the 1940s caused controversy. It showed a very common scene,

Photographer Carolyn DeMeritt is one of Charlotte's outstanding artists, whose subjects have evolved from landscapes to people. "Chelsea/ Star Mask, 1987" is from the Charlotte native's multimedia work, "When I was Little...I thought I Could Fly." For six years, DeMeritt photographed eight teenage girls as they grew through adolescence. The black and white photos accompany audiotapes of the girls who talk about their lives. In 1995, she produced "Give Me My Flowers," a look at women with AIDS.
PHOTO BY AND COURTESY OF CAROLYN DEMERITT

but one not discussed or certainly not captured for the public. The subjects are a young white woman being helped to get dressed for an elegant occasion with the assistance of a black maid, whose hands hooking the tiny, intricate back hooks of her mistress's "Merry Widow" lingerie are the only visible part of the maid's body.

More visible to the public were Wanda Montgomery's collections for the African-American Cultural Center which documented and exhibited works never seen in Charlotte. One Charlotte native, painter and sculptor Elsie Shaw, placed her work in unusual outdoor surroundings. Working from her studio in

Florida, she balances humor and serious content in her arresting sculpture of "Miss Ann and Dan," a woman wearing hat, coat, boots, and pocketbook leading her small dog Dan among the shrubbery in front of Belk Chapel on Charlotte's Queens College campus. Up the street at the intersection of Providence and Queens Roads is Shaw's statue memorializing the popular Myers Park character Hugh McManaway, who liked to direct traffic at that intersection.

Acclaimed artist Doris Leeper, also a Charlotte native, grew up in the Eastover and Elizabeth neighborhoods in the 1930s and attended Central High School. At five, she received a small magnifying glass as a gift from an uncle and became fascinated by sand, insects, and snowflakes. She sketched what she saw as a child as she walked around with "a little magnifying glass around my neck and looked at everything in great detail." While at Duke University studying to be a doctor, Leeper said, "I realized I was enjoying doing drawings of dissections more than I was enjoying the idea of blood and guts." She took a class with painter Charles Sibley, who encouraged her talent. In Atlanta, she worked as a commercial artist before taking up painting and sculpting full time in the 1960s. Her work has been commissioned and exhibited around the United States, and one sculpture, "The Reflection," was erected in 2000 on a public outdoor site in Charlotte's Fourth Ward. Leeper was also founder and executive director of the Atlantic Center for the Arts in New Smyrna Beach, Florida, where the emerging artists and master teachers gather and work in the ongoing residential studio center for the arts.

Charlotte native Charleen Swansea is a writer and much, much more. She grew up on Biltmore Drive. After college, and earning her M.A. at UNC Chapel Hill, she returned, married, had two children, and in the tiny laundry room of her Westminster Place house, she birthed a groundbreaking literary publication, the *Red Clay Reader*, a non-profit venture, in 1964. The teacher and former editor of *The Carolina Quarterly* set up shop as publisher and editor of *Red Clay Reader*, and in 1971, founded Red Clay Books.

The woman who became her business manager, Bobbie Campbell, a young mother of two, had worked in publishing in New York. Campbell recalls, "I got all dressed up to apply for a job with *Red Clay Reader* in my New York professional outfit. I put on my girdle, my best clothes. When I got there, laundry was everywhere. Her son Tom was home throwing up. It wasn't at all what I expected." Then why take the job? "The job was just what I needed. I was desperate, I was not made for motherhood."

She recalls that the mailing list occasionally got mixed up with the laundry, but *Red Clay Reader*, a hardback annual, published the new writings of some of the South's best writers very early in their careers. A New York literary review deemed it "easily distinguishable . . . an outsized hardback with brilliant storybook covers." Swansea published talented fledglings, often unknown, alongside heavyweight, recognized authors such as Harry Golden, Reynolds Price, May Sarton, Kate Millett, Romulus Linney, Stanley Kunitz, and Linda Pastan, whose work would attract notice to those in adjacent pages. She published Alice Walker's story "Sweet Jerome" in issue seven. Walker won the Pulitzer Prize for Fiction in 1983. Doris Betts's story "The Ugliest Pilgrim" appeared first in *Red Clay Reader*, then was included in Betts's collection *Beasts of the Southern Wild*. A subsequent film version of "The Ugliest Pilgrim" (retitled "Violet") won an Academy Award. A story by Charlottean Barbara Lovell published in Red Clay Books' *Love Stories by New Women* won a Pushcart Prize. Poems by A.R. Ammons, Julie Suk, and Marion Cannon accurately forecast their future success. "Every single issue helped launch at least a couple of really strong talents," said Swansea.

The Loving Book published by Red Clay Books on the subject of birth control sold so well that its profits financed the publication of four books of poetry. President Jimmy Carter bought and gave away thousands of copies to junior high students all over the country. Red Clay published 20 books and seven annual *Red Clay Readers,* which sold quickly and became collectors' items. The venture was so successful they had to quit. Swansea explained, "The purpose of the *Red Clay Reader* was to discover and publish deserving new writers. The book came into existence at a time when there was a renaissance of writing in the state, and after eight years we find we can no longer give such a quantity of work the special attention it deserves." They were receiving in one week as many manuscripts from writers seeking publication as they did their entire first year. Poems and stories poured in from all over the country.

Swansea, who had changed her name in college from Swanzey to the original Welsh Swansea, went on to organize and teach the poetry-in-the-schools program in Charlotte-Mecklenburg Schools, and to promote and foster talent wherever she found it, often pulling it from students whose innate talent did not seem evident. Dannye Romine Powell, a prizewinning poet and columnist for *The Charlotte Observer,* described her: "Charleen always believes you can do it. . . . She knows how to transmit that belief straight into your young heart."

After Swansea's second husband died in a tragic house fire while suffering from the mental effects of lead poisoning, Swansea began studying the mind and how it functions. Her research led her to found Mindworks, a business she designed to promote and understand brain power and memory. She led lively workshops throughout the country for corporations, teaching people how to improve thinking, to concentrate, and to learn faster. She accepted an invitation to the International Conference on Thinking in Hawaii sponsored by Harvard University.

At a Mindworks seminar in 1988, 230 members of Professional Secretaries International met at a South Carolina hotel for a session with Swansea. During one of the breaks, a dozen secretaries lined up outside the ladies' room. Two feet away stood the empty men's room. Swansea swished by, exclaiming, "Women, what's the matter with you? You've got to learn to think!" And she threw open the men's room door and five women followed her in. Swansea once told an interviewer, "I've always been two steps ahead of my time which is dangerous." The women's movement of the 1960s, 1970s, and 1980s was the optimum time for a woman like Swansea to be creatively and dangerously at large.

One young writer, Diane Oliver, rose to high acclaim very early in her life, but did not live to write further stories of her city, such as the one which won her first award. Charleen Swansea's *Red Clay Reader* published Oliver's important story "Neighbors." It was also published in *Sewanee Review*, appeared in *The O. Henry Prize Stories,* 1967, and remains in print in major anthologies of southern and black literature. The story artfully chronicled the experiences of the main character's young brother who is the first black student to attend a white school. The family is under seige. "He's going to be fighting them the rest of his life," wrote Oliver. "He's got to start sometime."

At age 22, Oliver won a scholarship to the prestigious University of Iowa Writers' Workshop and wrote other stories of the experiences of black families or young women caught in the southern civil rights conflicts of the 1960s as they struggled to get out or struggled to remain. A graduate of West Charlotte High School and UNC Greensboro, she was killed in 1966 in a motorcycle wreck in Iowa City.

Susan Ludvigson of Charlotte and subsequently Rock Hill, South Carolina, was not publishing her poems when the *Red Clay Reader* was up and running, but between 1975 and 2000, the homemaker, who became an award-winning poet and full professor of English at Winthrop University, published 11 acclaimed poetry books. She also won prestigious national awards including fellowships from the Fullbright, Guggenheim, Rockefeller, and Witter-Brynner Foundations, from the National Endowment for the Arts, and from both the North Carolina Arts Council and South Carolina Arts Commission. Rebecca McClanahan, who followed Swansea as director of Charlotte-Mecklenburg Poetry-in-the-Schools Program, is an outstanding Charlotte poet who retired young to write and teach poetry all over the country, and to publish a poetry and prose handbook for teachers and writers titled *Word Painting*. Her acclaimed books of poetry include *Mother Tongue* and *The Intersection of X and Y*. Poet Mary Kratt won the Brockman Poetry Book Award for *Small Potatoes,* the Peace Award for two history books, and continued to chronicle the people and places of Charlotte in numerous other books of history, biography, and poetry.

Three female novelists from Charlotte in the 1990s received special acclaim for their work. At the age of 23 Ashley Warlick, a Charlotte native, won the coveted Houghton Mifflin Literary Fellowship for *The Distance from the Heart of Things,* followed by *The Summer After June.* Warlick says, "I don't write to be a better person." But she admits that when her writing is good, "I slip inside the skin of someone else. I can have their life, their happiness, their good dogs, their romantic dinners, their long walks in the sunshine. When they argue, I win, because I play both sides. . . . The older we get, the fewer the clean starts we find waiting for us, but I can start over again and again, as often as I like, for my story, through my story, until I'm happy with what I've got. I can't think of another job in the world that offers a chance like that."

Award-winning poet Judy Goldman ventured into the realm of the novel with her first, *The Slow Way Back,* which was shortlisted for the Southeastern Booksellers' Association Annual Fiction Award. The young girl's story reflects in some details Goldman's own experience growing up Jewish in a small South

Carolina town in the 1950s and 1960s. As a columnist and essayist for National Public Radio, she grabs the reader and listener like this: "Yes, we lit Chanukah candles. And my mother and father, my sister, brother, and I chanted the captivating Hebrew blessings in hushed voices over the low flames. But if I'm to be honest, the holiday that made my heart hum like organ chords was Christmas." Or in a poem, "Between Losses:" "This morning you slid in beside me/and as I listen to our breath/I think of our wedding/and the two young people/who ran down the steps of my parents' house./ We thought that day was a conclusion./ Nobody told us it was simply a time/between losses, when rice was something/to be held in the hand/before letting it fly for the camera."

Popular mystery writer Dr. Cathy Reichs is also a professor of anthropology at UNC Charlotte. Her first novel, *Deja Death,* won Canada's Arthur Ellis Award for best first novel. Her second was *Deadly Decisions.* Her mysteries include fascinating details of investigations and use Reichs' expertise as a forensic anthrolopogist. She is a frequent expert witness in criminal cases and is on the board of directors of the American Academy of Forensic Sciences.

Charlotte native Gail Haley grew up on Montford Drive as Gail Einhart. Her drawing talents and storytelling ability set her apart as prestigious author and illustrator of 24 children's books, and illustrator of eight other books. For *A Story, A Story*, her retelling and illustration of an African folktale, she won the coveted Caldecott medal in 1971 for the most distinguished American picture book published that year in the United States. In 1976 she won the Kate Greenaway Award given by the British Library Association for *The Post Office Cat.* She is founder and curator of the Gail Haley Collection of the Culture of Childhood at Appalachian State University.

Novelist Judy Stacy of Mooresville in *Maggie Sweet* invented an intriguing coming-of-age story of middle-aged heroine Maggie who, against her husband's wishes, fulfills her dream to become a beautician.

It is rare indeed for a city, particularly a southern city, to have a successful female playwright, one who lives next door and who came from down the country road in the village of Waxhaw. Judy Simpson Cook's play *Country Songs* played to packed houses at the Spoleto Festival in Charleston. Her *Retreiving the Lamb* was premiered by the Charlotte Shakespeare Company and produced by theaters in North Carolina, Tennessee, Pennsylvania, New Jersey, and Texas. Five other plays displaying her comedic gifts have been performed and won awards as well. One lively one-woman play by Cook depicts the life and international activism of Charlottean Gladys Avery Tillett in *Gladys*, which was produced by Charlotte Repertory Theatre in 1995 to honor Tillett and celebrate Women's History Month.

Cook's newest, *Benedictions*, which had been a winner in the New Play Festival competition, premiered in 2001 by Charlotte Repertory Theatre. This ambitious, provocative work creates art out of the serio-comic experiences of Cook's regular involvement in the church, her own spiritual crisis, and her "sadness at the judgment, condescension and disgust aimed, in the name of God and the church, at one segment of our community." She was prodded into creating the play as a response to her mother's death and her dismay at the hate and vindictiveness expressed in Charlotte toward gays and AIDS during a local production of the Pulitzer Prize-winning play, *Angels in America*. She feels that "*Benedictions* was my attempt to find answers to many spiritual questions. The result for me was more questions—but questions I think we all ask and for which the answers may vary and evolve." Art requires daring, and Cook's play dared to draw the theater-goer into the hot conflict of faith and culture, and into the humor and pathos of human failure and triumph. In the religion-laced South, this is swampy ground.

Charlotte native Jacqueline Butler Hairston's musical talents have taken her and her compositions to America's far corners and beyond. As a composer/arranger, she had two of her spiritual arrangements premiered by Kathleen Battle at Carnegie Hall in 1993. Her works have been recorded by the London Symphony and Andre Kostelanetz Orchestras and by professional solo artists. Battle's 1996 Christmas CD, *Angels Glory*, recorded Hairston's arrangements. Her commissions include an arrangement for Leontyne Price's *Guide My Feet* and for outstanding choral groups throughout the country.

Hairston was honored at Hampton University's first Symposium for Black Women Composers in 1997 and is featured in the first edition of *Outstanding African-American Composers*. She lived in Charlotte until 1973 and received her musical training at the Julliard School of Music, Howard University, and Columbia University, where she earned a master's degree. She served as an invited master artist/teacher at the Atlantic Center for the Arts in New Smyrna Beach, Florida.

Before heading the music department at Merritt College in Oakland, California, she taught at Johnson C. Smith University. At Merritt College, she groomed an award-winning choir, The New Traveling Voices, and was artist-in-residence with the Oakland Youth Chorus as vocal coach and composer-arranger. More recently she directed the Mills College Jazz/Gospel/Pop Vocal Ensemble. She retired in the Oakland area and continues solo performances, composing, and faculty work at the University of Creation Spirituality founded by Dr. Matthew Fox. Hairston is a popular arranger for top artists and has received awards for her many years of work with youth and music education.

Two women emerge in recent history as important leaders in creative theater in Charlotte: Constance Welsh with her long-term dramatic and educational efforts with the Davidson Community Players and the touring Taradiddle Players, and Dorothy Masterson, known as the "grand dame of Charlotte theater." Welsh also had a hand in the formation of the bygone Charlotte Shakespeare Company and the thriving Charlotte Repertory Theatre. She taught at UNC Charlotte, Charlotte Country Day, Queens College, and Davidson Schoolhouse of the Arts. According to *Observer* theater critic Joann Grose, she tended a reliable theater grapevine, cooked for starving actors, invented small jobs to help them out with money, and "gave Tony and Oscar parties that qualified as performance art." She was a consummate critic and theater mother, often called "the best friend Charlotte theater ever had."

Dorothy Masterson, who was born in Pittsburgh and raised in Denver, got her first movie role at age 12. No one knows her exact birthdate. Her daughter said, "I've asked her and got different numbers. I think she was born around 1910." Age was unimportant to Masterson, born Dorothy Simpson, who dreamed of being a classic dramatic actress. She insisted that age had nothing to do with anyone's talent or career. She liked to keep the young people she taught guessing: "If they know everything about me, you lose all the magic."

She married a flashy salesman, Fred Masterson; taught and managed speech groups in cities in Colorado, Illinois, Alabama, and Texas; acted in California;

and moved to Charlotte in 1948. She was said to have been a director who would "squeeze every bit of theatrical blood from an actor." After only 10 days in town, she had landed a role with the Little Theater. She founded the Mint Theater Guild (which later became the Golden Circle Theater). She had also performed in 149 professional plays, appearing with Lee Marvin and Robert Reed. She learned to direct from Antoinette Perry, for whom Broadway's Tony Award is named. In Charlotte, she directed television commercials, had an interview show on WBT radio, taught at the Community School for the Arts, and held classes for the North Carolina School of the Arts. In 1970, she was named Outstanding Career Woman of Charlotte. Soon after, she was listed in *Who's Who in the United States* and *Who's Who of Women in the South*. Charlotte executives, preachers, and politicians came to her for private elocution lessons.

Besides her skill and awards, her personality is best remembered. Popular veteran actress Gladys Lavitan said, "She's tough in that she will not allow a sleazy performance." Actor Rudy Thompson recalls times when "if I had a hatchet in my hand, I'd have planted it in her skull." Thompson also remembers that "she was very delighted one time when someone called her a magnificent bitch." As director, her trademark was to precede her productions with an elegant sweep onstage where she would say a few dramatic words about the play and gaily announce, "And now, it's magic time!" just as the curtain went up.

Charlottean Charles Kuralt, who acted in a youth production directed by Masterson said, "She was wonderful, a taskmaster, a good director . . . a bit of a temper. She was professional; we were decidedly not."

CHAPTER TEN

$\mathcal{Y}$ou won't find her name on an official list of public servants, but during the 1950s–1970s, a remarkable woman named Anita Stroud gave a lifesaving legacy to small black children in the community housing projects where she lived. Stroud's influence changed lives. She stands as the "foster mother of a generation of underprivileged children." She is but one of many noteworthy female volunteers and professionals, whose record in Mecklenburg County is outstanding in the field of public service, i.e. judges, educators, physicians, public health nurses, skilled volunteers, or paid service coordinators. Passionate volunteerism for many Charlotte women through the latter part of the century often worked into a full-time commitment, community leadership, a paying job as head of a non-profit organization, or sometimes, as noted in earlier chapters, into elective office.

Born in 1900, Anita Stroud, a foundling on a Chester, South Carolina, plantation, was passed from one cabin to another, from one black woman to

Children called Anita Stroud (1900–84) "Miss Neet." In a small, donated trailer, her colorful storytelling and nurturing provided after-school and summer leadership and inspiration for hundreds of children in her low-income neighborhood. Her influence proved life-changing to many young African-American youth. She said, "I feel like if we were all in a ditch, and I happened to crawl out, I'd want to reach back and get somebody, if not but one, and pull him out, too."

REPRINTED BY PERMISSION OF THE CHARLOTTE OBSERVER

another. She did not know her parents' names, but she knew how it felt not to be loved. "Nobody cared nothing about me," she said. She had an idea, a dream of growing up and owning a farm that wasn't going to have the pigpen in the backyard, or chickens roosting under the house. She dreamed she would go around and get all the children to come and live on that farm.

Emily Herring Wilson in an interview with Stroud for the book, *Hope and Dignity*, quoted her saying that in later years, "I got the children, but no farm. I decided I was going to work to help other children who had to come up hard like I come up . . . children who were shoved around." Stroud remembered an elderly woman, a former slave, whom she knew growing up. "Granny Ann would tell us that good manners and good behavior would take you farther than any money you had. She always said, 'Whatever you do in this world, try to be somebody.'" In Stroud's childhood, a woman she had called Aunt Rhoda would come to the farm and hold Sunday School out on a hill under some cedars. From the newspapers pasted on the walls inside a cabin to keep out the wind, Aunt Rhoda taught the black farm children the alphabet. First, Stroud learned to spell "coffee." Then "Jello." Then she learned words from the Bible and an Uncle Wiggly book. As a child, Stroud would round up children to come and listen and learn from Aunt Rhoda.

Later, when some friends went to Charlotte to find jobs, Stroud went too. She worked in the homes of white families, doing housework and taking care of their children. She recalls that there were no toilets anywhere uptown for black shoppers. When the streetcar was full, and a white man or woman got on, Stroud and her friends had to get up and give them their seats. "And if you sat down beside one, you went to jail," she said. In the 1940s, she began, like Aunt Rhoda in her own childhood, inviting children from her low-income neighborhood to her small apartment so she could teach them. The children called Anita Stroud "Miss Neet." From her small wages earned as a domestic worker in white homes, she paid for school materials for the children—pencils, paper, crayons, books. Two large white churches in Charlotte, St. John's Baptist and Myers Park Baptist, focused on helping her efforts, and with the Sertoma Club, formed the Anita Stroud Foundation to receive donations. A trailer was purchased for her to use for her after-school Bible stories and instruction, crafts, and a clothing closet for clothing the children. Funds were gathered regularly to send 70 of her inner-city children to summer camp at William Umstead Park near Raleigh. Stroud went with them by bus to give them a rare three-week experience in the wooded outdoors.

In 1982, health problems forced her to close her trailer and retire. The University of North Carolina at Charlotte awarded her the honorary degree of Doctor of Humanities for her service to children. In one of her last days in her trailer, she said, "I feel like if we were all in a ditch, and I happened to crawl out, I'd want to reach back and get somebody, if not but one, and pull him out too. Let's all come out, if possible . . . get just one child and carry him along with you."

Caroline Love Myers never applied for a job. Jobs just found her. In 1975, to the great good fortune of many thousands of Charlotte's most needy people, one unusual job found Myers. It lasted for 25 years.

Born in Burlington, North Carolina, Myers grew up in Charlotte and earned a B.A. degree in math from Queens College. She says that in 1975, she was a member at Covenant Presbyterian Church in Charlotte when her minister, Dr. Doug Oldenburg, invited her to be director of missions. "I was working 10 hours a week helping the church reach out to the community. That was a time of recession, lots of need in the community and people coming for the discretionary fund that I had. I was also teaching math at CPCC, and I had worked before at Queens as registrar. Somebody from CPCC that I played bridge with said, 'Oh, you have a math certificate!' Very soon I was hired part-time. Teaching high school completion work at CPCC, I discovered I loved working with people rather than the math."

In 1976, the first full year of operation, the church's ministry gave money to nearly 3,000 families who had nowhere to turn. The food stamp office referred people to Myers. This new program didn't have food pantries and there weren't many places with efforts like Myers's. She recalls, "I knew I needed to learn more so I went to the Department of Social Services and asked the head of training there for social workers, 'Can I come and take your training you give to your new folks?' She said, 'I don't see why not,' so I did."

Then an effort began with four partners: the city, county, United Way, and the religious community. Myers was a representative from the laity. "We knew the faith community had a long-term commitment to keep doing for the poor, not just the unemployed. Through Covenant, we called together a small group from the Clergy Association and visited a crisis control ministry in Winston-Salem. We took a car full of us, brought back all their forms and expertise we could gather. I knew who was in the car and who was doing what already. I knew that the only person who would be able to be given to this with some level of commitment was going to be me.

"I think God was calling me out. With four kids I don't know why I was so receptive, but I was." Her children ranged in age from nine to 14, hectic years for a parent. About this time, her husband Mike also went from the for-profit world to work at CPCC. "We made changes at the same time. I encouraged him, and he encouraged me," she says.

"Crisis Assistance Ministry became a private non-profit that turned into a public-private non-profit. At first we worked under the 501(c)(3) non-profit status of the Charlotte Area Clergy Association." In 1985 they became a community-based organization, when both the county and the United Way provided operating funds and a building. "What we do," she said, "is put together packages of aid to help low-income people. We provide help, hope, and understanding. We listen to what is going on in a way that is caring and instructive. We're looking at life-threatening things like power disconnection and eviction."

Most of the people in the waiting room outside Myers' office were women. "Yes," she noted, "that is the face of poverty. We hear her situation, the cause of the problem, try to understand who she is in that predicament. Hopefully she brought good information that verifies her situation, like bills, paychecks that show she lost income, and we see what we need to do to help solve the problem. We give donated clothing. In 1975 there were about six clothing closets in various places. On Tuesdays, we sent persons to Hawthorne Lane Methodist, on Thursdays to Covenant. In 1978 we asked churches we were working with to come together as one large closet we could open daily. Still it is a feeder system where churches accumulate clothes and sort them."

Myers believes the reason she sees so many women as clients in crisis is that "women are the caregivers. We see the single parent phenomenon . . . and there is still a gap in pay levels between men and women. We have a database for jobs. Our clients write to us with the most beautiful stories. They say, 'Thank God for Crisis Assistance Ministry. The help you gave me made all the difference in my life which helped me and my child from being homeless.'"

Myers says, "I see the Almighty in the faces of the people we see." One was Sandra Washington whose letter appeared in *The Charlotte Observer* showing one face of the 25 years of assistance. In 1999, $4 million in financial assistance was distributed to help resolve 19,439 emergency requests. They received federal funds and funds from individuals, congregations, businesses, foundations, clubs, the city, the county, and Duke Power's Share the Warmth program. They distributed emergency grants and donated fuel oil. Sandra Washington described Crisis Assistance Ministry as "a big blessing for the people and families of Charlotte."

Myers retired as executive director in 2000. For the woman who is laid off and whose heat costs more than her disability check brings in, the helping organization Myers nurtured into being stands ready to help. And the woman who thought she wasn't eligible for food stamps, but learned from Myers that she was indeed eligible, can thank Caroline Myers and the extensive teamwork she fostered.

Elizabeth Randolph's mother wanted her to be a teacher, so "Libby" recalls: "I grew up knowing I could be a teacher. All of the six Randolph children grew up knowing they were going to college. She taught out in the county [near Raleigh] and when she came home, we had dinner and then we got out our books and our homework and sat around the table and studied." Randolph affirms that the black teachers and black preachers were the most respected people in their community. "The entire community looked up to the teacher. . . . I can't think of anything else that was available that I could do with my college education but teach. There certainly were not any other jobs that black people could aspire to. If you didn't get a job teaching, you went to the post office or did something that was menial."

Randolph worked a Depression-era WPA job to pay her way through college. After graduating from Shaw University in Raleigh in 1936, she taught near Asheville, in Wake Forest, and in Burlington before coming to Charlotte in 1944 to teach high school English at the segregated West Charlotte High School. She hadn't really planned to come to Charlotte until a colleague said, "A teacher like you ought to be in a place like Charlotte. . . . Charlotte pays a supplement." Charlotte's supplement to teachers' salaries was the highest in the state. With her teaching salary, Randolph was able to put a younger brother and sister through college. During summer breaks, she went to summer school for four years at the University of Michigan to earn her master's degree. She chose Ann Arbor "following a man I was in love with," she recalls.

After she had taught 14 years at West Charlotte, school superintendent Dr. Elmer Garinger asked her to become principal of the new University Park Elementary school near Johnson C. Smith University. She protested, "I'm a high school teacher. I don't know anything about elementary schools!"

Garinger countered, "The principalship is a leadership position. Your job is to create a climate where teachers can teach and students can learn." Randolph was being offered a pioneering professional coup for a black woman in 1958. Charlotte schools were segregated and not yet consolidated with the county schools. The changes of integration and consolidation would soon come with Randolph in position for both leadership and change. She would supervise her first white faculty members as desegregation began. One of her fellow teachers had watched her professionalism and told her admiringly, "You won't last here long."

Her experience in smaller, rural schools had given her perspective. Everywhere she had taught outside Charlotte, the educational and instructional materials were insufficient. She said, "In each one of those towns, the black schools got the leftovers from white schools. White students got the new books coming from Raleigh. I did not expect to see it in Charlotte but I did. . . . Teachers had to have fundraisers just to buy supplies they needed. In those days before desegregation, black and white were separate but unequal in everything."

Randolph was told by her teacher she was the first black person to earn school administrative credentials at UNC Chapel Hill. She went for two summers and commuted on Saturdays during the school year. In 1967, she was moved to the central office of the school system to become the county's first African-American woman to act as a school administrator and only the second African-American in that capacity. Gradually blacks were brought into the administration. To be part of the decision-making process was a milestone, because she said, "Under segregation, black persons didn't even go to the central office unless they were janitors."

As administrator, she used federal Title I funds to start the system's first kindergartens, which were later used as models for state kindergartens. In the 1960s, only private kindergartens existed and many of these were in churches. In 1976–77 she was one of a four-person management team, who acted as the school system's interim superintendent. Up until her retirement in 1982, she was associate superintendent of the system. Governor Jim Hunt awarded her North Carolina's Order of the Long Leaf Pine. One colleague recalls that for many years, "Lib was on more boards than anybody."

She also worked with the YWCA and as an advisor to a Y-Teens girls' club at the segregated West Charlotte High School. There were two YWCAs in Charlotte at the time. The large YWCA for whites located on East Trade Street (since 1914) had been a major outlet for young women, offering classes, working girls' residences, and the city's first swimming pool for women (1921). The black chapter, which began in 1918, was called the Phillis Wheatley Branch for Negroes, one of the oldest of its kind in the United States. This branch YWCA was named for a young black poet who was born in Africa and was shipped as a very young girl to a Boston slave market where she was purchased by John Wheatley. He encouraged her talent. Her poems were first published in London in 1773.

June Kimmel "comes when she is called." She is another woman who specializes in sharing her expertise with women. As western director for the North Carolina Council for Women, she has in the 1990s, according to League of Women Voters president Mary Klenz, connected with many groups and has "had the most ongoing campaign against violence toward women. As an unheralded advocate for women and women's issues, she educates and supports women on tough issues, and often travels the western region of the state to do training and work with different groups." For the league, she worked as advisor and co-sponsor for panels on issues such as health-care reform, environmental, and other issues. In 1995, she won the Charlotte Women's Commission's Susan B. Anthony Award for work to achieve equality and rights for women and their families.

Dianne Ward English's position as point woman or catalyst for key public-service actions in Charlotte shows how she sees important needs and works effectively to meet them. As executive director of the Community Building Initiative, she worked with Charlotte leaders to focus the community on matters of race, ethnicity, equity, and inclusion for all the city's citizens. Between 1980 and 1997, she was an organizer, advocate, and executive director for Mecklenburg Ministries, establishing Bridge Builders, a group which links congregations of different races and faiths with the mission of offering compassion and seeking justice. She developed Youth Breaking Barriers, a summer learning program for young people of different races, religion, and socioeconomic backgrounds. She was a primary organizer of the Emergency Winter Shelter and is a founding board member of the Center for Urban Ministry, which provides services and shelter for the homeless.

English says, "My father trained as a CPA. My mother was an intensely spiritual but practical woman. I went into the family business, the business of social change by organizing, advocating, or positioning an issue."

English may have also taken a page from the life book of "Dolly" Tate, who was born in Union, South Carolina and lived in Charlotte from 1938 to 1940 and from 1941 to 1991. Tate was the optimum Charlotte advocate for children and youth, and she received armloads of awards for her services, including the Governor's Award for Volunteer Work and Organizational Administration. She founded the Davidson-Cornelius Child Care Center and the Council for Children, but her earliest focus was on the problem of adolescent pregnancy, first with the Florence Crittenton Home as president, but further in establishing a teenage pregnancy program (TAPS—Teen-Age Pregnancy Services) to address the needs of teenage girls who discover they are pregnant and are without resources or training to cope.

The problem was particularly alarming at the time because pregnant girls were not allowed to attend public school. TAPS service offers continuing education for expectant teenage mothers, as well as academic coursework, vocational courses, counseling services, career counseling, health education, social services, and a nursery. It was first set up at the Florence Crittenton Home and in 2001 is on Central Avenue.

With the Council for Children, Tate was assisted greatly by legislator Louise Brennan as they worked for better day care and for improved standards. The council became a United Way agency and serves as an advocacy group for research and education on all children's needs both locally and nationally. When Tate moved near Davidson, she worked for hospital care for teenage parents in the Huntersville hospital.

A woman who shares Tate's long-term concern for children is Cynthia Marshall. She founded and directed the Communities in the Schools of Charlotte Mecklenburg (formerly Cities in Schools) to aid in dropout prevention. The organization is part of the nation's largest dropout prevention network. She was also the founding board president of the Family Support Center, and like numerous other women cited, moved from being Junior League president to stalwart leadership in the public-service community.

Under the leadership of Susan Hancock Sewell as first paid executive director, Habitat for Humanity of Charlotte became the largest affiliate in the country, the first to complete 100 houses, and also the first to build a house entirely constructed by women.

Kimm Jolley began work in 1985 as executive director at International House, which was founded in 1981. It first was called Community College of International Ministry, organized by people who wished to support the international students at CPCC.

From their first small office in St. John's Baptist Church, they moved into the mansion next door and expanded outreach programs to the wider international community. Her efforts and those of many Charlotteans have bridged cultural differences to help the region appreciate the variety which enhances a healthy city. Their motto is, "International House—where Charlotte welcomes the world."

Pat Grigg, at a Women's Commission dinner, was presented with a miniature giraffe, awarded for sticking her neck out for women in Mecklenburg County in her efforts on behalf of justice and equality. The Charlotte native became director of the Women's Commission in 1989, and is a graduate of Johnson C. Smith University and UNC Chapel Hill. The commission she heads has helped thousands of women find jobs and retrain for new jobs, has worked with crisis-oriented cases of domestic violence, and has partnered for grants to aid women through workshops and seminars.

Waiting outside an office at the commission, a visitor overhears this advice to a fledgling job applicant, a "displaced" woman who has been out of the workforce a while and hopes to return: "Find two most important reasons why he should hire you—reasons important to him—ones that are zinging to his bottom line. Know specifically why he should hire you for this particular job." And as the female client leaves the office, the interviewer calls out to her, "Let me know how it is going." The commission works with over 400 job orders from area companies. They help assess a woman's skills and help her prepare a resume and get ready for job interviews. Most of the women who come are intimidated by interviewers and lack confidence.

Deborah Guibault, the commission's transitional employment coordinator, is a social worker who was a displaced homemaker herself, divorced with two small children. In her mid-30s, she moved to Florida to be with her mother and to create a new life. "It gave me empathy and a true understanding of being out there by yourself, trying to support your kids," says Guilbault. Having worked in employment training for 15 years, she sees the applicant from the employers' point of view as well as the applicant's.

Lucy Bush belongs to a new generation of Charlotte women who are raising the public consciousness to meet community needs. The 48-year-old president of the Swann Fellowship is committed to racial and social justice and to reaching across racial borders. The fellowship, organized in 1997, takes its name from Presbyterian missionaries Darius and Vera Swann, who were the first African-American missionaries to be assigned outside of Africa. Their assignment prior to their return to Charlotte in 1964 was to India, where they saw firsthand through their missionary experience the value of an integrated society.

In 2001, Bush was the assistant director of the Friendship Trays program, involved with it 16 years as a volunteer and eight as an employee. She serves on the Charlotte Housing Authority Board of Commissioners, which places her in a knowledgeable seat to work for goals of justice, equity, and fairness. Former board of elections chairman Bill Culp describes her as one "from the white side of the fence who has been most active in reaching across the fence in various ways." But without the leadership of Ann Elliot the extensive Friendship Trays program may never have gotten off the ground. She became concerned in 1976 that homebound citizens were not getting hot meals. In 1990, 300 persons received daily meals thanks to 700 volunteers, and the expanded program continues.

Mary Harper and fellow professor Bertha Maxwell-Roddey were a visionary team of two. They felt a need for a way to honor the life and times of African-Americans in the Charlotte community. Plantation houses were being spruced up, publicized, and toured. Homes of the wealthy were researched and the lives of their owners described in detail. Oral historians interviewed the white movers and shakers of the city, who became well chronicled in books, articles, and in the public mind. But there was no center, no group, no program to celebrate African-American lives, art, artifacts, and stories.

Harper developed the idea for such a center while working on her doctorate from Union Institute while she was teaching English at UNC Charlotte. In an interview for *The Charlotte Post* she said, "One of the points of the doctorate program was to develop something that would bring about change in the community." She was concerned about "the lack of interest in our culture. There was an interest in historical preservation in Charlotte, but it was a matter of whose interests were being preserved. It seemed that everything in our community was being torn down. So we came up with the idea of a cultural center to provide a place to teach the aesthetic dimension of our culture." Roddey knows Charlotte well. She was the first black principal in an all-white Mecklenburg County school, and she developed the Afro-American Studies department at UNC Charlotte.

Harper, Roddey, a 36-member advisory board, and Samuel Jeeter began the work of spotlighting African-Americans. The center moved into a series of offices including Spirit Square Center for the Arts. "Our goal was to be a repository of knowledge that someone could come to and find information about African-Americans," said Harper. The center, which was named the Afro-American Cultural Center, was to present, promote, and preserve African-American art, culture, and history and to increase the awareness, appreciation, and understanding of African-American cultural traditions among the citizens of Charlotte-Mecklenburg, the region, and the nation.

The board chose to work with the city of Charlotte to acquire the old Little Rock AME Zion Church on East Seventh Street in uptown Charlotte. The congregation had moved into a large, modern facility next door. The distinctive old church had been built in the early twentieth century in a thriving neighborhood, which housed both blacks and whites and supported two large black churches. The old church was designed by J.M. McMichael, a leading architect of white churches in the Carolinas, and of other important Charlotte buildings such as Spirit Square and the church that became the Great Aunt Stella Center. The building was synonymous with African-American history and memories. And it was sitting empty, but dangerously in the path of a major street-widening project. The Little Rock Church next door, and cultural and community groups worked together to raise $1.1 million in pledges in 20 days, money that would go toward the cost of renovations. The space included an Attic Theater, two levels of gallery space, and an outdoor amphitheater. One of the directors of the Afro-American Cultural Center was Wanda Montgomery, whose significant leadership and vision was, says Harper, true to the center's founding mission.

The two women's dream came true. The center hosted exhibits, interviews, performances, and celebrations of the work and lives of African-Americans as well as collaborating with the local schools, the Museum of the New South, and the Mint Museum. One former board chairman said he considers the center "a community living room."

The neighborhood of First Ward, which is home to the Afro-American Cultural Center, was also the location of a major infusion of Bank of America funds for investments and leadership in constructing a wide variety of new housing for residents, and for providing community facilities for the neighborhood. This bank also made major changes in another formerly black neighborhood, Third Ward, when it planned its $350 million Gateway Center and surrounding projects, reorienting and giving a new face to the West Trade entrance into the city from I-77. The person the bank called on for input and neighborhood history in Third Ward was Mildred Baxter Davis. Bank of America CEO Hugh McColl paid Davis this tribute: "She helped guide us, so we didn't make stupid mistakes for that neighborhood."

In an editorial at Davis's death in 1999, *The Charlotte Observer* praised her efforts to keep another old, inner-city neighborhood from being crassly swept away by development. "She was gracious and dignified," reported the *Observer*, "but she also was determined that Charlotte's uptown revival should value diversity and include people already living in the area. The Committee to Preserve Third Ward, which she helped found in 1981, worked with the city, developers, and what's now Bank of America to achieve those goals. She preferred to build consensus, but when necessary, she could firmly defend her neighborhood's interests."

When developers and NationsBank (now Bank of America) broke ground for the 15-acre Gateway Village for offices, shops, residences, and parking, Davis was too weak to walk very far. McColl arranged for a golf cart and escort to bring her to the event and to drive her around. "No one was too important to her," said Darrell Williams, a county commissioner. "She probably got as much done laying in the bed talking on the phone as people who are 100 percent healthy."

Baxter held only one public office, soil and water conservation commissioner, but her stature in the community made her a formidable leader. Trained as an elementary school teacher, the Charlotte native was one of the founders of the Black Political Caucus. Savvy Charlotte politicians called her up. U.S. Congressman Mel Watt (D-N.C.) of Charlotte consulted her to gauge the community pulse. "You certainly wanted her blessing if you were going to be a candidate, and you wanted her advice if you were going to be a campaign manager. You wanted her on your side," he said.

Although Charlotte had prominent female attorneys from the 1920s onward, there was a period during the 1940s, 1950s, and 1960s when female lawyers were rare. Lelia Alexander seems, according to the 1954 Charlotte phone directory listing, to be the lone female, working as a sole practitioner in her office in the Law Building and living on Dartmouth Place in Myers Park. With the 1960s and 1970s rise of the women's movement and the incursions of young women to medical and law schools, many that had recently opened their doors to women, Charlotte saw numerous attorneys in skirts, before pantsuits for women were acceptable.

In the twentieth century, only two female attorneys were elected president of the Mecklenburg County Bar Association: Carrie McLean in 1925–26 and Nancy Norelli, 1999–2000. In 1968, attorney Claudia Watkins (later Claudia Watkins Belk) was elected district court judge, a first for Mecklenburg County. Some of the lawyers who followed were perhaps inspired by the remarkable success of a neighboring female lawyer and judge, the legendary Susie Marshall Sharp (1907–1996), the fourth female law graduate at UNC Chapel Hill. She began practice with her father in Reidsville in 1929. She became the first female city attorney in the state, the first woman in the state to sit as Superior Court judge (1949), the first woman on the North Carolina Supreme Court (1962), and the first woman in the country to be elected Chief Justice of a state Supreme Court (1974).

Other female attorneys in Charlotte elected to serve as district court judge were Marilyn Bissell (1984, 1988, 1992, who had served four terms in the N.C. House and two as county commissioner); Resa Harris (beginning in 1982 and following); Yvonne Mims Evans (1992 and following), who was one of the first black women elected district judge in the state; Elizabeth Currence (1996 and following); Jane Harper (1990 and following); and Rickye McKoy-Mitchell, Nancy Norelli, and Averil Sisk (elected in 2000).

In the 1970s, Yvonne Mims Evans, fresh out of law school, went to the Polk County courthouse to handle cases for her law firm. She walked confidently into the courtroom in her three-piece suit and moved toward the area designated for attorneys' seating. A sheriff's deputy stopped her saying, "You can't sit here. Lawyers only." She remembers it well, especially years later as a sheriff's deputy announces her own entry as district court judge into her courtroom.

Sara Parker of Charlotte was elected to the North Carolina Court of Appeals (1985, 1989) and to the North Carolina Supreme Court (1992, 1996, 2000). She is known as a wise judge and formidable campaigner. Julia Jones was elected Superior Court judge in 1990. Jones's philosophy as a judge was "to give every person all the opportunity the law allows." Jones, who died of a recurrence of ovarian cancer in 1999, grew up in Shelby, graduated with a B.A. from Queens College, an M.A. from Appalachian State University, and a law degree from Wake Forest University Law School. In Charlotte, she practiced with a law firm for 11 years, paralleling her vocation with her love of folk dancing, hiking, and meditation. She felt called to her work as Superior Court judge, but was too ill to run for re-election. Her personal bout with illness and chemotherapy while serving on the bench made her wonder, "I've had cancer. I can't believe people are fussing like this. I'd like to take them out behind the barn and explain what's important in life. And I realized this *is* what is important to them. It's their life and their case. I could even listen to the guy who told me, 'Sure I'd had 12 beers and two quarts of white lightning, but I knew what was going on!'" When Jones was leaving to go for gene therapy to fight the recurring cancer, a group of her friends hung a wide array of blue jeans across her front porch with a sign, "We're giving you our jeans. Now go make it work!"

Shirley Fulton says, "My son started kindergarten the same day I
started law school, a real challenge for both of us." Subsequently the South
Carolina native came to Charlotte in 1982 as a single parent to work as
assistant district attorney. She progressed to become Charlotte's resident
Superior Court judge, beginning in 1988 and continuing. Her outstanding
public service work in founding the Wesley Heights Community Center and
as co-founder of the Queen City Congress marks a long commitment to
community building.

PHOTO BY J. ALLEN WILLIAMS

192

Since North Carolina has no female federal court judges, Shirley Fulton, the resident Superior Court judge, is the highest-ranking senior judge in Charlotte and has served since 1988, re-elected in 2000. Fulton came to Charlotte in 1982. She had been practicing law in Durham after Duke Law School and decided to take a job with the district attorney's office in Charlotte, since she was a single mother of a son about seven years old.

She recalls growing up in Kingstree, South Carolina, on a low-country cotton and tobacco farm. She graduated from high school at 16 and went to North Carolina A&T University in Greensboro, got married at 18, had a son when she was 20, and worked for about five years in a registrar of deeds office before deciding to go to back to school to finish her degree. Then she headed to law school. She recalls, "My son started kindergarten the same day I started law school. That was a real challenge for both of us. My sister came to live with us during the time I was in law school, so she is like his second mom. During that time she was his first mom."

When she looked into the Charlotte job, she felt it offered a structured schedule that allowed time to be with her son. District attorney Peter Gilchrist in interviewing her for the job of assistant district attorney had asked, "Where do you see yourself 10 years down the road?" Fulton says, "I had not thought 10 years down the road. I was too busy trying to make it on a day-to-day basis. But I said, 'I'd like to be a judge.' Gilchrist said, 'Well, we'll work toward that.' So I moved to Charlotte."

"When the first judgeship became available, Peter asked me about it. I declined to seek it because I didn't feel I was ready, or that my son was ready for me to do that. He was about 10. A few years later another position became available, and I did seek that one. He was 14 then. I got appointed by Governor Martin to complete an unexpired term as a district court judge." Later after a lawsuit changed the selection of judges from appointment to election and when electoral districts were drawn, she ran for superior court judge. While serving in that position, she had her first bout with breast cancer. She walked away clean from that first bout, then had a recurrence in 1995, a mastectomy, chemotherapy, radiation, and a stem cell transplant. She was out for a year recovering, then was re-elected and went back to work in January 1997 full-time as a judge. But she decided also to do something else she had been considering. She enrolled in the Queens College Executive MBA program. Her father died in the interim, delaying her studies at Queens, but she finished her MBA in 1999.

Fulton remarried. She was invited to join the Junior League, and she did. She and her husband moved into the Wesley Heights neighborhood, a 1910s neighborhood of some ragged, unkempt areas, but solid housing stock. Fulton thought the houses were gorgeous. "I saw an opportunity to make a difference in a predominantly black neighborhood because I had never had the experience of living in one, because I grew up out in the country. We moved there with the commitment to save houses, revitalize the neighborhood. The neighbors had been working on organizing and drafting articles of incorporation. My husband is also a lawyer and we said, 'We could help.'" Incorporation allowed them to file for Title I C3 status. They had a neighborhood festival, started meeting with city folks and police officers. Fulton said, "Some of the same people that sold drugs on street corners, I saw them in court. They were always very polite. 'Hi, Miz Fulton. How you doin'?'"

But the drug dealers moved on after the neighborhood organization targeted and purchased houses owned by out-of-state landlords. Neighborhood leaders sought out people interested in becoming homeowners, neighbors who could be hired for renovation. They got a total of five houses, and because of other things happening on the corridor between their neighborhoods and up-town, Fulton says, "The market has taken over." The organizing group and neighbors promoted a greenway, which won a "City Within A City" matching grant and was adopted as part of the master plan. The city began to maintain it. The reclaimed blocks of houses became homes. The area became a neighborhood proud of itself. Perhaps her most challenging civic accomplishment has been the founding of the Wesley Heights Community Center and her service as co-founder of the Queen City Congress, Inc., a coalition of Central Charlotte neighborhoods.

While eating a salad at her three o'clock lunch hour, Fulton told a story which answers the large question of where she got the will and determination to haul herself out of a low-country tobacco and cotton farm and become a catalyst for change:

There was a funeral director in Kingstree who was generally responsible for my going to college. He started taking me and a group of my friends to the state capitol, to lunch with a U.S. Senator, and just exposing us to different events. Virgil Dimery's goal was for me and my three friends to go to college. We did. All four girls. He took me and my parents the first time.

Also, one of my high school teachers, the chemistry teacher, would make sure I got to events when my parents wouldn't take me at night. She made sure I got there safely. The teachers were all black. I went to a segregated school. This was before integration. A segregated school limited my exposure, but gave me mentors who knew me all my life and didn't mind disciplining me as though they were my parents, and telling my parents!

I find a similar relationship in my current neighborhood with these kids. There is a boy about nine next door, who lives with his mother, a single parent. He went to Washington Heights Youth Camp, a summer camp not far away. He had been giving the teacher some difficulty, and it happened she had the community police officer in that day. She called me about the boy and I said, 'Put him in the police car and send him to me.' So he spent the day with me in my courtroom. We call him the 'village kid.' His second mom is a woman across the street now in Wesley Heights. Mattie Marshall has devoted her life to making sure the neighborhood kids are exposed to many new things. She has taken some from almost drop-outs to honor roll students.

CHAPTER ELEVEN

*I*f the frequent report is true that Charlotte, until about the 1980s, was a thoroughly "good old boys' town," where men had the power, respect, and made the big decisions, then it was up to women to prove what women could do in the public arena. In a city where money talks, where money and the earning of more money evoke optimum power and respect, then women needed to make money, not just inherit it. Women needed to raise money and lots of it for good causes and public enhancements. And they did.

Marcia Simon remembers how she learned fundraising, which she views as "one more step in the progression of women to become equal." She looks back at how women got the vote, gained the ability to control their reproductive systems, joined the work force in droves, were admitted to and came to outnumber men in many of the professional schools, fields once dominated by men. "Women have excelled in all areas of life," says Simon. "As we have become more economically independent, we have begun to give money away.

No longer do women have to 'ask permission' to be philanthropic." Simon recalls,

> When I began raising money in the 1970s, I was scared to death. Women I knew were fearful of making a direct solicitation . . . anything other than going door to door or writing a note to ask for five or 10 dollars. Organizations traditionally had called on women to handle this. In the arts community, women were asked to head the neighborhood drives. And it took an army.

> I came to realize how much easier it is to raise funds from a few people and ask for more. Rolfe Neill asked me to be a vice chair of the Arts and Science Council fundraising drive when he was chair in 1979. Hugh McColl served as the other vice chair. . . . As a 'returnee' to Charlotte, I didn't realize at the time that I was in 'high cotton.' I began working on the drive when I was six months pregnant. One colleague told the story many times of my planning my cesarian around the fund drive dates. It's not altogether true, but it made a good story. In 1979, the goal was $350,000, a real reach, we thought. In 2001, we just made $10 million.

> I enjoyed fundraising. When I started my consulting firm in 1980, I was hired as a professional to organize drives at Spirit Square. I learned quickly that it is difficult to fundraise simultaneously as a professional and then as a volunteer. I made a conscious decision then to only fundraise in the community as a volunteer.

Simon, a businesswoman who owns an upscale clothing store in Myers Park, says:

> To be successful in fundraising, you must be a 'giver' yourself before you ask others. Charlotteans are very civic minded and give generously to community needs. Newcomers are often told, 'This is what you do here.'

> Summit House, a home we started in Charlotte for non-violent women offenders and their young children, had all the elements for a successful fundraising effort. These women would go to prison and be separated from their infant children if this program did not exist. Now these women can stay with their children and have the opportunity to start life over again. At Summit House, donors could see where their

money goes. They can come and see a newborn and what we need in our house—a classic case for fundraisers. I took one prospective donor to the house. I picked her up and took her home. I asked her for $25,000. It is difficult to hear yourself get 'the ask' out of your mouth. She wrote a check out of her household checkbook for $25,000!

Simon, who has lived in Charlotte most of her life, returned from San Francisco in 1974–75. Someone called and asked her, "Make a call for me. Someone's not coming through for me." Simon said, "I felt I couldn't do it. But I called him back. I took a business division, called one on one and did a real good job."

Is it necessary in fundraising for a woman to have lived here a long time? "Yes, it helps," she agreed. "I am essentially a native, was born in Erwin, North Carolina, because my mother went home to give birth and the hospital in Dunn was full. We lived on Knollwood Road, and I went to Sharon Elementary School where young Billy Graham had gone. There must have been 10 Jewish kids. Evangelists would come into the classroom there. They challenged us to memorize New Testament Bible verses and win prizes. Jewish kids were good at this. We memorized the verses and won prizes until our parents found out what we were doing.

"I grew up in two worlds. I am Jewish, but also a southerner. I was one of the first Jewish women in the Junior League and the first in the Y-sponsored Girl Ambassadors at Myers Park High School. I was in one of the first classes to integrate at Myers Park. Two black students came. I was brought up to believe in the importance of social justice. It is one of the essentials in the Jewish way of life." This background is a vital impetus in Simon's philanthropy and fundraising.

Sally Dalton Robinson's enthusiasm and absolute belief in the causes she promotes are legendary and thoroughly contagious. A native of Charlotte and lifetime resident, who attended Charlotte's public schools and Duke University, Robinson has extensive connections with Charlotte movers and shakers and is well known for her leadership and communication skills. In addition, she and her husband Russell have contributed to and worked for myriad local causes including UNC Charlotte, the Arts and Science Council, and the Mint Museum. When her junior high school English teacher, Anne Batten, approached her in 1989 to coordinate the organization and support of a history museum, Robinson said yes. With hundreds of phone calls, she rallied support, funds, and a strong founding board. The Museum of the New South was born, a regional museum exploring area history from 1865 to the present.

Celebrating its 10th year in 2001, this museum achieved an impeccable record of both popular and scholarly multicultural and historical programming and earned star-quality rating in public opinion. Robinson had been told at the outset that the task was formidable, but she is not easily discouraged. In 1997–98 Robinson chaired the effort that raised over $8 million to renovate the museum's building and to install the core exhibit in 2001. The Museum of the New South with a membership of over 720 expanded its uptown site, and created a permanent core exhibit, "New City, New South" with a $200,000 grant from the National Endowment for the Humanities.

Prior to the museum effort, Robinson, as former Charlotte library board chair, had led the successful drive in 1989 to raise $554,000 to help equip the new $11.4 million uptown library building. Her appeals to friends, families, businesses, and foundations garnered important new local support for the library. After all, civic philanthropy had created the library in the early part of the century, when iron magnate Andrew Carnegie gave $25,000 to the first library building in Charlotte in 1903.

Robinson is a member of the Queen's Table, a private group which gives funds to purchase major art works for the city. Her further interest in art raised $25,000 to erect a sculpture by Doris Leeper, a Charlotte native and internationally acclaimed artist whose commissions include IBM in Atlanta and the Orlando International Airport, exhibitions in New York, the National Museum of American Art in Washington, and Wadsworth Athenaeum in Hartford. Robinson worked with Suzanne Fetscher of the Tryon Center for the Arts to locate a space for the Leeper sculpture, which was installed in the spring of 2000 on the wide lawn of Edwin Towers, a public housing project for the elderly in Fourth Ward.

Deborah Small Harris, the great-granddaughter of a Maine sea captain, grew up in Charlotte in the Eastover neighborhood and on Sharon Lane, attended Charlotte Country Day School and Myers Park High School, and earned her B.A. at UNC Chapel Hill in religion. When she graduated in 1969, she told her fiancé, Charlottean Johnny Harris, that she was going to New York. "You don't want to marry me until I get this out of my system." There she shared an Upper East Side apartment with sorority sisters and worked as an assistant to a diplomatic correspondent at the United Nations. Because she wanted to earn her living independently, she also modeled to make ends meet. She came home, married, had three children, and became involved in cultural and Junior League projects. She served as president of the Arts and Science Council board, Junior League president, board president 1977–78 of Charlotte Drug Education Center, and chair of the Mecklenburg Drug and Alcohol Commission. (Harris was the second Arts and Science Council female president, following Harriet Cuthbertson, who was the first president in 1977.)

Like many civic leaders, Harris was aware of a large need in Charlotte. The problem appeared in 1975 as a brief item in a consultant's report. When strong arts supporters, lawyers Mark Bernstein (Charlotte Symphony) and Sydnor Thompson (Charlotte Opera), objected that the current Cultural Action Plan for Charlotte-Mecklenburg did not include a performing arts center, the consultant suggested that the acoustics in Ovens Auditorium be improved. But in 1979, the chamber of commerce formed a committee to include a potential arts center site as part of a $300 million office tower project which NCNB was building on the Square. In 1981 however, the voters rejected a $1.5 million bond referendum to buy land for an uptown arts center. As incoming chair of Charlotte-Mecklenburg Arts and Science Council, Deborah Harris was undeterred, making the performing arts center a priority. And in 1985, Belk Store Services, NCNB Corp., and Charter Properties donated the potential arts center site as part of a $300 million NCNB office tower project.

In 1987 city manager Wendell White named a task force led by Deborah Harris to represent the city in negotiations for a North Carolina Performing Arts Center at Charlotte. The North Carolina legislature approved $9.5 toward the Center. In November, 1987, Charlotte voters approved a $50 million bond issue 2–1. "They called us the giant vacuum cleaner," Harris was quoted in the *Atlanta Journal-Constitution*, referring to their ability to attract funds. "They thought we were going to go in and sweep up all the money. But we used the analogy of the large ship in the ocean—it just raises the level." *The Charlotte Observer* described her as the elegant, model-thin woman who prods

CEOs from her Volvo's car phone while waiting to pick up her kids from school. Not surprisingly, in 1987 Harris, president of the board of the North Carolina Blumenthal Center for the Performing Arts, was named Charlotte's Woman of the Year.

Harris kept a list in her $1.99 spiral notebook and used it constantly. Hugh McColl, CEO of Bank of America, remembered how Harris "might call and say 'I've been waiting to hear the result of this.'" She was persistent. She would call McColl and other CEOs daily until they completed whatever they agreed to. Cesar Pelli, the outstanding international architect who designed the office tower/arts center project, became accustomed to her attention to detail, "She was interested even in the minutest details of the project. By now, I can't separate her ideas from mine; they have grown inextricably together." Her concern included the colors of the trim and the stage curtain, wanting the hall to be warm and inviting.

McColl recalls, "There's a certain shyness about her but not when she's on a project." Always elegantly dressed and coifed, she was unaccustomed to direct, personal criticism such as she received when the project became a public issue. Before the city council voted in 1987 on the arts center bonds, fellow board member and *Observer* publisher Rolfe Neill worried she would add to the criticism that the center was elitist if she dressed with her usual elegance. He advised her to dress down. She said, "I wore a black suit and no jewelry except my wedding ring. It didn't bother me a bit. At that point, I took advice from anyone who would give it to me."

When the bond issue passed, the funding was found, and the center opened in 1992, Harris refused to take credit. "One of the main things I've learned in the projects I've worked on is that it takes teamwork to make something happen . . . a lot of people, and a lot of working together." But others know how she helped it happen. Dr. Jonnie McLeod describes one of her talents. "She makes people feel good." And Judith Allen, the first executive director of the North Carolina Blumenthal Center for the Performing Arts, testifies, "She's a powerhouse. We're talking energy and motion."

The name on the performing arts center is a consummate example of remarkable philanthropy. Herman and Anita Blumenthal's generous gift toward the achievement of the center was so outstanding that the center was named for them. It is only one example of the Blumenthals' investment in the arts in Charlotte and North Carolina.

An essential ingredient in getting others to donate time, energy, and money is to give generously yourself. Deborah Harris and her family have been excellent civic examples for several generations. Her husband's family inherited through his grandfather, North Carolina governor Cameron Morrison, and Morrison's wife, Sara Ecker Watts, heir of a Durham fortune, several thousand acres of Mecklenburg County land, which they developed to become Southpark and Ballantyne. The Harris family has been consistently one of leadership and philanthropy in Charlotte and in North Carolina. Angelia Morrison Harris, Deborah Harris's mother-in-law, gave away millions, including the 15-story Commerce Center building to Covenant Presbyterian Church, $10 million for a foundation, and 18.3 acres for the Harris YMCA. Angelia Harris's daughter, Sara Harris Bissell, carries on the family tradition of generous philanthropy.

Author and historian David Goldfield reflects on southern cities and their first families: "Through the decades, a relatively small but growing group of families has exercised economic and political power. One of the perks of that position is that you get to set the community's priorities. And one of the benefits for the community of having a local elite is that they do have a civic consciousness." Charlotte is most fortunate to have a growing number of such families and individuals, who exercise a strong commitment to community and create imaginative uses of wealth for the public good.

An individual who exemplifies this generosity is one of Charlotte's few female, large-company CEOs, Dale Dick Halton, who is president and board chairman of Pepsi-Cola Bottling Co. of Charlotte. In 1988, *The Charlotte Observer* described a dinner in Moscow, where Halton was honored for her company's increased sales. Sitting with her husband Phil and other winners, she listened at dinner to a male bottler from Oregon direct questions to her husband. "How many routes do you run?" he asked Phil Halton. He answered, "I don't know. Ask her," pointing to Dale sitting next to him, "she's the bottler." Halton has learned to keep her sense of humor handy in the male-dominated arena of Pepsi bottling. "We see a lot of this at conventions. Somebody will start talking to Phil and just ignore me absolutely. We have fun with it."

Dale Halton grew up with Pepsi-Cola much more closely than her thirsty peers. Her grandfather owned the early Pepsi franchise in Charlotte, beginning in 1905 when he opened Charlotte's first Pepsi plant in back of a blacksmith's shop on West Trade Street. Halton grew up watching him and her grandmother, father, mother, and aunt involved in the business, which seemed an extension of their home. She became president in 1981, managing sales in seven counties. As businesswoman and philanthropist, she donated handsomely to scholarships and other projects at UNC Charlotte. The Dale F. Halton Arena opened on campus in 1996.

In the first seven years after she became president of her company, her overall sales increased 60 percent and profits jumped 600 percent. Dale Dick Halton knows Pepsi. It is a family tradition. In 1905, her grandfather Henry Fowler opened Charlotte's first Pepsi plant behind a blacksmith's shop on West Trade Street. (Pepsi had been invented by a druggist in New Bern in 1898, and at first was called Brad's Drink. Halton's was the nation's first Pepsi bottling franchise.) After Henry Dick married Fowler's oldest daughter, Dale and her sister were born. With her parents, Dale Dick lived in Florida, then moved back to Charlotte in 1947 and attended Agnes Scott College in Atlanta. She became treasurer of Pepsi in Charlotte in the early 1970s. When she divorced in 1980, she took over running the company, which her ex-husband had managed after her father's death. Although she had no business experience, she had watched her grandmother, mother, and aunt involved in the Pepsi business, and often went to the plant as she was growing up.

The company was struggling, so she and Darrell Holland, second in command in the business, worked out a recovery plan for reinvestment, cost cutting, and addressing high employee turnover. When the company recovered, she turned her business sense to the community—to the Charlotte Symphony, the N.C. Dance Theatre, and her largest project, UNC Charlotte, where she gave large donations and support.

Her grandfather, Henry Fowler, was a staunch supporter of UNC Charlotte's founder, Bonnie Cone, and Halton determined to continue his investment at the university, which became a campus of the University of North Carolina system in 1965. Halton's scholarship support in her grandfather's memory sends up to 25 students abroad to study. Since about 1980, she has been contributing to the athletic program at UNC Charlotte. In 1996, the Halton Arena—with a $1.2 million donation from Halton—hosted its first game. The Dale F. Halton Reading Room in the university library is her gift to the library expansion, and her gifts supported the sculpting of the gold miner statue at the entrance to the university. She is an avid fan of UNC Charlotte's basketball team, the 49ers. "I'm the crazy lady in the stands," she says. "I have to teach the referees every game that my 49ers don't foul."

Halton recalls meeting the wife of a West Coast bottler who mistook Halton for a homebody. The woman was fascinated that Halton ran the family business.

She told Halton that her husband was running her family's bottling business back in Oregon. She was full of questions—"How did you do it? Our girls are getting old enough. I've been thinking about going down to the office." Halton said, "Maybe I encouraged her to go find out what it's all about. Several things like that have happened. I feel like maybe one of the reasons I'm here is to encourage others."

Mary Lou Babb knows how to raise money. She has no inherited wealth, so her journey is perhaps more typical of the volunteer path of a parent or good neighbor who often makes fine things happen in a community.

Mary Lou Davis and her twin sister Nancy moved to Charlotte with their parents when the girls were in the eighth grade. They had been in a Catholic boarding school near their parents' home in Pinehurst. Moving to Charlotte and going to Piedmont Junior High School was severe culture shock. Instead of saying, "Yes, ma'am" to teachers, she had been used to the nuns, who rapped her knuckles, and whom she addressed, "Yes, sister." Later, with scholarships, she took a commercial course at UNC Greensboro, and came back to work at *The Charlotte Observer*. She got a job as secretary to the general manager and was bored to death. So she moved to the newsroom to the city desk where she worked four years for men. "All men," she said. "I was the only woman on the city side then." The society or woman's department was another department at the time. "About 1957 another girl was hired as a reporter to write about food, society, and gardening. I was asked to do a social column called 'Under 21.' I worked later for Wachovia before getting married. That's the last time I had a paying job."

She and her husband Jim Babb lived at first in Starmount off South Boulevard. It was, she says,

> everybody's first house. Loads of children. And it was where I first started volunteering on a door-to-door basis. The symphony had a new director, and they were trying to get new members and sell season tickets. I remember going up and down my block touting the symphony, then the Jaycee Jollies, the Heart Ball selling raffle tickets. Jim was involved with politics, and I did a lot of volunteering in the

Democratic party. I was on the campaign cabinet of Betsy Kelley, who ran for school board. Liz Hair got me involved in a lot of things. During that time I had four children. Every Thursday I had help, so I could go out and do my thing.

When we moved to Kingswood and had our fifth child, my volunteering began in schools, kindergarten, PTA, room mother, socials, then Girl Scouts. Brownie leader, all four daughters went through Brownies. When we lived on Edgehill Road, I served as PTA president at Myers Park Elementary, at Alexander Graham, and at West Charlotte. All those barbecues. All that phoning. An exchange program. I was always involved with the Symphony Guild, the Designer House, not taking major jobs, but when the girls and Jimmy started going off to school, time opened up a little for me. And I remember Gwin Dalton asking me to chair the Home and Garden Tour of the Mint and I was not even a member then. Then I chaired their antique show. And now I am going in as chair of the board of the Mint for a two-year stint (2000–2002).

I served on the state arts council for six years. When they asked me, I said, 'You don't want me, I have no background in arts across the board.' But my ability, I guess, is in fundraising, which is why I am asked to help. It has been so rewarding. I have done a lot of lobbying of legislators for annual funding, the funds we get annually to distribute for grants, such as sending arts educators to low-wealth counties for educational purposes.

When asked how she got to be good at fundraising, Babb replies,

I am not good at it, but the only thing I am probably good at is in connecting people, just knowing whom to call and maybe find the person who has a passion for something that connects with the Mint or Symphony. I don't have any hang-ups about calling to ask for a meeting with someone. Lots of people do not like to do that because they know why we're coming. Of course they know why we are coming! But most people are very kind about it and willing to listen to you if they know you, like you, or care about what your project is.

The most I have asked for is about $50,000. We have to do a lot of work educating folks why we need it, why they should be a part of it. Push their passion button. We have to get them excited. It's fun. You are dealing with personalities. I am not a financial person.

As president of the PTA at Alexander Graham Junior High, we had a meeting in the 1970s that everybody came to, and it was so noisy. We talked about how we could get ceiling tiles put up, so it might make a difference. I thought Jim was going to be there, but it was opening night of the World Series, and he took off to Philadelphia with our son. I was left high and dry. I didn't know how I was going to pull off that meeting by myself. When I got there, I remember we were electing the officers. I was supposed to ask for a motion, but I forgot to do it, and all of a sudden it occurred to me that with all those people there, it was a perfect time to raise the money for that ceiling. So I said, 'You know what? We can have this fabulous project, and we can get it done tonight. Every family here is going to buy a tile for the number of children they have. I have five, so I am buying five tiles.' So they signed up at 10 dollars a tile. We made enough money that evening to tile our ceiling.

When asked about her strategy for raising money, Babb says quickly, "Often it's a seat of the pants strategy. Your own adrenalin has to be running for it to happen. You should give money to a project yourself. If you have 100 percent commitment of your board moneywise, you tell people you have this.

"I have spent 40 years as a volunteer, all in Charlotte. People ask me, 'Why are you still doing this?' I like it. You meet so many neat folks, and there are things I want to accomplish." A week later, Babb received the Marie Rowe Award for Volunteerism.

Charlotte's cavernous Merchandise Mart, which a few weeks earlier seethed with an orgy of regional shoppers touching and tasting cookies and cheeses, buying beeswax candles, pottery, plants, and personalized framed poems, looks entirely different for this occasion. It is two weeks before Christmas 2000. The great, high barn narrows within walls of red fabric to section off a stage and Christmas tables for 1,000 women who are the Good Friends.

Lunching at tables of 10, on box lunches of turkey, dilled Havarti cheese, greens, and Rudolf Red potato salad, these extremely well-dressed women are gathered to give. The group began in 1987 and on this December day, there is hardly a Christmas sweater in sight. Charlotte women started this charity organization, which meets only once a year, "after watching 70 years of Good Fellows' lunches from the sidelines." The women's monetary gifts had been accepted for years, but only men could be members, so women were seated on the edge of the room, not at the tables. The men's raucous, generous Christmas rally for charity had begun in 1917 as the Men's Benevolent Association. They changed their name in 1919 to Good Fellows.

So four well-connected Charlotte women, Catherine Browning, Alice Folger, Sally Saussy, and Patty Norman started their own charity group and called it Good Friends. The women who attend are young and old, black and white, working women, volunteers, and stay-at-homes, all gathered to listen to Christmas music of a women's choir and bells, and the brief, high-drama presentation of the plight of three separate women whose needs are great. The funds go to those who fall through the cracks of other emergency services, to those who need help and have exhausted all other agencies and resources. Mary Lou Babb brought eight friends and two of her daughters to fill her table. Kathy Shonts filled hers with educators from Discovery Place.

On each table is a small white bucket for folding money and change so you can "empty your pockets," as they suggest. "Every penny we raise this day will be returned to the community. Your dues go to putting on this occasion," says founder Browning as she welcomes the crowd. A jovial male Santa shouts as he bursts through the curtains, "Here's your chance to play Santa Claus! Just add another digit to that check." All checks go into a separate container on the table and then along with the cash, are gathered by Santa's rowdy helpers from each table. The funds will be distributed through a special account with Mecklenburg County's Social Services Department. In 1991, $77,000 was raised, and in 1996, more than $126,000, outdoing the men's Good Fellows group for the first time.

Jill Flynn, senior vice president of First Union National Bank, leads off with the story of 42-year-old Linda, a divorced mother of four, living in a crime-ridden neighborhood, who works for a janitorial service. After her job, she hosts a weekday volunteer haven in her neighborhood for after-school neighbor children. She greets them, listens, and helps with their homework because she believes, "children need to know someone is waiting for them when they come home from school." Two other eloquent speakers follow, the Reverend Jane Summey Mullennix, outreach minister at Myers Park Presbyterian Church, and Emily Zimmern, executive director of the Museum of the New South. Each has a story of a woman or girl in dire need who will benefit with others from the funds raised by Good Friends on this one occasion. "Let the light of your caring shine forth," urges Zimmern. And the women do just that, contributing $135,000 in the wink of an eye.

There are all sorts of ways to raise money, and women have historically put their particular spin on the effort. For decades, the way that African-American communities, particularly the churches, raised money for church buildings was to hold a fish fry, selling fish sandwiches. Or they held an ice cream supper, selling bowls of hand-churned ice cream. Women cooked and fed and cleaned up at these and all the fellowship dinners held to raise money. Or they brought homemade desserts and fried chicken or handmade crafts to sell at a church or school bazaar.

Rose Leary Love tells of one conscientious woman who spent a sleepless Sunday night waiting for the bank to open so she could deposit the money made at a particularly successful Ebenezer Baptist Church effort. Professional people and laundresses had come forward to contribute a remarkable $1,000 for church expenses. Mrs. Ethel Wyche took the money home and "sat up all night with a pistol by her side to make sure that no harm came to the money with which she had been entrusted."

Other examples are volunteer "room mothers" at public schools who raised money for supplies or band uniforms, while churchwomen raised funds for a missionary and his wife whom the church sponsored abroad, or for the young people in the church to attend a church conference in the mountains, or to buy a church bus. Charlotte women developed sophisticated money-raising schemes, such as antique and house and garden shows, a musical show called the "Follies" with a cast of talented members and local dignitaries with a professional director, or the ever-popular tour of a designer house. One popular event was the fashion show, which the Junior Women's Club of Charlotte and several other groups have raised to a fine art. In 1960, the Junior Women's Club's annual "Serenade to Autumn" raised $3,500 for charities. By 1990, the event featured not only music and the modeling of beautiful clothes, but also a guest designer and popular entertainer, which that year netted $78,000 to benefit the Shelter for Battered Women, Habitat for Humanity, and other community charities.

The "gala" rose in a class all its own as a Charlotte charity fundraiser masterminded by women. Particular women became known as experts in this field, such as Patty O'Herron, Gwin Dalton, Sara Bissell, and Pepper Dowd. Dowd has chaired "galas," and is known as a strong leader who can guide any board or Charlotte venture. When asked what a "gala" is, one woman who has attended many, described it:

> Always cocktails, food, incredible flowers, music, put on by lay people with somebody to head it up who is often professional or semi-pro. Table arrangements are a big thing. This subject requires more discussion and thought than many other elements. It is important to have exotic arrangements and to auction them off to pay for the charity event. The idea is to get lots of people to come and pay $300 per person, to get corporate tables where the corporation pays for a whole table and sends its people there. Ten people per table times 10 tables nets several thousand per table. Often there is dancing or an auction where the objects auctioned might be lunch with Hugh McColl and a walk through the bank, or a seat at NASCAR and a ride around the track in a car, or a vacation home for a week or weekend. At a gala you get lots of wine and everybody's feeling good and then you just start bidding. It goes real well. For such highly organized events, it takes hordes of women. The planning is incredible. It is a way for women who haven't been in the business world to be creative, and to display executive and administrative ability.

The meetings to organize events require a standard hierarchy of women who agree to concrete, assigned tasks, and reportage to someone higher up. The committee chair gets people to meet at her house for lunch to get to know them and for them to get to know each other. A genuine effort is made to make everyone feel important. It is essential to do your assignment well. The women so involved often become friends for life and when another event comes along to be organized, they know whom to call and what their specialty is. At the Mint, for example, there is a huge pool of volunteers who can as a whole make a very significant contribution.

Peggy Culbertson, a community activist who served two terms as chair of the Planning Commission and six terms on that commission, has experience as a fundraiser for Johnson C. Smith, for the Mint, for political candidates, and as North Carolina chair of the campaign to raise funds to start the National Museum of Women in the Arts in Washington, D.C. Culbertson is an art collector also. When she and her husband saw a painting they liked, they called a knowledgeable collector, Billie Holladay, to check out its value.

On Holladay's recommendation, they bought the painting, but Holladay in return collected Culbertson's interest and fundraising involvement in the birth of Washington's National Museum of Women's Art. As chair of the North Carolina group, Peggy Culbertson gathered women in the state to support the effort to raise the consciousness of women and the public as to the history and excellent works by women artists who had heretofore been ignored. Culbertson, Jean Gaskin, Sally Van Allen, and Ann Maxwell contacted many women to attend lunch at the Charlotte Country Club. Holladay came to speak and the next day she spoke to the Friends of the Mint. The drive for the Women's Art Museum in Washington was successful, as was the related traveling exhibit which was shown throughout the state. The museum is in a landmark building, a former Masonic Temple near the Smithsonian Museums.

Culbertson's long-term work with the arts and civic affairs gives her perspective on how fundraising has historically happened in twentieth-century Charlotte:

When it comes to arenas, stadiums, banks, it's the men. Also politically, it's men raising big political money. Men generally do it differently. They are used to politics and starting new arenas. Men have a network in which they find out who's willing to give what. They pay back each other. But the museum and art type things have been largely spearheaded by women as at the Mint, the Blumenthal Performing Arts Center, the Museum of the New South. There are always women who were well-connected and non-threatening to men. 'It's just the arts, a little museum. Yes, we knew her grandparents. It must be fine.' It's been primarily arts related when women are fundraisers. Women working together in large groups have become institutionalized, like for the symphony. They work as a team there and for galas and bring in people from many miles away to see people's homes.

The general consensus is that the trick in raising money for female, first-time political candidates is to "get in there in office and show you're capable and then the money comes easier." Of course, this means that the initial effort for women to get elected to office is a huge obstacle, which requires enormous volunteer organization and grassroots contacts, such as Liz Hair describes in Chapter Six.

Often, a philanthropist with a particular interest, such as Sara Belk Gambrell whose family is interwoven into the successful mercantile and social history of Charlotte, chooses to give to a personal project of interest, such as the Charlotte Museum of History, which operates a visitor museum and the Hezekiah Alexander homesite. Lucille Puette Giles and her sister Mary Liz Francis have followed the significant, philanthropic example of their parents by giving generous donations, often anonymously. Giles's bequest in her will may be the largest ever given for unrestricted charitable purposes to the people of Mecklenburg County.

One focused, high-profile benefactor was Marie Rowe. Her major gifts and leadership included colleges, the Republican Party, Charlotte Symphony, and in 1993, she gave $100,000 to Opera Carolina. At the time, this was one of the largest personal donations to a performing-arts group in Charlotte history.

CHAPTER TWELVE

By the 1990s, great changes occurred for women in Charlotte and through-out America. For their writing, Toni Morrison, an African-American woman, had won the Nobel Prize for literature and Alice Walker won the Pulitzer. The divorce rate and the age of first marriages rose appreciably; married women and women with preschool-age children increasingly entered the work force; day care became widely available; and official scrutiny of sexual harrassment altered the attitudes of the workplace. The influence of women in the election of Bill Clinton and the confrontation between Anita Hill and Supreme Court nominee Clarence Thomas produced an enormous "genderquake."

Breast cancer research and treatment, rape prevention awareness, and the abortion rights controversy at the turn of the century remain highly visible and audible in the American public mind. Young women in well-paid jobs cannot perhaps imagine an era 30 years past when women in public office, the board room, the executive suite, and the television anchor position were rare or totally absent. Whether one agrees with it or not, whether one recognizes it or not, the feminist revolution since the 1960s has thoroughly altered the national consciousness. So these examples of Charlotte women who have risen remarkably to the top show what different paths they have followed.

Freda Hyams Nicholson says that one teacher in her high school in mountainous Swannanoa, North Carolina, convinced her that college was possible. Nicholson says, "I probably wouldn't have gone to college had it not been for my chemistry teacher who said, 'We can get you into nursing school.' That one person made the difference in my life."

And how different her life has been! Nicholson retired at the end of the year 2000 after 27 years working in science museums, 20 of those as CEO of Discovery Place in Charlotte. Discovery Place is a premier hands-on science museum, which she and her staff got off the ground and developed into one of the top 20 museums of its kind in the country.

Instead of relaxing into retirement at age 65, she began immediately a prestigious two-year term as chairman of the board of the Washington, D.C.–based American Association of Museums. On the ballot for her election, she was unopposed.

Today's Charlotte Woman quotes the director of development at Discovery Place, who worked with her for 15 years: "Freda is team-oriented, a technically oriented person, but very creative. You don't find those traits together very often. Although she's fairly quiet, when it comes to business she's very savvy, one of the best businesswomen I know. Freda not only knows what she wants, but knows how to get what she wants."

The unusual path of her career is a wonderful route, filled with surprises. She earned her nursing degree (R.N.) at St. Joseph's School of Nursing in Savannah, Georgia, married a surgeon in 1956, and moved to Charlotte when he started his practice. She went back to school and got her B.S. in nursing at Queens College in 1959 and earned her Master's in Education, Supervision, and Administration at UNC Charlotte in 1976. Somewhere in between she had six children.

She recalls having a lot of administrative duties in nursing, where you have nursing assistants, orderlies, and people working under you. "At the Nature Museum I became a guild member because my four little boys loved to hang out there. I had no intention of working there. I was teaching in the nursing field at the time." She recalls Nature Museum founder, Laura Owens, who had realized the need for a children's museum initially. Owens was able to convince the right people to help her with that, primarily the Junior League and the Lions Club. And Charlotte Kelly had given her own money and aroused the people around her to make a planetarium happen at the museum.

"Jonnie McLeod and Charlotte Kelly approached me about taking on the health classes at the Nature Museum because Jonnie was going to do the drug education center. I said, 'Jonnie, I don't know how to do that.' Between the two of them, those two powerful women, I had no choice. That's how I got involved in putting together the Hall of Health with TAM, the transparent anatomical mannequin, and was teaching classes. These two women were both wives of physicians, [Jonnie also a physician herself] and I was able to get lots of volunteers through the Medical Auxiliary. We started teaching formal classes for the Charlotte-Mecklenburg Schools at that time. We used the models to educate the children about their own human bodies. And it is still required for every fifth grader. They come to Discovery Place now. The same teacher teaches every fifth grader that same class. We call it Growth and Development."

Russ Piethman, director at the Nature Museum, felt Charlotte needed an interactive science museum uptown. Plans and funds were gearing up, with Nicholson working on an exhibit for that, when the museum board felt different leadership was needed for the large shift in scale and budget to Discovery Place. Dean Colvard was the board person in charge when he came to Nicholson's office and said, "I don't have anybody else to do this. You are just going to have to do it temporarily." Freda said she would do it for a short while. She recalled,

I was actually not working a 40-hour week; by then I was at 30 hours because I had six children at home. They started a search and at the end of six months, Colvard said, 'Give me your resume, you are going to apply.' . . . The board asked me to take the position as president and CEO, which I did in January 1981. Through the sheer determination of the staff, we carried it through. People said, 'Oh you will never open.' But we did it. We opened.

But when we were trying to get it open, I got up at four a.m. That's when I did my grocery shopping, and luckily Harris-Teeter was open all night. Often I would be down here at four in the morning and see the winos and all. It used to drive my husband wild, but it was the time I could get the most done. When Dean Colvard asked me to take this on temporarily, we had a family vote around the table as to whether I could or couldn't. Even Stuart, who was six, voted. They voted that I should do it. When I took it permanently, they voted again. They wanted me to do it. It was a family decision from my husband right on down.

The decision to put the museum on North Tryon Street had been a radical one because it was a questionable, run-down area where Nicholson recalls, "It was not unusual at 5:30 to look out the window and see the prostitutes at work on the corner of Seventh Street."

When asked about difficulties as a female leading a science museum, she said: "There was an association of science museum directors. I thought I should apply for that. I did and didn't hear anything. I thought, 'I'll send it in again.' No response at all. Finally the director of the Franklin Institute, Joel Bloom, said at a Museum of Science Directors' meeting, 'Come on, we are getting ready to go to the directors' luncheon.' I said, 'Joel, I am not a member.' He said, 'What do you mean? You are not a member! Why didn't you join? Join!' So I told him and he got Vic Danilo, CEO of the Chicago Museum of Science and Industry, and the two of them took me into that luncheon. The man who was chairing it at that time said, 'Oh, we don't know what happened. It's fine. It's fine. She's now a member.' That was about 1983–84, because I applied for three years before they finally opened the door."

Sometimes, Nicholson recalls, "it was difficult doing contracts and negotiations. We do the planetarium program for the science museums in Singapore, and it would always take quite a few meetings before they really believed I was the person who would finally sign the contract. Without those two men, Danilov and Bloom opening doors for me, I would have had a lot more trouble. They got me into the Exhibit Collaborative. They said, 'You need to be here.' They were friends of Russ Piethmann, so a lot of it goes back to him."

Another of Nicholson's valuable skills is a talent for raising money for Discovery Place. "I like to raise money. I like to make matches whether they are people matches or money matches. If you can try to identify a company or person who would have a personal reason for wanting to be attached to this project, then it is fairly easy. I guess part of my success in working with the state is in pointing out how the facility is used by people from all over the state, and then it matches. The whole development department looks at the benefits the company receives from giving money to Discovery Place. What would it mean to their families? In the case of Ike Belk, our largest donor, he always honors Carol [his wife]. He knew there was a need to build this parking deck, that he had grandchildren himself, and it would benefit them. We put it all on paper, and we didn't have to ask anything more. He just wrote me a check for a million dollars."

A key ingredient is personal contact. She says, "With legislators, I have to go Raleigh to their offices. I see legislators from everywhere, because we have kids who come from everywhere. We take little mementos from here, so when the legislators are drinking their coffee they see Discovery Place in their mug. I try to personally go and meet with them and tell them that this many students came from Carteret County. If we can, we get a photo of [each county's] kids getting off the bus."

Securing major exhibits and IMAX films that draw great crowds and promote Discovery Place are high priority. She says "If you saw the film, The Dolphins, we got a credit at the end of the film for Discovery Place. By investing a little money in the film, I had the privilege of reviewing all the science. If it didn't have a lot of science in it, I could call on my colleagues who also had invested and say, 'Look, we need to do something about this, it is not something we want our names on.' In the case of The Dolphins they welcomed every bit of help we could give them."

The board chairman, who had the task of finding Nicholson's successor, said, "Freda has been a visionary who has built Discovery Place into one of the premier science centers in the country. She's not just well-known here, but worldwide." Among her many high honors is North Carolina's Order of the Long Leaf Pine.

During the six years Ruth Gwynn Shaw spent as the new president of Central Piedmont Community College, Charlotteans realized she was an exceptional leader. Coming to the largest community college in the Carolinas as its first female president in 1986 from the presidency of El Centro College in Dallas, Texas, she became a highly visible community activist. In 1992, she was soon lured to the private sector by Duke Power Company as vice president for corporate communications. Duke (now Duke Energy) is a global energy company with over $29 billion in assets in 2000, headquartered in Charlotte, which provides electric service to about two million customers in the Carolinas.

The Danville, Virginia, native holds a Ph.D. in educational administration and master's and undergraduate degrees in English from East Carolina University in Greenville, North Carolina. In 1997, she was named executive vice president and chief administrative officer at Duke. Shaw is adept at creating firsts. In a city where prominent men have most often led fund drives, she has chaired campaigns for the United Way, the Arts and Science Council, the Boy Scouts, the YWCA, and the 1995 school bonds campaign. She served on the 1999 blue ribbon task force to determine needs for the university and community college systems and was chosen the 1996 Businesswoman of the Year. In 1992 North Carolina's governor awarded her the Order of the Long Leaf Pine.

When she first arrived at Duke, she admits she "didn't understand why electricity wouldn't just run out on the floor when you pulled the plug." As the 1993–94 president of the Charlotte Rotary Club, she altered the brief, traditional "health and happiness session" which usually consisted of members' telling stories or jokes about their wives, girlfriends, or other females. She encouraged them instead to use the time to share business or personal experience.

At the age of 10, Shaw geared up her businesslike ambitions by saving money she earned babysitting and breaking ponies at a Greenville stable in order to buy a horse. "I learned that often the work that pays the least is really the most challenging work, the most underappreciated." At 14, she wrote columns for the local newspaper about high school events. Paid by the column inch for her writing, she is sure this is what led her to be somewhat verbose.

She was succinct however in 1997, when she spoke for 27 other Charlotte business leaders and their employees in public opposition to the county commissioners' withdrawing controversial funding from the Charlotte-Mecklenburg Arts and Science Council. The commissioners subsequently chose not to reappoint Shaw to the Charlotte-Mecklenburg Public Library board of trustees. As she predicted, several of these commissioners were defeated in the following election. Shaw has proved to be one of Charlotte's strongest, most articulate leaders. To promote future leadership in others, the Duke Foundation, which she heads, gave $4.5 million to the Lynwood Foundation in 2000 to pay off its mortgage and focus on a program to develop community leaders in the year-long Lee Institute.

Shaw's mother remembers early signs of her daughter's initiative. At age three, she invited several elderly ladies in her neighborhood to her house for a birthday party. They came. But there was no party planned, so her mother Frances Gwynn invented refreshments and admired her daughter's spunk. "She's always taken initiative and responsibility," she said.

When Judy Rose was acting athletic director at UNC Charlotte, she attended the Sun Belt Conference meetings as UNC Charlotte's representative. When her official position was announced at the conference, she recalled, "You could hear a pin drop. It was like I had, or like UNC Charlotte had shattered their world. And the announcement said, 'Furthermore, she will from now on be attending these meetings because who we are going to name will be in a dual position, and he will not be able to attend. So she will be spokesperson for us on this level.' Dead silence. I remember they were all making plans for dinner. Nobody asked me. It was kind of uncomfortable. This is probably where I developed my philosophy of how am I going to deal with this in this setting. Nobody in this group—and most men don't—liked a pushy broad, somebody acting like a female activist. You don't automatically have respect. You just gotta earn it. You just listen. Don't be pushy, I was telling myself, and somebody said, 'You're going to go with us, aren't you?' And I did."

Judy Rose came a long way to get to that dinner. She had begun her career at UNC Charlotte in 1975 right out of graduate school as a coach of women's basketball and tennis. She had been associate director of athletics since 1985. In 1990, Chancellor Dr. James H. Woodward appointed her the university's director of athletics. Sources agree that he knew what his appointment of Rose would accomplish: "Success across the board." Rose was just the third woman in NCAA history to spearhead a Division I athletics program.

At North Carolina State University, where Jim Valvano served a dual role as both men's basketball coach and athletic director, drug testing problems arose among the players, causing UNC's board of governors to end the policy of allowing this dual role in the UNC system. Consequently Jeff Mullins, who had served as UNC Charlotte director of athletics and men's basketball coach from 1985, was asked by the UNC Board of Governors to relinquish his dual role. Rose's promotion was the result of this new policy. In doing so, the university viewed the change as "giving the university two exceptional leaders within one system."

Rose recalls that "everybody was just up in arms about it because Jeff is a really good guy. Jeff called me in and said, 'I've been thinking about this. Judy, it's not a bad deal for me. I get the same amount of money as I'm getting paid. You're doing all the administrative stuff anyway. I won't feel guilty if I've been away if I'm just basketball coach. I'm recommending you to be athletic director.'"

Judy went home and said to her husband, "Ken, I need to talk to you. Put that stuff down." He came over and sat down, and she told him of Jeff's news that she was to be offered the athletic director's job. He said, "That's great! You've been doing it anyway. And now you'll have the title and the money that goes with it." Judy says,

> I still don't believe I did this, but I said, 'I don't know if I want it.' He said, 'What do you mean you don't know if you want it? You have been doing it. Jeff has been coming to you asking to spend money because you control the budget. Why wouldn't you want it all?' I guess it was nerves. I always knew I could pass the buck and say, 'No, you can't do this. And Jeff has said you can't do this.' I always had someone I could push it to.
>
> I asked Jim Woodward, 'When you announce this and it is going to make a big splash that UNC Charlotte has named a woman, that's going to make news because it is not being done in the profession. Are you going to support me after that announcement? Are our philosophies in sync?' Jim was great. I couldn't have asked for a better boss or

someone with more progressive thinking. It did scare me. If it was just to make this splash, I'd be in the news one day and probably be out in less than a year for not being able to be successful on the job.

Rose saw a large challenge in the changing profession of directing an athletic program. "Years ago it didn't have the fundraising element it does today or quite as much business element. It was funded through the university and you were not responsible for raising scholarships. When I came on board, the university's philosophy changed a little bit. The fundraising became imperative because of the needs of the program and state funding. . . . I'd never done this before. Woodward's expectation for community involvement of senior level administrators increased tenfold, twentyfold . . . he expected deans, department heads, and the athletic director to be very visible, active, and involved in this community."

Judy Rose came through. Since her promotion, six UNC Charlotte teams have advanced to NCAA play, as well as individuals from the sports of women's cross-country, women's track and field, and men's golf. Thirteen conference championships were won. UNC Charlotte climbed from the Sun Belt Conference to the Metro Conference to its new home in Conference USA. Brand new facilities for athletics were added to the campus through wide local fundraising: the Halton Arena in the new Barnhardt Student Activity Center, the Irwin Belk Center for men's and women's soccer and track and field, and the Wachovia Fieldhouse with locker rooms and coaches' offices for baseball, softball, and soccer. Rose was instrumental in attracting two NCAA basketball "Final Four" tournaments to Charlotte, (one for men's teams, another for women's teams), both highly successful events, which increased Charlotte's image and visibility. Rose was instrumental in attracting the NCAA soccer tournament to Charlotte, as well as regional basketball and soccer tournaments, the German track team entry in the 1996 Olympics, and the National AAU's Junior Olympic Games, which brought more than 10,000 athletes and thousands of families and friends to Charlotte. She was the first woman to serve on the NCAA men's basketball tournament committee, planning three years of post-season tournaments. In 1997, she was awarded the Citizen of the Year Award in the university city area for her leadership in improving the region's public profile.

Rose is the first to acknowledge her fortunate timing. But it is clear that she had the key background, talent, energy, and readiness for opportunity when it arrived. How this young southern woman from a small town came by this is an intriguing story.

Judy Wilkins's mother died of colon cancer when Judy was 15. With five siblings, Judy feels that event "shaped who and what I am, and what I do." The three oldest were away at college, so the three youngest, who were in junior and senior high at home in Blacksburg, South Carolina, formed a team early on to cook breakfast and dinner, to grocery shop, to study, and play sports. "I was kind of forced into trying to balance all of that," she recalls. As their mother had done, they cooked southern-style meals for their dad's business guests from his company's head office in Chicago. With Judy's sisters, "if you had something important to do, I would do your part, and if I had something important to do, you'd do mine. We did not have telephones in our rooms. We had one television we shared in the den. One stereo. Dad said, 'Y'all are gonna have to just work it out.' We were forced into that kind of teambuilding in the family."

Judy Wilkins played basketball from grade seven up and in college at Winthrop where she got her B.S. in physical education. At the University of Tennessee she got a graduate assistantship coaching the women's basketball team under coach Pat Head. "Also, while I was there, Title IX really hit big time, so when it was time to graduate, all the girls in our class had all these opportunities, which had not been available before because all these schools had to create women's athletic programs. . . . Schools which received any federal funding for athletics or for academic programs had to comply. . . . I think that a lot of where I am and what I have been able to do is because of timing."

She came to UNC Charlotte in 1975, a very young university then. Her lifelong dream had been to coach basketball, not necessarily in college. She student-taught basketball at a junior high in Rock Hill when she got her teaching certificate. When she took the job at UNC Charlotte, teaching women's basketball and tennis at the college level, she thought she "had died and gone to heaven. The $8,000-a-year salary was not an issue because at that time, you could make it." In addition to this job, she taught a physical education class each semester, and worked in intramurals. Judy became coordinator of women's athletics, women's basketball coach, and taught. The teaching fell away when she later became assistant athletic director and women's basketball coach. Her duties were over both programs, men's and women's.

As the university grew in enrollment and jobs expanded, she was given the choice of full-time women's basketball coach or women's athletic director. Her team had a very successful women's basketball season, but she chose the job as women's athletic director. This put her in an experienced position when the unexpected division of duties was made in Jeff Mullins's job as athletic director and men's basketball coach. Rose says,

> I admit I have used some of the southern stuff. At a meeting I could tell this man was turned off because I was a woman. I realized his daughter was at Winthrop, a good field hockey player. I said, 'I know your daughter Susie at Winthrop. Tell me what's she doing.' And he pulled out the stops after that. He took a personal interest in me from then on. It is a matter of personal style and relationship. A woman in this business can't come on as threatening. But now this has softened. They have more respect because women have proved they can do the job.
>
> I studiously dress very feminine. Long hair. My sister said to me when I went up to Winthrop to major in physical education, 'Don't you come back here walking like a man.' I had long hair all through college. I always try to have curl. Even buying suits, a skirt and jacket, I am very conscious of wanting to look feminine. I like being a woman.
>
> At the first conference I went on, it was an away trip. They hesitated to tell me about it. 'We meet at Amelia Island,' they said. 'What's the problem?' I asked. They said, 'We share condominiums. Three-bedroom condos.' I asked, 'Do the bedrooms have private baths?' 'Yes,' he said. Well, I have no problem with that. But when I got there, I had my own three-bedroom condo.
>
> Then when we went out to dinner, they drove back to park at their condo and didn't offer to take me to mine, which was a good way through the woods at night. Not to drive me there, or to walk with me, so I was mad, but I got out my key and literally ran through the woods. I called my husband on the phone and told him how mad I was. He said, 'Listen. We don't know what to do with y'all! If somebody had offered to walk with you, you would have been like

"Oh. Uh-oh!" So,' he said, 'you have to educate us. Tell us what you want.' That taught me a lot.

Whenever Rose gives talks out in the community in Charlotte or surrounding towns to groups of supporters or civic groups, she gets questions about the problems she meets as a woman high up in the athletic education echelon. She says that there have been very few difficult moments, not more than a handful during her tenure at UNC Charlotte.

Difficult moments should be rare to a woman who can muster the support of Charlotte's movers and shakers as she did, persuading the powers that be to honor Charlotte's bid to join Conference USA. She enlisted CEOs Hugh McColl, Bill Lee, Ed Crutchfield, Jr., and real-estate entrepreneur Johnny Harris. McColl said, "I just did whatever Judy asked me to do. I made a few phone calls to some of the schools in the conference. I was glad to do whatever I could, because Judy has been tremendous for UNC Charlotte athletics."

The chairmanship of the Charlotte Chamber of Commerce has been a star-quality recognition of influence and achievement throughout the twentieth century. The forerunner of the chamber was the Greater Charlotte Club, founded in 1905, which enlarged into the Charlotte Chamber of Commerce in 1915, both created to arouse civic pride, provide leadership and information, and to promote improvements, all the time rousing the citizens and others to "Watch Charlotte Grow." With former chairmen selecting the new chair, it was for almost a century Charlotte's pre-eminent civic men's club. An editorial in the *Observer* in 1960 viewed the chamber as a major asset, saying, "Charlotte is run, primarily and well, by its chamber of commerce. The fact is not wholly applauded."

Nowhere had Charlotte's growth been more evident than in the 1990s, when the chamber included many female businesswomen as members and committee volunteers, but it had long been speculated whether or when the chamber would finally elect a female chair of its board of directors.

Carroll Gray, chamber president, and Nelson Schwab, the 1994 chair, said a female chair was possible in the near future. Schwab said, "We have a lot of women members . . . a lot of minority members, large companies and small companies. We are just trying to be responsive." Gray noted that a fourth of the businesses joining the chamber were owned or represented by women and that more women were involved and active in programs. "Absolutely, a woman could make chair." High profile contenders with substantial chamber involvement were described in *The Charlotte Observer*: Joan Zimmerman, Dee Ray, Karen Smoots, Elaine Lyerly, Muriel Helms, and Paula Newsome. County commissioner and library board chair Patsy Kinsey and others such as real estate-firm owners Bonnie Widenhouse and Sandra Townsend had served on committees or the chamber board over the years. Reports were that the chamber, like the city's business community, had realized in the 1990s that the old order of all-white-male leadership could not continue, and that there were women well qualified to lead.

Historian Dan Morrill cites this sort of awareness and change as a major theme in the last half of the century. It is a radical departure: "the demise and erosion of the old white male elite's total domination of Charlotte-Mecklenburg. Even more dramatic is the emergence of African-Americans for which school integration is the key." African-Americans began to rise in corporations and in membership in formerly all-white bastions. Women, that other minority— both white and black women—were on the rise as well. .

In 1993, Muriel Helms became a member of the chamber's nine-member executive committee and chaired the group's key public affairs division. In 1995, Helms was the first female chair ever chosen for the chamber's prestigious board of directors. She was 51, president and co-owner of Prudential Carolinas Realty, a 35-branch full-service real-estate firm with 950 sales associates in the Carolinas. A chamber volunteer since 1978, she came up through the ranks, chaired several important chamber events and committees, and was serving on the executive committee. Helms said of her prospects, "I don't wave banners. I just take advantage of opportunities."

Close on the heels of Helms's election came the election of Sharon Decker to chamber chair in 1998. Decker, a native of Albemarle, had been a Charlotte area resident since 1985, and was first president of the Lynnwood Foundation. As such, she had been instrumental in the restoration of the Duke Mansion (White Oaks) and in developing the William States Lee Leadership Institute at that location. She had worked 17 years prior with Duke Power and was the youngest and first female vice-president in Duke history. While chamber chair, she focused on regionalism and building relationships with surrounding counties. Subsequently she accepted the presidency of the Doncaster Division of Tanner Companies in Rutherfordton, commuting from her home in Belmont.

As keynote speaker for WomanFest in 1998, Decker gave 400 women and girls some tips on how women can lead balanced lives. "Keep a gratitude journal and write down four things you are grateful for every day. Find a quiet space daily and take five minutes or more to be still. [She said when her children were small, she sat in her closet next to her shoes, to grab quiet time.] Believe in yourself: Whatever you are and whoever you are, you're great."

Sixteen-year-old Dorothy Cowser Yancy stepped off the Greyhound bus on West Trade Street in Charlotte in the fall of 1960. She had ridden all the way from her home in Alabama to join the freshman class at Johnson C. Smith University and would stay to earn her degree in history and social science. She little dreamed when she left to earn an M.A. in history at the University of Massachusetts at Amherst, then a Ph.D. at Atlanta University in political science, and taught at numerous colleges and as professor at Georgia Tech, that she would in the 1990s become the first woman president of her alma mater, Johnson C. Smith.

In 1994, university trustees elected her the 12th president of the university. It was time for a bold venture forward, and Yancy's choice certainly emphasized that vision. During her first five years as president, JCSU received unprecedented grants from many large foundations, including the Duke Endowment, the Andrew W. Mellon Foundation, UNCF/Lilly Endowment and the Kresge Foundation. She spearheaded the final phase of the Fifty Million Dollar Campaign, which was begun by Charlotte corporations and prominent community leaders, taking it to $56 million.

Under Yancy's leadership, JCSU was the first HBCU (Historically Black Colleges and Universities) to become an IBM ThinkPad University. Planning and implementing the technology to carry out this program was remarkable, a feat that put JCSU in the big league of progressive schools in the United States.

In the fall of 2000, it became one of only 400 schools in the nation that was fully computerized. During her tenure, historic Biddle Hall, which is on the National Register of Historic Places, is to be restored as well as the George and Marie G. Davis house, a historic faculty house across from the campus.

Yancy has taught classes in urban politics, African-American history, U.S. government, race relations, labor policy, unionism, and collective bargaining. She is certified in labor arbitration and mediation and serves on arbitration and mediation panels. She sees JCSU, founded by Presbyterians shortly after the close of the Civil War to train black teachers and preachers, entering the new century with its new $4.5 million technology center. She sees the university "at the forefront of training and teaching our students the skills necessary to use technology successfully in the marketplace. We have no choice. The issue at JCSU is to successfully prepare our students for change in the new century. We dare not fail. Our students cannot be victims of the digital divide, but must be prepared to ride the wave of technology to new levels of success."

Yancey joined a remarkable coterie of outstanding Charlotte leaders in the 1990s, leaders who head their prominent organizations, leaders who are also women.

Some of these outstanding newcomers to town forged important niches for themselves as soon as they arrived. Gloria Pace King took over in 1994 as president of the United Way of Central Carolinas, after being chosen over 175 other applicants. A registered nurse from Cleveland, she was the president and CEO of the Visiting Nurse Association of Cleveland, Ohio, from 1981 to 1988, and subsequently, senior vice-president of community investment and resource management for the United Way Services in that city. She met her challenge in Charlotte with 65 employees by creating an astounding 21% increase in 1997, and 10% more in 1998. Both increases were twice the national average. In 2001, the drive, representing 95 agencies, exceeded the $35 million goal by $1 million.

King feels that her career as a nurse prepared her. "It teaches you that the whole object of what you're doing every day is to improve the quality of life." King's father was a postal worker and her mother a day-work domestic. When her father bought a Tastee-Freez franchise, she began work at age 11, learning how to run the frozen-custard machines.

Leaders who are key female professionals in major arts endeavors are Harriett Sanford, hired in 2000 as president of the Arts and Science Council, and Judith Allen, president of the Blumenthal North Carolina Center for the Performing Arts. Sanford arrived from Atlanta, where for two decades she played a dramatic role in shaping the development of Atlanta's cultural programs and institutions. In 1991–2000, she directed the department of arts and culture for Fulton County and managed the largest publicly funded arts program in Georgia. Her challenge in Charlotte was to raise the ASC goal for 2001 of $10 million. She succeeded.

Judith Allen arrived in Charlotte during the summer of 1990 to oversee the construction and opening of the ambitious North Carolina Blumenthal Performing Arts Center. Her title was president of the center, which also took on management and programming for Spirit Square (an education center housing Performance Place theater in uptown's renovated First Baptist Church).

Allen's route to Charlotte and to arts administration was a circuitous one. Prior to 1990, she was managing director of the Bushnell Performing Arts Center in Hartford, Connecticut, and served as director of the Fine Arts Center of the University of Rhode Island. At one point, she worked as a secretary. As a single mother with two children, she worked in the personnel (human resources) department of a hospital. The Rhode Island native has a bachelor's degree in psychology from the University of Rhode Island.

Beginning in 1996, for the first time Charlotte's city manager was a woman. Pam Syfert had worked six years as deputy city manager under city manager Wendell White, and before that as assistant city manager, budget director, evaluation supervisor, and program analyst/research assistant. She had also taught part-time at Michigan State University and at UNC Charlotte. She earned her M.A. in political science, state, and local government from Michigan State, and graduated from the Program for Senior Executives in State and Local Government at Harvard University in 1990.

Raised outside of Omaha, Nebraska, she moved to Charlotte in 1968 when her husband took a teaching job at Queens College. For her, the "first woman" thing is no big deal. She said in 1996, "Charlotte is a city full of women in important jobs." At a panel on women and leadership held at the Museum of the New South, Syfert passed along her dad's best, plain-spoken advice, "Don't let the bastards get you down." In one of her jobs for city government, she was largely responsible for developing the plan that cut the city's multi-layered government structure from 26 to 13 departments. "Rightsizing" she calls it. And she is credited with developing a customer-service center where citizens can get prompt answers to municipal questions.

White, her former boss, called her "a very strong manager." One city councilman testifies, "She can't be rattled." Colleagues consistently praise her fairness and ability to delegate. One neighbor says Syfert's yard often wins Yard of the Month in their Dilworth neighborhood, but that Syfert's husband does it all. "She's a good delegator. She runs her home just like she runs the city. The trains run on time on Myrtle Avenue."

⚜

Crandall Bowles at the turn of the twentieth century steers the largest ship propelled by a woman in the area. Crandall Close Bowles's family company, the southern textile giant which began in 1887 with a single cotton mill, underwent major changes to meet its second century as Springs Industries, Inc. Bowles became chairman of Springs's board of directors and chief executive officer in 1998, and since then, has built a team about which onlookers say, "Springs has found its soul." Bowles is the fifth generation of the Springs family to lead the company.

Springs has manufacturing facilities in 13 states and marketing and distribution subsidiaries in Canada and Mexico with annual sales of $2.2 billion. They are a leading manufacturer and marketer of home furnishings including bed, bath, and window fashions marketed under the names of Wamsutta, Springmaid, Dundee, Bali, and Graber and licensed textiles depicting Harry Potter.

Stock analysts in the 1990s described Bowles's effort to "kick Springs into high gear. . . . What has changed is the corporate attitude, the way Springs sees the world—and the speed with which it acts." *The Charlotte Observer* reported in late 1999 that "Bowles preserved the heritage of a company that helped make Carolinas history while imbuing it with the focus, talent and vigor to compete in a fast-moving, unforgiving marketplace." Bowles is credited with "bringing a different style of leadership, a willingness to communicate with anybody in the

After working as financial analyst with the Springs Company in 1973 and serving as its president until 1992, Crandall Close Bowles became president and CEO of the southern textile giant, Springs Industries, Inc. in 1997. The South Carolina company, which was founded in 1887, has manufacturing facilities in 13 states and is a leading manufacturer and marketer of home furnishings including bed, bath, and window fashions marketed under the names of Wamsutta, Springmaid, Bali, and Graber.
COURTESY OF SPRINGS INDUSTRIES, INC.

company. People in the plants see it too." But the changes cut deep, slicing the overall work force, largely from divisions which the company closed or sold. The company also modernized and made operational changes. The new executive leadership encouraged new ideas and cost-cutting competitiveness while striving to keep quality products and to retain respect for the Springs heritage.

Bowles is the great-granddaughter of founder Leroy Springs and great-great granddaughter of co-founder Samuel Elliott White, who together began the nineteenth-century Fort Mill Manufacturing Company. Bowles earned a bachelor's degree from Wellesley College and an MBA from Columbia University, working her second year at the UNC Chapel Hill Kenan-Flagler Business School. She also worked two years as a statistician at Morgan Stanley & Co. in New York.

Bowles began in 1973 as financial analyst with The Springs Company, and was president of the privately held management company until 1992. She rejoined Springs Industries, Inc., in 1992 as executive vice president-growth and development, became president and chief operating officer in 1997, and chairman and chief executive in 1998. She is the daughter of Anne Springs Close, who founded the Palmetto Conservancy Fund and worked to create the Palmetto Trail, a mountains-to-sea hiking trail in South Carolina. Bowles and seven siblings founded the Anne Springs Close Greenway in honor of their mother. The Greenway's 2,300 acres act as a natural woods and farmland buffer in the Catawba River and Nations Ford area between Fort Mill and Charlotte.

Leslie Winner grew up in Asheville, earned her law degree at Northwestern University School of Law, then clerked one year for U.S. District Judge James McMillan. After representing low-income clients with Legal Services of the Southern Piedmont, she joined the Charlotte law firm of Ferguson, Stein, Watt, Wallas, Adkins & Gresham.

By 1997 Winner was 47, living in Charlotte with a husband, an eight-year-old daughter, and an outstanding record of having served three terms in the North Carolina State Senate, representing Charlotte. Although passionately committed to the issues of public education, civil rights, and women's issues, she resigned her seat in order to eliminate the arduous, constant commute to

Raleigh, which kept her from sharing more actively in the early years of her daughter Lily.

The decision led to her next job offer in 1998, an appointment as top attorney for Charlotte-Mecklenburg Schools. Two years later, the president of the North Carolina University system, Molly Broad, made a surprising announcement in Chapel Hill. Leslie Winner was appointed vice president and general counsel of the 16-campus University of North Carolina system. As the university system's senior legal officer, she would counsel the system's president, board of governors, and senior university staff. Broad said, "Leslie Winner brings to the University of North Carolina a rare combination of legal expertise, experience in the halls of state legislature and deep knowledge of the complex policy issues now facing all of higher education."

Winner said, in her usual unassuming, plain-style response to interviewers, "I think I was chosen because I was the only one with an empty plate and probably because I knew something about the legislature." Part of Winner's background is an egalitarian view going back to growing up Jewish in Asheville, where her friends' families were members at one of Asheville's two country clubs, which did not welcome Jewish members. The experience of exclusion has had a lifelong impact, and gave her, as she says, "a taste of what it felt like to be an outsider." Winner took to the senate floor on Rosh Hashanah (the Jewish New Year) and Yom Hashoah (the day to remember those who died in the Holocaust) to deliver short speeches about the importance and meaning of these holidays. She says, "Those were probably the most listened-to, well-received speeches I ever made."

Winner credits others who gave her confidence, "I owe a lot to people who have supervised me and have put me in situations I wasn't ready to handle."

Emily Zimmern developed leadership skills as she managed and led many groups of men and women from across the United States for the United Jewish Appeal conferences, fund campaigns, and international relations efforts with Israel and Eastern European countries. When the job came open in 1995 for a director of Charlotte's new Museum of the New South, founded in 1991, she applied. She after all had a B.A. cum laude in history from Vanderbilt University, an MBA from Queens College, and an M.A. in American diplomatic history and East Asian studies from Vanderbilt. She taught junior high school history, was an executive with *The Birmingham News*, and raised funds for the Charlotte Jewish Federation, Planned Parenthood of Greater Charlotte, and the Mecklenburg Medical Auxiliary Endowment.

She got the job. As executive director of the Museum of the New South, she directs operations of a museum dedicated to interpreting the diverse history of the South since the Civil War, with a focus on Charlotte and the surrounding Carolina Piedmont. Under her leadership, an array of outstanding programs and grant-supported projects has infused the community, and expansion funds and plans have created the renovation and addition to the existing uptown museum, which reopened in October 2001.

When Jennie Buckner visited Charlotte as vice president of news for Knight-Ridder (parent company of *The Charlotte Observer*), she had her small daughter Katie and her nanny in tow. Part of Buckner's demanding job was to travel around to various Knight-Ridder newspaper cities and oversee news and editorial operations of the company's 10 largest newspapers and its Washington bureau. Buckner recalled speaking with Rich Oppel (*Observer* editor at the time), who was to pick her up at the airport, and asking if he would stop on the way and buy some Pampers. "That's different," he remarked.

When Oppel moved from Charlotte in 1993, Buckner was promoted to Oppel's job as *Observer* editor-in-chief, the first woman to hold that position. The *Observer* is the Carolinas' largest newspaper. The *Observer* is also where Buckner began her newspaper career as a summer intern in 1968. The Kentucky native graduated with honors from the Ohio State University School of Journalism.

One other woman held a top job at the *Observer*, but came to the position of publisher by a very different route. That is a story Mrs. Curtis B. Johnson (Irving Harding McGheachy Johnson) often told on herself. She was on an airplane from Charlotte to New York, when she got into conversation with the man sitting next to her. After he learned that she was from Charlotte, he said, "I knew two brilliant men from Charlotte. One was a Presbyterian preacher and the other a newspaper publisher." Mrs. Johnson replied, "Yes, and I married both of them."

Observer historian Jack Claiborne writes that in the years after her husband's death, Irving Johnson gained control of the *Observer* just before her 65th birthday. She had a visionary conscience, and Claiborne credits her with giving the *Observer* in the 1950s, "the courage to welcome the racial revolution." Johnson was the daughter of a Davidson College professor and had been the tour guide for James B. Duke in the 1920s when he visited Davidson College and decided to include Davidson in the Duke Endowment.

This chronicle is only a beginning. The few women described here are representative of an American rise of woman-power in many fields, but most have yet to command in more than token terms the leadership of large national organizations or companies. At the year 2001, an astounding number of women in the Charlotte area own their own businesses and run them successfully.

A tide of young artistic talent is also visible. The city teems with women for whom creative service to mankind is their daily bread. As shown in the preceding pages, for every woman who received Charlotte's Woman of the Year award, there are many more who qualify. For every woman and organization mentioned, there are a hundred more who are equally worthy.

Improving on the wave of women's accomplishments moving into the twenty-first century, optimally these women leaders will mentor other younger women who come behind or beside them. The 2000 census shows Charlotte as the second fastest-growing city of its size in the nation, advancing approximately 29% in growth during the decade since 1990. Hopefully, the women who have lived here many years will continue to reach out to newcomers of different racial, class, and ethnic backgrounds. Since its earliest days in the 1700s, Charlotte has assimilated newcomers well and benefitted greatly from them. The new challenge is one of vast and exciting proportions.

In the twenty-first century, the selected stories of the few "pioneers" in this century-long chronicle may provide inspiration and celebration. In this brief history, the dominant theme has been women helping and mentoring others. "Lifting as we rise," will certainly be the continuing test of women's character and of Charlotte's future.

SELECTED RESOURCES

Archives

North Carolina Collection, University of North Carolina at Chapel Hill, Clipping File.

Southern Historical Collection, Wilson Library, University of North Carolina at Chapel Hill: Interview transcripts in the Southern Oral History Program Collection (#4007) by James LeLoudis and Alice Evitt, Charlotte, 1979, H-162, and Edna Hargett, Charlotte, 1979, H-163; by Allen Tullos with Willie Mae Honnecutt, Charlotte, 1980, H-166.

University of North Carolina at Charlotte, Library Manuscript Collection: Papers of Annie L. Alexander, Wilkes Family, Bonnie Ethel Cone, and Louise Brennan.

Books:

Banner, Lois. *Women in Modern America: A Brief History*. Fort Worth: Harcourt Brace, 1995.

Blythe, LeGette and Charles Brockman. *Hornets' Nest: The Story of Charlotte and Mecklenburg County*. Charlotte: Public Library of Charlotte and Mecklenburg County, 1961.

Cranford Profiles: The First Hundred Years of a Charlotte Book Club. Charlotte: Public Library of Charlotte and Mecklenburg County, 1992.

Gaillard, Frye. *A Dream Long Deferred*. Chapel Hill: UNC Press, 1988.

Hall, Jacquelyn Dowd, ed. *Like a Family: The Making of a Southern Cotton Mill World*. Chapel Hill: UNC Press, 1987.

Kratt, Mary ed. *The Imaginative Spirit: Literary Heritage of Charlotte and Mecklenburg County*. Charlotte: Public Library of Charlotte and Mecklenburg County, 1988.

Kratt, Mary and Thomas W. Hanchett. *Legacy: The Myers Park Story*. Charlotte:
Myers Park Foundation. 1986.

Lawrence, Elizabeth. *Gardening for Love: The Market Bulletins*. ed. Allen Lacy.
Durham: Duke University Press, 1987.

Love, Rose Leary. *Plum Thickets and Field Daisies*. Charlotte: Public Library of
Charlotte and Mecklenburg County, 1996.

Making A Difference: Women of Mecklenburg. Charlotte: Charlotte Branch, American
Association of University Women, 1980.

Powell, William S. *Dictionary of North Carolina Biography*. Chapel Hill: UNC Press,
1979-96.

Randolph, Elizabeth S. and Patricia Ryckman. *An African American Album: The Black
Experience in Charlotte and Mecklenburg County*. Charlotte: Public Library of
Charlotte and Mecklenburg County, 1992.

Rosen, Ruth. *The World Split Open: How the Modern Women's Movement Changed
America*. New York: Viking, 2000.

Sloop, Mary T. Martin with Legette Blythe. *Miracle in the Hills*. New York:
McGraw Hill, 1953.

Smith, Margaret Supplee and Emily Herring Wilson. *North Carolina Women Making
History*. Chapel Hill: UNC Press, 1999.

Watkins, Charlotte. *Women of the Years, 1955-96*. Charlotte, N.C., 1996.

Wilson, Emily Herring. *Hope and Dignity: Older Black Women of the South*. Temple
University Press, 1983.

Interviews

By Mary Kratt in 2000 and 2001 unless otherwise indicated. With Martha Alex-
ander, Mary Lou Babb, Mary Thomas Burke, Lucy Bush (telephone), Sarah
Bryant, Elizabeth Clarkson (1978), Kathleen Crosby, Peggy Culbertson, Shirley
Fulton, Susan Green, Hilda Gurdian, Elisabeth Hair, Ann Hammond, Sis
Kaplan, Aurelia Liston Law, Ruth Ava Lyons (telephone), Jonnie McLeod,
Caroline Myers, Freda Nicholson, Betty Chafin Rash, Maggie Ray, Judy Rose,
Ella Scarborough, Betty Seizenger (telephone), Marcia Simon, Sarah Stevenson,
Charlene Swansea (telephone, 1987), Ann Thomas, Minette Trosch, Bea
Wallas, Charlotte Watkins, Carrie Winter, and joint interview with
policewomen Mickey Casey, Cheryl Williams Horner, and Gail Sloan.

Oral histories with professional women of Charlotte and Mecklenburg County,
conducted by Jennifer Greeson for Museum of New South, Charlotte, North

Carolina, in 1993. These interviews included Theresea Elder, Eudora Garrison, Liz Hair, and Elizabeth Randolph.

Vertical Files

Robinson-Spangler Carolina Room

Other sources

Author's files.

League of Women Voters Commemorative Program Journal, 1995 and 2000.

Replies to questionnaires sent in 2000 to Women of the Year Award winners and vitae supplied by subjects.

The Charlotte News, The Charlotte Observer, Today's Charlotte Woman, Charlotte Magazine, North Carolina State Bar Quarterly, Southern Textile Bulletin.

WOMEN OF THE YEAR

Beginning in 1955, WBT Radio of Charlotte honored an outstanding woman in Charlotte-Mecklenburg with the Woman of the Year Award. When WBT ended its sponsorship in 1991, the former honorees chose to continue the tradition of annual selection. Since 1999, Bank of America, Duke Energy, Springs Industries, Museum of the New South, and WFAE Radio have co-sponsored this annual award.

The data that follows is selective and by no means includes all community service and awards.

Martha Bedell Alexander (Mrs. James Frosst) b. 1939 in Jacksonville, FL. B.S., Florida State Univ.; M.A., UNC Charlotte. Char. resident since 1970. Four children. Elected to the N.C. House of Representatives for four terms (1992–2000), focusing on health-care delivery, education, campaign finance reform, and health and human services. Served as executive director of the Charlotte Council on Alcoholism and Chemical Dependency (1981–93). Was chaplain's assistant at Presbyterian Hospital (1977–81), after retiring as an assistant librarian and elementary school teacher. Involved in various civic, community, and church activities on a local, state, and national level. Served as chair of the Companion Diocese for the Episcopal Diocese of N.C. and as a member of the Global Mission Commission for the Diocese. Received numerous awards for advocacy in political reform and social services, including the 1994 Legislator of the Year award from the Alliance for the Mentally Ill, the 1996 Woman of Courage Award from the N.C. Chapter of NOW, the C. Odell Tyndall Award from the N.C. Rehabilitation Association and the 1999 Advocate of the Year award from the National Association of Social Workers. Woman of the Year 1993.

Mary Lou Davis Babb (Mrs. James G.) b. 1935 in Pinehurst, NC. Attended UNC Greensboro. Char. resident since 1948. Five children. Served on the National Conference of Christians and Jews. Served on the Housing Authority Scholarship Committee and as a member of the board of the Crisis Assistance Ministries. Was instrumental in the organization of the Women in Transition Program, providing housing and education to women in need in the community. Served on the board of the YWCA for six years and was board president for two. Led one of the most successful financial campaigns for the Mint Museum Auxiliary; elected Mint Museum board chair in 2000. Continues to be an influential advocate and fundraiser for the arts and education as member of Center Stars of the Performing Arts Center, Good Friends, and Johnson C. Smith Committee of 100 Women. Woman of the Year 1995.

Lurlene Barnhardt (Mrs. L.E.) b.1912 in Mt. Gilead, NC. Attended UNC Greensboro. Char. resident from 1930 until 1997. Served as member of the Mayor's Community Relations Committee. Chosen in 1960 as Churchwoman of the Year by the Methodist Church and served as president of the Western N.C. Conference Women's Society of the Methodist Church in 1966. Served as fourth president of the Charlotte Pharmaceutical Auxiliary in 1941 and president of the Charlotte Women's Club in 1947. Served on the board of the YWCA and was a member of the Charlotte Chapter of the National Conference of Christians and Jews. Served as a member of the Commission on Ecumenical Affairs and in 1977 as a delegate to the White House Conference on Aging. Woman of the Year 1963.

Louise Smith Brennan (Mrs. Stanley L.) b.1922 in Chester, SC. B.A., UNC Charlotte; M.A, UNC Chapel Hill. Char. resident since 1946. Three children. Elected member of the N.C. House of Representatives, achieving passage of bills that improved the quality of life for mentally retarded children, troubled youth, women, and the elderly. Served as past president of the Mecklenburg County Democratic Party, was a founder of the Charlotte Women's Political Caucus, and leader of the Mecklenburg County Democratic Women's Club. Honors include Distinguished Rotarian in 1998, 1991 UNC Charlotte Hall of Fame, Charlotte Alumni Association Distinguished Service Award 1989–1990, and Outstanding Legislator of N.C. in 1981–82. Served on numerous community boards and was a leader in many political organizations that addressed needs of children and women. Was member and elder of Caldwell Memorial Presbyterian Church, adjunct professor of Political Science at UNC Charlotte, and businesswoman. Woman of the Year 1982.

Mary Thomas Burke b. 1930 in Westport, County Mayo, Ireland. B.A., Belmont Abbey College; M.A., Georgetown Univ.; Ph.D, UNC Chapel Hill, Nat'l Board certified therapist, N.C. licensed professional counselor. Char. resident since 1949. A Roman Catholic nun and educator. Recognized for the compassionate and humanitarian spirit that distinguishes her activities as a teacher, lecturer, counselor, writer, and friend. As professor and coordinator of counselor education at UNC Charlotte for the past 20 years, provided invaluable leadership to the development of their M.A. in Counseling Department. Sister Mary Thomas's involvement in the National Summit of Spirituality in Counseling helped to develop the standards to have this aspect of life integrated into university programs on a national level. As a community leader, consultant, and mentor, helped to develop 15 or more human services agencies and programs. Received many awards including the B'nai B'rith Anti-Defamation Human Relations Award in 1978, the 1995 Humanitarian Award from the National Conference of Christians and Jews, and the Counselor of the Year Award in 1998 from the American Counseling Association. Woman of the Year 1979.

Sarah Brownlee Bryant (Mrs. James Robert, Jr.) b. 1922 in Charlotte, NC. Attended UNC Greensboro, Queens College, Ellis Business School, CPCC. Lifetime Char. resident. Two children. Founded in 1972 and was twice elected president of Planned Parenthood of Charlotte, an organization focused on building responsible parenthood. Responsible for directing the organization's growth, raising funds, and traveling extensively to build support. Served on national board of Planned Parenthood, the local and national boards of Florence Crittenton Homes, the Children's Theatre, the YWCA, and others focusing on the needs of young children and the arts. Received community awards for her service in these areas. Woman of the Year 1972.

Bonnie Ethel Cone b.1907 in Lodge, SC. B.S., Coker College 1928; M.A., Duke Univ. Char. resident since 1943. Taught math at Central High School in 1946, when Charlotte established its first state school offering college-level courses to veterans returning from World War II. Worked as a part-time teacher and became the center's director the next year. Served as the center's president when it became Charlotte College and was a skilled advocate in its rise to become a major university. Assumed the position of acting chancellor until 1966, when she became vice chancellor for student affairs and community relations until her retirement at age 66. Known as a tireless advocate and the mother of UNC Charlotte, serving long after her retirement as professor emeritus. Served as a member of the Governor's Commission on the Status of Women and on the Carlyle Commission in 1960 to study education beyond high school. Received numerous local, state, and national honors and awards, including the 1965 Liberty Bell Award, the prestigious University Medal from the board of governors of UNC, and honorary degrees from Coker, Wake Forest, Duke,

Mt. Holyoke, Queens College, Davidson College, and Belmont Abbey. Woman of the Year 1956.

Elizabeth Moon Conard Corkey, M.D. (Mrs. Harold) 1903–1995, b. in Philadelphia, PA. A.B., Grinnell College, Phi Beta Kappa; M.D., University of Michigan; M.P.H., UNC Chapel Hill. Char. resident from 1955–95. Two children. Taught at Shanghai Medical School in China under the auspices of the American Friends Committee until her marriage in 1935 to the Reverend Harold Corkey, a Presbyterian minister. Continued her missionary work in China before WWII as a physician delivering and taking care of babies. Following Pearl Harbor she and her family were held by the Japanese at Weishein Internment from 1942 to 1945, where she cared for over 1,700 prisoners. Upon her return to Charlotte, served as assistant medical director of the Charlotte-Mecklenburg Health Department (1960–68) and as medical director of the Community Health Association from 1968 until her retirement. Was an early advocate for birth control and well-baby clinics. Was a founding member of the Charlotte Friends Committee and president of the Business and Professional Women. Served as a member of the Charlotte-Mecklenburg Community Relations Commission and the Downtown Charlotte Association. Was a leading advocate for the mental retardation community, serving on the advisory board for the Mecklenburg Mental Health Authority and as president of the Nevins Vocational Training Center. Was president of the YWCA. Woman of the Year 1960.

Kathleen Ross Crosby (Mrs. Joseph C., Sr.) b.1925 in Winnsboro, SC. B.S., Johnson C. Smith Univ.; B.M., Bank Street College of Educ., NYC. Char. resident since 1946. Two children. Had a long career in advocacy and education as an area superintendent with the Charlotte-Mecklenburg Schools until her retirement in 1986. From 1957–67, taught at Lincoln Heights Elementary, while serving as a systemwide educational television teacher. Appointed as the institutional director of Headstart training, District 6, N.C., and then the in-service specialist for early childhood education, CMS, before becoming principal of Billingsville Elementary. Received the B'Nai B'Rith Human Relations Award in 1974. Inducted into the NCAAP Hall of Fame for outstanding community service. Member of board of governors for UNC system. Appointed honorary lifetime trustee for UNC. Awarded honorary Doctorate in Humane Letters at Johnson C. Smith and Queens College. Woman of the Year 1976.

Harriet Hampton Cuthbertson (Mrs. Rennie) 1933–1995, Charlotte, NC. B.A., Agnes Scott College. Lifetime Char. resident. Four children. Served as first female president of the Arts and Science Council. Her tireless efforts secured funding from the National Endowment of the Arts for the Arts and Science Council, making Spirit Square, NCNB Performance Place, the cultural arts programs, and Discovery Place a reality. Woman of the Year 1980.

Sharon Allred Decker (Mrs. Robert L., Jr.) b. 1957 in Albemarle, NC. B.S., UNC Greensboro. Char. area resident 1985-99. Four children. Served as the first female chair of the Charlotte Chamber of Commerce, while working as the first president of Lynnwood Foundation. Was instrumental in overseeing the 1999 restoration of White Oaks, the Duke Mansion, and developing the William States Lee Leadership Institute there. Worked for 17 years prior to the Duke Mansion in the public utility industry with Duke Power Company and became the youngest and first female vice president in Duke Power's history. Joined Tanner Companies as president of the Doncaster division in 1999. Chaired and served on many community boards in Mecklenburg and Gaston Counties. Spoke frequently in public and on television as a regular host on WTVI's "Carolina Business Review" about leadership skills, values, and personal balance. Woman of the Year 1998.

Carla Eloff DuPuy (Mrs. S. Stuart) b.1947 in Bellefountaine, OH. B.A., Univ. of FL, attended Queens College. Char. resident since 1972. Two children. Served as chair of the Mecklenburg County Board of Commissioners for three terms (1984–90). Led a series of successful bond campaigns, where voters approved the largest packages ever passed in Mecklenburg County. Was co-founder of the Carolina Counties Coalition and appointed by the governor to chair N.C. Development Council. Served on N.C. Environmental Management Council, two terms on State Board of County Commissioners, and was also on National Association of County Commissioners' community and economic development committee. Employed as director of environmental affairs for Crescent Resources, Inc., a business group of Duke Energy Corporation. Worked previously as director of public affairs at Carolinas Healthcare System, and later, as director of development for Sprint. Remains involved in community boards, volunteer organizations, and civic and professional groups, having served as chair of Children's Theatre, Charlotte Chamber of Commerce environmental concerns committee, and Public Library Board of Trustees. Woman of the Year 1989.

Ruth Moss Easterling, b. 1910 in Gaffney, SC. B.A., Limestone College. Char. resident since 1947. Completed her 12th term in 2000 at age 89 as Mecklenburg's representative in the N.C. General Assembly (1977–00), where she worked to improve the quality of care for children and the elderly, introduced bills to reform divorce, alimony, and equitable distribution laws, as well as the bill that established

Smart Start under Governor Hunt's Child Enhancement Program, and sponsored bills to collect child support, improve the environment, fund the arts, and strengthen consumer-protection laws. Worked as executive assistant to the president, Radiator Specialty Co. 1947–78. Appointed to the Governor's Commission on the Status of Women by Governor Sanford in 1964 and received the Order of the Long Leaf Pine that year for her leadership. Appointed in March 1972 to the Charlotte City Council until the end of the term. Since 1964 has received numerous awards for her advocacy for women and children. Served as president of the National Federation of Business and Professional Women. Described in the *Raleigh News and Observer*: "Her religious faith, her life and her politics are completely enmeshed." Woman of the Year 1964.

Thereasea Clark Elder (Mrs. Willie) b.1927 in Charlotte, NC. RN, Lincoln Hospital School of Nursing, Durham; and Public Health Cert., UNC Chapel Hill; Urban Studies Cert., Johnson C. Smith Univ.; Gerontology Cert., Livingstone College. Lifetime Char. resident. Two children. Since her retirement from the Mecklenburg Health Department in 1989 has arranged sickle-cell testing and worked with breast-cancer patients. Educates the African-American community about HIV/AIDS, providing information and recruiting volunteers to help those who are ill. Founder of Greenville Community African American Historical Society. Received many awards, including the 1987 Sojourner Truth Award, the Martin Luther King, Jr. 1992 Humanitarian Award, and the James G. Curran Award from the Mecklenburg Medical Society in 1995. Continues passionate service on community boards and committees dealing with public health, African-American history, and race relations. Woman of the Year 1995.

Dianne Ward English (Mrs. Roger) b. 1944 in Easton, MD. A.B., UNC Chapel Hill; graduate work at Univ. of GA. Char. resident since 1973. Three children. Serves as executive director of Community Building Initiative, an organization that focuses community leaders on issues of race, ethnicity, equity, and inclusion. Established Bridge Builders, as former executive director of Mecklenburg Ministries (1991–97), another organization that built lines of communication between congregations of different races and faiths. Developed Youth Breaking Barriers, a summer program for children of different socioeconomic and ethnic backgrounds. Helped to organize Emergency Winter Shelter. Was a founding member of the board of the Center for Urban Ministry, an organization that provides care for the homeless. Serves on the board of Florence Crittenton and the Bethlehem Center. Woman of the Year 1999.

Martha W. Evans (Mrs. Charles) 1910–1979, b. in Philadelphia, PA. B.A., Boston University. Char. resident from 1946–79. Was the first woman elected to the Charlotte City Council (1955–59), blazing the trail for women to be elected to higher office. Ran two unsuccessful but strong races for Charlotte mayor and later became the first woman to serve in both houses of N.C. legislature. Focused on kindergarten education and childcare as well as higher education, helping to make UNC Charlotte the fourth campus of the consolidated UNC system. Helped create legislation concerning auto inspections, parental control, responsibility for air rifles, and mental health, basically revamping the N.C. mental health laws. Was by profession a physical therapist with postgraduate work at Columbia, Johns Hopkins, Lafayette, Duke, and St. Louis Universities. Was first winner of Woman of the Year award in 1955.

Jill Stewart Flynn (Mrs. Fletcher Smith) b. 1945 in Brooklyn, NY. B.A., Salem College; M.A., Univ. of Alabama. Two children. Char. resident 1945–68 and since 1977. Organized the first Habitat for Humanity house constructed entirely by women. Founded Good Friends, an annual holiday event that raises money for needy families and individuals. Established Seigle Avenue Partners, a ministry of Seigle Avenue Presbyterian Church that focuses on education and leadership for families in the economically challenged Piedmont Courts/Belmont neighborhood. As member of Women Executives for Community Service, helped to establish WINGS (Women Initiating and Nurturing Growth Through Scholarships). Served on the board of trustees of Central Piedmont Community College, Salem College, Foundation for the Carolinas, and Charlotte-Mecklenburg Education Foundation. Retired senior vice president of organization effectiveness at First Union. Woman of the Year 2000.

Tempie Franklin (Mrs. Ernest Washington Jr.) 1906–1975. b. in Louisburg, NC. B.A., UNC Greensboro. Char. resident from 1934 until her death. Two children. Served as president of the Mint Museum board of trustees (1964–65), when she single-handedly was responsible for raising $250,000 to secure the M. Mellanay Delhom Collection of Ceramic Art for the Mint Museum and the city of Charlotte. Was honorary chairman of the 1975 Seminar on Historical Pottery and Porcelain. Died days before this event. Served on the Charlotte Memorial Hospital Auxiliary, Charlotte Garden Club, YWCA Board, Charlotte Nature Museum, Children's Theater, and was chair of Camp Latta for Girls during WWII. Woman of the Year 1967.

Shirley Louise Fulton (Mrs. Leon Orr, Jr.), b. 1952 in Kingstree, SC. B.S., NC A&T Univ.; J.D., Duke Univ.; M.B.A., Queens College. Char. resident since 1982. One child. As assistant district attorney and most recently senior resident Supreme Court judge, worked to improve the function of the courts in Mecklenburg County. Received the 1998 Judge of the Year Award from the N.C. Association of Women Attorneys. Founded the Wesley Heights Community Center and co-founded the

Queen City Congress, Inc., a coalition of Central Charlotte neighborhoods. Served as president of both organizations, helping to revitalize Central City neighborhoods. Awarded Person of the Year by Omega Psi Phi Fraternity and Zeta Phi Beta Sorority. Continues to work in all phases of improving the court system by helping to found the Children's Law Center and serving on the boards of the Boy Scouts, Charlotte Drug Education Center, and United Family Services. Woman of the Year 1998.

Susan Peck Green b.1949 in Rock Hill, NC. B.A., UNC Chapel Hill, graduate work at N.C. State and Stanford Univ. Char. resident since 1962. Served two terms as Mecklenburg County commissioner with focus on land use, transportation, and neighborhood advocacy. During her terms as commissioner (1980–84), directed county manager's budget of $250M and workforce of 2,600, initiated the first-ever public appearance period at each board meeting, providing an opportunity for citizens to be heard on any subject; adopted innovative recycling, resource recovery, and toxic waste disposal technologies; and pioneered child daycare certification and workfare alternatives for parents. Described in *The Charlotte Observer*, "A fine record: One in five who made a difference." Was Democratic primary winner of N.C. 9th District of U.S. House of Representatives in 1983 and national finance director of 1990 U.S. Senate campaign. Received Distinguished Democrat Award in 1984, and N.C. and U.S. Jaycees awards for Outstanding Women in Government in 1985. Woman of the Year 1984.

Elisabeth Green (Liz) Hair (Mrs. Samuel C.) b. 1920 in St Louis, MO. B.A., Wellesley College. Honorary Doctorate of Humanities, Queens College. Char. resident since 1949. Four children. Activist for women and children and advocate for the arts and environment. Was the first woman elected to Mecklenburg Board of County Commissioners and served as chair for three years. Was instrumental in the establishment of an Area Mental Health Board. Was the primary force behind the Cultural Action Plan that turned uptown's old First Baptist Church into Spirit Square. Served as chair of the N.C. Urban Counties Committee and member of NACO Tax and Finance Steering Committee. Was first chair of the Women's Political Caucus, state chair of the Democratic Women's Political Caucus, and chair of the Charlotte Board of Elections (1960–72). Considered instrumental member on the Carlyle Commission in 1962, which established statewide community colleges and made Charlotte College, the UNC Charlotte predecessor, a four-year institution. Woman of the Year 1975.

Jacqueline Butler Hairston b. in Charlotte, NC. Julliard School of Music, B.M. Ed, Howard University; M.A., Columbia Univ. Char. resident until 1973. One child.

Recognized for her unselfish, creative contribution to the community at large as a music teacher in the public schools, especially teaching underprivileged children. Worked as assistant professor of music at Johnson C. Smith University. Headed music department at Merritt College, Oakland, CA. Known nationally as a composer, musician, and producer. Presently an Oakland/San Francisco-based professional pianist, multi-talented ASCAP composer/arranger for nationally known vocalists, including Kathleen Battle and Leontyne Price. Featured in *Outstanding African-American Composers* and *Music by Black Women Composers*. Woman of the Year 1971.

Deborah Small Harris (Mrs. John William) b. 1947 in Charlotte, NC. B.A., UNC Chapel Hill, graduate work at UNC Charlotte and UNC Greensboro, finance and accounting and executive management at the Wharton School. Lifetime Char. resident. Three children. Spearheaded one of the most ambitious private fundraising efforts in Charlotte to create the N.C. Blumenthal Performing Arts Center in 1987. Was president of the Junior League of Charlotte and the Charlotte Drug Education Center. Served as chair of the Arts and Science Council for their first million-dollar campaign. Has served on numerous boards of UNC, Wake Forest, and Davidson as well as the National Center for Learning Disabilities in New York City, and the Foundation for the Carolinas. Continues as advocate and volunteer for numerous social services and educational organizations in Charlotte. Awarded Order of the Hornet in 1992. Woman of the Year 1987.

Helen Hunter (Mrs. Ernest B.) 1902–1978, b. in Wilmington, NC. B.A, Hunter College. Char. resident 1930–78. Two children. Was active in state and local civic affairs, serving as the president of the N.C. Congress of Parents and Teachers (1947–49), the president of the N.C. Mental Hygiene Society (now the Mental Health Association) and as chairman of the N.C. Mental Health Council. Served as chair of Education for Responsible Parenthood and vice-president for N.C. Family Life Council, N.C. Health Council and N.C. Conference for Social Service. Was honored by the Mecklenburg Board of County Commissioners upon her retirement from the county social services board in 1974. Helped to obtain the remainder of the WPA funds for the State Art Museum and for a traveling art exhibition in public schools across the state. Served as the first female elder at Covenant Presbyterian Church. Continued to be an active volunteer with Girl Scouts, the YWCA, the N.C. Symphony Society and at the libraries of Queens College and UNC Charlotte. Woman of the Year 1958.

Sis Atlass Kaplan (Mrs. Stanley) b. 1933 in Chicago, IL. B.A., Rollins College. Char. resident since 1965. One child. Served as chair of the Governor's Crime

Commission for N.C. and chair of the Criminal Justice System of Mecklenburg County. Led the committee responsible for the construction of the new courthouse and intake system. Was recipient of the 1994 Mecklenburg County Bar's Liberty Bell Award for her efforts. Employed currently as president of Leader Newspaper, Inc., after almost 30 years as a producer in the radio and TV industry. Served on the chamber of commerce, Urban League, and as president of the National Radio Broadcasters Association from 1980–84. Continues to serve on community boards that focus on the needs of children, education, and the arts, including Teen Health Connection, the board of visitors at Davidson College, and the N.C. Blumenthal Performing Arts Center. Woman of the Year 1994.

Charlotte Abbott Kelly (Mrs. Luther W., Jr.) 1897–1988, b. in Flat Rock, NC. B.A., Wellesley College. Lifetime Char. resident. Four children. Worked as astronomer and planetarium director for the Children's Nature Museum, where she organized classes for children, teachers, and civic groups, making the museum a pioneer in the field of astronomy. Founded the Charlotte Astronomy Club. Served on the board of Children and Family Services and was president of the Wellesley Club. Was founding member and trustee of the Charlotte Unitarian Church where she was church pianist and first president of the Women's Alliance. Lost her sight before her death but not before she had introduced the wonders of the universe to many in the community of Charlotte and surrounding counties. A star is named for her. Woman of the Year 1965.

Gloria Pace King, b.1945 in Cleveland, OH. R.N., St. Alexis Hospital School of Nursing; B.A., Cleveland State University; M.B.A., Baldwin Wallace College. Char. resident since 1994. Two children. As president of United Way of Central Carolinas since 1994, mobilized significant community support resulting in major increases in the organization's annual campaigns, led efforts for organizational improvements among United Way's member agencies which became models for UW agencies nationwide. Serves as a community volunteer and advocate for numerous boards including Leadership Charlotte, Belmont Abbey College, Mecklenburg Partnership for Children/Smart Start, the chamber of commerce, and the advisory board of Carolinas Healthcare System. Woman of the Year 1998.

Cynthia Blythe Marshall (Mrs. Thomas Styles) b. 1943 in Washington, DC. B.S., UNC Greensboro; M.S., Univ. of PA. Char. resident since 1945. Two children. Chaired a child advocacy effort for the Junior League, focusing on family and work-related issues affecting women, child abuse and neglect, foster care, childcare and learning disabilities. Founded and directed Communities in Schools of Charlotte-

Mecklenburg, (formerly Cities in Schools,) an organization that is part of the nation's largest dropout prevention network. Was founding board president of the Family Support Center and served on the Child Care Resources board, United Way social planning council, Mecklenburg County Youth Services Action Board, and Mecklenburg County Committee for the Prevention of Child Abuse and Neglect. Was president of the Junior League of Charlotte. Woman of the Year 1988.

Julia Watson Maulden (Mrs. Paul R.) b.1913 in Wilmington, NC. B.A., UNC Greensboro; M.E., UNC Charlotte; D.H.L., Queens College. Char. resident 1960–91. Four children. Served as a member of the Charlotte-Mecklenburg Board of Education for eight years strongly advocating desegregated schools and equal education. Served on local, national, and international boards of girl scouting for 30 years, including being president of the Cabarrus Girl Scout Council. Worked as a French teacher and translator of French documents for the United Nations. Helped to overcome poverty and prejudice by serving as first executive director of Charlotte Habitat for Humanity, as a missionary for the Peace Corps in Zaire, and later in Haiti, leading Presbyterian youths in a mission to improve the quality life in Haiti called the "Integrated Rural Development Project." Received Liberty Bell Award 1977. Woman of the Year 1973.

Jonnie Horn McLeod, M.D. (Mrs. Leslie) b. 1923 in Lucedale, MS. B.A., Newcomb College of Tulane; M.D., Tulane Medical College; internship and residency at Charity Hospital of New Orleans. Char. resident since 1954. Four children. Worked as professor emeritus of human services at UNC Charlotte since 1993, as professor since 1975. Founded the Charlotte Drug Education Center, where she was director 1971–1975. Founded the Open House Drug Counseling Service, now McLeod Addictive Disease Center. Served as consultant in health education for Charlotte-Mecklenburg Schools since 1960, incorporating the sex-education program she created, which is now outlawed. Served as president of the Mecklenburg Medical Society and chair of the Governor's Council on Alcohol and other Drug Abuse among Youth. Received the 1996 Liberty Bell Award, the 1995 Distinguished Service Award by UNC Charlotte trustees, the 1990 Nat'l Conference of Christians and Jews Silver Medallion Humanitarian Award, the 1980 Davidson College Honorary Doctor of Science Award, and the 1979 B'Nai B'rith Humanitarian Award. Cited in 1972 among "Charlotte 23" top citizens as the medical person who contributed the most to Charlotte. Woman of the Year 1969.

Caroline Love Myers (Mrs. Michael G.) b. 1933 in Burlington, NC. B.A., Queens College; graduate courses, including not-for-profit management cert. at UNC

Charlotte. Lifetime Char. resident. Four children. Founded and directed Crisis Assistance Ministry making her the most visible and consistent advocate for the poor. Served on the board of directors for Travelers Aid and Loaves and Fishes. Serves as advisory trustee at Queens College, board member of Legal Services of Southern Piedmont, steering committee member of the Homeless Services Network, and chairperson on the boards of the Emergency Financial Assistance Network for Mecklenburg County and National Fuel Funds Network. Served as ruling elder at Covenant Presbyterian Church (1986–92). Received the 1999 Humanitarian Award from the Nat'l Conference for Community and Justice and the 1994 Liberty Bell Award from the Mecklenburg Bar Association. Woman of the Year 1985.

Freda Hyams Nicholson (Mrs. Henry H., Jr.) b. 1934 in Asheville, NC. R.N., St. Joseph's School of Nursing; B.S., Queens College; M.Ed, UNC Charlotte. Char. resident since 1955. Six children. Served as president and CEO of Discovery Place, Inc. (Nature Museum, Discovery Place, and Museum of Coastal Carolina) 1981–2000, transforming a hands-on museum with its beginnings at Charlotte's Nature Museum into one of the nation's premier science museums, its location and success becoming the launching pad for a thriving uptown cultural district. Received honorary Doctorate from Queens College and outstanding alumna award from UNC Charlotte. Is president of the Association of Science-Technology Centers and chair of the American Association of Museums. Received the Lifetime Achievement Award from the Charlotte Convention & Visitors Bureau, the 1995 Pegasus Award of the Charlotte chapter of the Public Relations Society of America, the Order of the Long Leaf Pine by the State of N.C., and in 1994, the Public Service Award by the governor of N.C. Woman of the Year 1981.

Cyndee Gibson Patterson (Mrs. Robert Michael) b. 1950 in Akron, OH. B.A., Purdue Univ.; M.B.A. courses at Queens College. Char. resident since 1979. Three children. Was instrumental as chair of the Arts and Science Council in the outcome of the 1997 public-funding debate, and in the establishment of the Community Building Task Force that received national recognition and became a model for other communities. Served four terms on the Charlotte City Council (1985–93) and as mayor pro tem (1989–91). Developed and implemented plan for the consolidation of Uptown Charlotte Development Corporation and CCA Division of Chamber, leading to creation of the new organization, Charlotte Center Partners. Created and developed the Info Charlotte Marketing Center of the Chamber of Commerce. Founded Jazz Charlotte and First Night Charlotte. Co-founded SpringFest. Serves as President of Lynnwood Foundation in Charlotte and Founder and President of Patterson Blake, Inc., which plans and implements large corporate events. Woman of the Year 1997.

Elizabeth Schmoke (Libby) Randolph (Mrs. John Daniel) b. 1917 in Farmville, NC. B.A., Shaw Univ.; M.A., Univ. of Mich.; Prof. Diploma, UNC Chapel Hill. Char. resident since 1944. Served as associate superintendent for curriculum and program development in the Charlotte-Mecklenburg Schools and national president for supervision and curriculum development. Was former assistant superintendent, principal, and classroom teacher. Was a member of the National Association of Administrative Education, the committee for state evaluation of teachers, the Charlotte-Mecklenburg Hospital Authority, and a life member of NEA. Considered one of the most renowned African-American educators locally and nationally. Served long after her retirement on boards of Davidson College, Queens College, School Workers Federal Credit Union, and the Museum of the New South, and as chair of the Charlotte-Mecklenburg Public Library and N.C. A&T University. Woman of the Year 1978.

Betty Chafin Rash (Mrs. J. Dennis) b. 1942 in Atlanta, GA. B.A., UNC Greensboro; M.P.A., UNC Chapel Hill. Char. resident since 1965. Two stepchildren. Served as member of the City Council (1975–81), becoming the first female mayor pro tem (1977–81). Worked as associate dean of students at UNC Charlotte and served as director of corporate relations at Queens College, where she developed and directed a woman's leadership program. Served on the steering committee for finance, administration, and intergovernmental relations of the National League of Cities and on the boards of the N.C. Center for Public Policy Research and the N.C. League of Municipalities. Operates her company, Betty Chafin Rash/Public Affairs, est.1983, and has been the executive director of Central Carolina Choices, a regional collaborative serving the 14 counties around Charlotte since 1997. Remains involved on many levels in the community, serving on the chamber of commerce, the Charlotte-Mecklenburg Housing Partnership, and boards focusing on the arts and education. Is active in numerous political campaigns for candidates and bond issues. Woman of the Year 1979.

Margaret Whitton (Maggie) Ray (Mrs. Tom) b.1942 in Charlotte, NC. B.A., Agnes Scott; M.A.T., Brown University; Post grad, Winthrop and N.C. State Univ. Lifetime Char. resident. Two children. Was chairman of the Citizens' Advisory Group that successfully drew up an alternative desegregation plan for Charlotte-Mecklenburg Schools, ending the impasse created by *Swann vs. Board of Education* over busing and desegregation. Taught biology for 20 years (1976–1996) in the public schools and is currently working on her Ph.D. in zoology at N.C. State. Served on the board of trustees of CPCC and the League of Women Voters. Woman of the Year 1974.

Sally Dalton Robinson (Mrs. Russell M., II) b. 1934 in Charlotte, NC. A.B., Duke Univ., Phi Beta Kappa. Lifetime Char. resident. Three children. Played major role in the Mint Museum's 1985 expansion that opened the Mint to Randolph Road and provided a home for the Harry and Mary Dalton collection of paintings and prints. Was chair of the board of directors of the Public Library of Charlotte-Mecklenburg, and later chair of the capital fundraising campaign that helped finance the uptown library. Was founder and first chair of the Museum of the New South and principally responsible for its community and corporate support (1992–2000), overseeing a capital campaign that raised over $8,000,000. Was first woman to serve as senior warden of Christ Episcopal Church. Serves as Duke University trustee. Serves on local and state boards, including the N.C. Humanities Council and the National Humanities Center. Received the Arts and Science Lifetime Commitment Vanguard Award in 1996, UNC Charlotte's Distinguished Service Award in 1998. Woman of the Year 1988.

Mae Lebby Smith Rogers (Mrs. Gayle) ca.1915–1980. B.A., Queens College. Lifetime Char. resident. Four children. Served as president and board chairman of the YWCA, leading the effort that chose the site and built the Park Road facility. Served as a member of the national YWCA until 1963. Founded the local and state Family Life Council and was president of Women of the Church at Myers Park Presbyterian Church. Served on the board of trustees of Queens College. Was chair of the 1974 YWCA capital campaign that raised $1,500,000 to build a gymnasium and replace the tennis courts. Woman of the Year 1962.

Judith Wilkins Rose (Mrs. Ken) b. 1952 in Spartanburg, SC. B.S., Winthrop College; M.S., Univ. of Tenn. Char. resident since 1975. Assistant director and director of athletics at UNC Charlotte since 1990. As director attracted two NCAA basketball "Final Four" tournaments to Charlotte. Developed UNC Charlotte women's basketball and tennis programs. Conducted and participated in clinics for high school coaches and a community service program for department of athletics. Has been responsible for several major fundraising efforts at UNC Charlotte raising over $15,000,000 to build three significant athletic facilities. Received 1981 YMCA Sports Woman of the Year award. Selected as Administrative Woman of the Year by UNC Charlotte in 1984 and 1991. Was member of the executive committee of the 1997 Junior Olympics held in Charlotte and chairperson for USA Conference for Athletic Directors in 1996–97. Recipient of the 1999 Pegasus Award. Woman of the Year 1996.

Susan Hancock Sewell (Mrs. William) b. 1954 in Berger County, NJ. Attended Columbus College, GA, and Northern VA Community College; Cert, not-for-profit management at UNC Charlotte. Char. resident 1968–93 and since 1997. Three children. Was leading advocate for affordable housing, serving as the first paid executive director of Charlotte's Habitat for Humanity. Led the organization to become the largest affiliate in the U.S., the first affiliate to complete 100 houses, the first to build a home in 24 hours, and the first to complete a house built entirely by women, giving Charlotte national attention. Became director of U.S. Affiliates for Habitat for Humanity in 1993 and later project director of IMPACT Habitat, an internal study of the whole project. Selected in 1997 to be the executive officer of Florence Crittenton Services, a residential facility for unmarried, pregnant women. Serves as a full-time volunteer promoting the availability of affordable housing. Woman of the Year 1990.

Ruth Gwynn Shaw (Mrs. Colin Stuart) b. 1948 in Danville, VA. B.A., magna cum laude, ECU; M.A., ECU; Ph. D., Univ. of Texas at Austin. Char. area resident since 1986. Two children. Served as president of Central Piedmont Community College (1986–92). Was first woman to serve as the general chair of the United Way of Central Carolinas 1989 campaign, raising $16 million. Served as chair of the United Way board of directors and of the Arts and Science Council. Was the first woman to serve as president of the Charlotte Rotary. Continues to serve on various boards, focusing on literacy and workforce issues. Is currently executive vice president and chief administrator of Duke Energy Corporation, serving on the policy committee and as president of the Duke Energy Foundation. Her many awards include the Order of the Long Leaf Pine from the State of N.C. in 1992, the Charlotte Business Award in 1995, and Women in Communication, Inc.'s Award for Communication Excellence in 1997. Woman of the Year 1991.

Marcia Weinstein Simon (Mrs. Paul) b. 1946 in Erwin, NC. A.B., Syracuse Univ.; M.A., New York State Univ. Lifetime Char. resident. Two children. Former teacher and social worker. Was first woman vice-chair of Arts and Science fundraising drive. Involved in advocacy efforts for the arts for over 20 years, helping to create local "one percent for art" ordinance adopted by city and county in 1980. Served as chair of Cultural Action Council for the Chamber of Commerce. Was early advocate for women offenders. As Summit House trustee and board chair, helped to raise significant funds to create a fiscally sound organization. Is considered fundraising and marketing expert. Served on the boards of the Foundation for the Carolinas, the Charlotte Jewish Foundation, the World Affairs Council, the Charlotte-Mecklenburg Education Federation and the Charlotte Women's Political Caucus. Was chair of the boards of the Arts and Science Council, Planned Parenthood, Charlotte Chapter of Hadassah, and vice-chair and founding board member of the Museum of the New South. Received

Jane Odom Award. Founder and president of Paul Simon for Women. Woman of the Year 1997.

Sarah Mingo Stevenson (Mrs. Robert Louis) b. 1925 in Kershaw County, Heath Springs, SC. Attended CPCC. Char. resident since 1940. Two children. Involved in Parent Teacher Association for 40 years, helping to integrate the black and white PTA councils. Was elected to serve as the first African-American president of the Charlotte-Mecklenburg Council of PTAs and a member of the board of NCPTA. Was the first black female elected member of the Charlotte-Mecklenburg Board of Education (1980–88). Received the NCCJ Certificate of Brotherhood, the NAACP Legal Defense Fund Outstanding Award, the 1980 Omega Psi Phi Citizen of the Year Award, the National Association of Negro Business and Professional Women's Clubs, Inc. Sojourner Truth Award in 1980, the Order of the Long Leaf Pine from the State of N.C. in 1985, the Community Relations Committee's Martin Luther King, Jr. Service Award in 1986, the 1992 Liberty Bell Award, and the 1998 Women's Equality Day Award from Mecklenburg County Women's Commission. Woman of the Year 1992.

Dorothy N. (Dolly) Tate (Mrs. John A., Jr) 1917–1991, b. in Union, SC. B.A., Sweetbriar College. Char. resident 1938–40 and 1946–91. Two children. Was a leading child advocate founding the Council for Children, Teen-Age Pregnancy Services (TAPS), and the Davidson-Cornelius Day Care Center. Served on the N.C. Child Advocacy Institution Board, the Charlotte-Mecklenburg Hospital Authority, the Siegle Avenue Cooperative Board, the N.C. Day Care Legislative Study Commission, and Community School of the Arts. Received the Governor's Award for Volunteer Work and Organizational Administration, and the first Dolly Tate Award from the Council for Children in 1982. Was co-recipient with her husband, Jack, of the NCCJ Award in 1986 and the 1987 Alexis de Tocqueville Award from the United Way America in Washington, DC. Woman of the Year 1983.

Ann Davis Thomas (Mrs. Edward) b. 1933 in Tyler, TX. B.A., Univ. of Texas, summa cum laude, Phi Beta Kappa. Char. resident since 1956. Two children. Served as chair of the County Board of Social Services. Was president of the Junior League of Charlotte, helping to found Youth Homes, Inc., and the Drug Education Center. Was the first woman appointed to the Civic Center Authority (1974–79) and the first female chair of the Social Planning Council of the United Way. Served one term on the Mecklenburg Board of County Commissioners. Was vice president, director of corporate contributions and community involvement at First Union Corporation (1980–95). Continued her career as community volunteer, serving and leading on dozens of community boards that focused on government issues and the organization and implementation of Charlotte's social services. Woman of the Year 1977.

Gladys Avery Tillett (Mrs. Charles) 1892–1984, b. in Morganton, NC. B.S., UNC Chapel Hill. Char. resident 1919–84. Three children. As the daughter of a state Supreme Court justice, she began her own political career in the early 1910s, while attending the Women's College in Greensboro. Was a strong advocate even then for women's suffrage; helped to organize the student government and served as its first president. After receiving another bachelor's degree in political science from UNC Chapel Hill, married Charles Tillett, a Charlotte attorney devoted to progressive politics. Organized the Mecklenburg County League of Women Voters in 1919 and began a lifelong career in the Democratic Party educating and empowering women all over the world. Selected in 1943 by President Roosevelt to be vice-chair of the Democratic Party, and in 1944, was the first woman to address the national convention. Appointed by President Kennedy in 1961 to be a U.S. Representative on the United Nations Commission on the Status of Women. Before her return to Charlotte, had traveled all over the world with the United Nations, visiting government officials and women with the sole purpose of helping them improve the quality of their lives. Her influence and advocacy for women's rights continued until her death in Charlotte in 1984. Woman of the Year 1961.

Beatrice S. Shapiro Wallas (Mrs. David) b.1915 in N.Y., NY. B.A., Hunter College, NY. Char. resident since 1941. Three children. Served as president of League of Women Voters, member of the Model City Commission, and was active in the Association of American University Women. Was pre-school director at Temple Beth El. Worked to help start Hospice in Charlotte. Served six years as member of board of Planned Parenthood. Woman of the Year 1959.

Ruth Hayden Wanzer (Mrs. Charles T.) 1895–1987, b. in Baltimore, MD. B.A., Goucher College. Char. resident 1927–87. Three children. Served as president of the League of Women Voters, leading a movement in 1964 to expand the organization across the state. Chaired the Urban Renewal Community and the United Nations Workshop for the Joint Council on International Affairs and the league. Was instrumental in organizing the Charlotte chapter of the American Civil Liberties Union. Served as state president of the N.C. Mental Hygiene Society, president of the Charlotte Parent Teacher Association, state president of the American Association of University Women, and director of the women's division of the Community Chest. Was a founder and president of the Little Theatre of Charlotte. Woman of the Year 1966.

Charlotte Metcalf Watkins (Mrs. Carlton Gunter, Sr.) b.1921 in Coffeyville, KS. Attended Kansas State University; RN, St. Luke's School of Nursing, Kansas City, MO. Char. resident since 1946. Four children. Served as president of the N.C. Congress of Parents and Teachers, where she presided over the unification of the NCPTA and the N.C. Congress of Colored PTAs. Appointed by President Nixon in 1969 to the Cabinet Committee on Education and Desegregation. Obtained the first U.S. grant for the national PTA to prepare teachers, parents, and youth in seven states for desegregation. Was a member of the National Conference of Christian and Jews, the Charlotte Area Fund, and the Council on Alcoholism. Served as the first president of the Charlotte Jaycettes in 1950. Woman of the Year 1968.

Louise Cameron Watkins (Mrs. James Z.) 1904–1996. b. in Greenville, NC. A.B., Winthrop College; graduate studies at Columbia University. Char. resident 1927–96. One child. Served as dean of the School of Christian Mission and Women's Society of the Methodist Church. While president of the N.C. Congress of Parents and Teachers in 1957, campaigned against the Pearsall Plan that would have allowed communities to close their schools in event of desegregation. Woman of the Year 1957.

Edyth Farnham Winningham (Mrs. James Lyndon) 1900–1994, b. in Arthur, ND. A.B., North Dakota University; M.A., UNC Chapel Hill. Char. resident since 1947. One child. Taught high school in North Dakota, Greensboro, and Wilmington before joining the teaching staff at UNC Greensboro, and later the University of Wyoming and UNC Wilmington. Joined the staff at the Charlotte Center of UNC in 1947 as their first political science professor until her retirement in 1967, when she became professor emeritus. Considered an early pioneer of UNC Charlotte for her efforts to create lasting ties between UNC Charlotte and the community of Charlotte. Founded the UNC Charlotte University Forum Council, bringing prominent speakers and leaders to the university. At age 84, returned to UNC Charlotte to teach international politics. Woman of the Year 1970.

Carrie Bess Cole Winter (Mrs. Carlton Vernon) b.1930 in Lexington, NC. B.S., Appalachian State Univ.; M.S., Univ. of SC; special graduate work in bacteriology at Emory Univ.; M.P.H., UNC Chapel Hill. Char. resident since 1960. Two children. Served as President of the PTA Council during the school desegregation process. Founded the PTA Thrift Shop. Served three four-year terms on the Charlotte-Mecklenburg Board of Education (1976–88), receiving national attention for the openness of her coordination for the superintendent search while chair. Participated in national education conferences, serving as the N.C. representative to the National

School Board Association. Was an organizing member of the Mecklenburg Council for Adolescent Pregnancy, Partners and Teen Health Connection. Served on the advisory board of Public Health, UNC. Received cash reward as research bacteriologist with Communicable Disease Center in Chapel Hill and Atlanta, for her pioneering work with fluorescent antibody techniques in the rapid identification of bacteria. Was appointed chair of the Charlotte Tree Advisory Commission. Woman of the Year 1986.

Velva Whitescarver Woollen (Mrs. Thomas Hayes) b. 1939 in High Point, NC. B.S., Salem College; M.T., Duke Univ. Char. resident since 1944. Four children. Served as chair of the Charlotte Housing Authority for six years and is considered a leading advocate for the economically disadvantaged, initiating programs in Charlotte for "family self-sufficiency." Was elected to the city council in 1983, served six terms. Served on numerous community boards including CanCare, Alexander Children's Center, and Blumenthal Performing Arts Center, and as chair of Science Museums of Charlotte, Spirit Square, and Salem College. Served as president of the Charlotte Junior League. Received the Order of the Long Leaf Pine from the state of N.C. for her work on the State Job Training Council. Elected ruling elder and clerk of session at Covenant Presbyterian Church. Woman of the Year 1998.

INDEX

Errata/Corrections to *New South Women: Twentieth-Century Women of Charlotte, North Carolina*

- Page 8, lines 26/27: Jane Wilkes' daughter-in-law, Mrs. J. Renwick Wilkes, became one of the first three Charlotte women to hold public office — not Jane Wilkes herself.
- Page 9, lines 6/7: Jane Wilkes' daughter-in-law, Mrs. J. Renwick Wilkes, was one of the first female public officials — not Jane Wilkes herself.
- Page 41, lines 12/13: ...Charlotte architect Martin E. Boyer, Jr. — not Miles Boyer.
- Page 60, line 2: Sims died in 1961 — not 1962.
- Page 87, line 2: ...there were still 88 one-race schools in Charlotte... — not 81.